CLIMATE REALISM

The only meaningful way to understand climate change and wider environmental harm is to begin with the facts. We need an honest assessment of what is working and what is not. The challenges are significant: carbon levels in the atmosphere are still rising, a genuine energy transition has yet to begin, and global energy demand is expected to rise sharply. Renewables remain expensive, nuclear power is costly, and carbon offsets are often little more than modern indulgences. Simultaneously, there is no clear route to sustainable growth. Some place their faith in technology or use offsets to ease their consciences, but this is wishful thinking. Written by one of the UK's leading commentators on energy policy and climate change, *Climate Realism* offers a radical reassessment of our current position. It argues that we must face the real cost of pollution we create and shows how to avoid wasting the years ahead.

Sir Dieter Helm is Professor of Economic Policy at the University of Oxford and Official Fellow in Economics at New College, Oxford. He is a renowned economist and author of *Legacy* (CUP, 2024), *Net Zero* (2020) and *Natural Capital* (2015). He was knighted in 2021 for services to the environment and energy.

'Dieter Helm makes a persuasive case that the argument about climate change needs to change. Two camps – the optimists and the pessimists – have become entrenched but neither have the virtue which Helm recommends, which is realism. This is a bracing reminder that we need to confront the costs of transition and make sure that we enforce the principle that the polluter must pay.'

Philip Collins, *Prospect* magazine

'Dieter Helm wants us to challenge our settled views on what it will take to set the economy on a sustainable path. In *Climate Realism* he argues for testing policies that aim to reduce carbon consumption, which, inevitably, requires us all to pay more for our use of nature. Uncomfortable as this will be, the alternative is worse.'

Diane Coyle, University of Cambridge, author of *The Measure of Progress: Counting What Really Matters*

'Dieter Helm is the most challenging and consistently iconoclastic thinker on climate, nature and energy of his generation, and *Climate Realism* shows why. With characteristic wit and forensic logic, he challenges many of the comforting assumptions of the climate orthodoxy: that an energy transition is under way, that renewables are cheap under any market arrangement, that 'clean energy' is a meaningful category, and that various technological get-out-of-jail cards (CCUS, DAC, hydrogen and geoengineering) will magically solve everything. Helm makes a compelling case that the problems we face can only be solved if we are willing to build economies around the stewardship of nature, which will involve tough political decisions. This book is a must read for anyone interested in climate change, economic policy, energy, and politics.'

Arthur Downing, Octopus Energy Group

'*Climate Realism* is at times bracing. It is often uncomfortable. You might not agree with every sentence, but it will make you think. And thinking clearly is still the first step we need to take on our global warming journey. Reading this book is a very good use of precious time.'

Chris Giles, *Financial Times*

'Dieter Helm has written the kind of book the climate debate badly needs: clear-eyed about the science, unsparing about policy failures, and refreshingly free of jargon. Some of his conclusions will be contested, and rightly so – that is how serious arguments advance. But the questions he forces us to confront, above all why thirty COPs have failed to curtail rising CO2 levels, cannot be ducked. Read it, argue with it, then think again.'

Charles Godfray, University of Oxford

'Dieter Helm is the single most authoritative and impressive thinker on energy and the environment in Europe today. He is bracingly honest, intellectually fearless and morally compelling. It is impossible to think seriously about climate change, net zero and our politics without reading this brilliant book.'

The Rt Hon Michael Gove

'Dieter Helm refuses the comfortable consensus and makes you think. *Climate Realism* is a bracing challenge to the assumptions underpinning 25 years of climate policy: that there is a 'transition', that renewable energy is 'clean' or 'cheap', and that territorial targets work. You will not agree with every conclusion – I don't – and I suspect Helm would be disappointed if you did. But anyone serious about actually reducing global warming must reckon with this book and its ideas. System costs do matter, atmospheric concentrations are not (yet) budging, and the politics is heading in the wrong direction, just when we need to move the needle on emissions, and fast.'

Cameron Hepburn, University of Oxford

'As formidably well-informed as he is incisive, Dieter Helm understands – and explains – the nexus of economics, policy, technology and science better than anyone writing about climate issues anywhere in the world. Agree or disagree with his analysis, you cannot afford to ignore it.'

Edward Lucas, formerly *The Economist*

'No one is a more astute critic of current approaches to the environment and climate crises than Dieter Helm. In his new book, Professor Helm argues cogently that there is no easy fix: climate change is everyone's responsibility. Until we accept that sustainable growth can only come from sustainable production and consumption, and until we accept that it is the current generation's duty to restore the natural infrastructure we have destroyed, we are destined to be seen by future generations as very poor ancestors indeed!'

René Olivieri, Chair of the National Trust

'Dieter Helm has written a sweeping book that might be more aptly entitled, 'Hard Truths and Hard Choices'. One may not agree with the author on every count. But skepticism about current policies ultimately gives rise to a clarion call that we recognise that more of the same will not regenerate the natural environment.'

Paula Reynolds, NED, GE Vernova and National Grid

'In a world of pollyannas and cassandras, deniers and zealots, Dieter Helm is something rarer, but a lot more useful: a realist. Amid ferocious culture wars, this book is unusual. Helm commits what is heresy for those on one side of the debate: he accepts climate change is happening, is worrying and is serious. He also commits a heresy for the other side: renewables, he argues, have proven very costly and, so far, not terribly effective. This book might be depressing, but it is important – and maybe we need to face reality.'

Tom Whipple, *The Times*

DIETER HELM

CLIMATE REALISM

FACING THE FACTS ABOUT ENERGY

CAMBRIDGE
UNIVERSITY PRESS

CAMBRIDGE
UNIVERSITY PRESS

Shaftesbury Road, Cambridge CB2 8EA, United Kingdom

One Liberty Plaza, 20th Floor, New York, NY 10006, USA

477 Williamstown Road, Port Melbourne, VIC 3207, Australia

314–321, 3rd Floor, Plot 3, Splendor Forum, Jasola District Centre, New Delhi – 110025, India

Cambridge University Press is part of Cambridge University Press & Assessment, a department of the University of Cambridge.

We share the University's mission to contribute to society through the pursuit of education, learning and research at the highest international levels of excellence.

www.cambridge.org
Information on this title: www.cambridge.org/9781009880619
DOI: 10.1017/9781009880602

When citing this work, please include a reference to the DOI 10.1017/9781009880602

First published 2026

A catalogue record for this publication is available from the British Library

A Cataloging-in-Publication data record for this book is available from the Library of Congress

ISBN 978-1-009-88061-9 Paperback

To Sue and the next generation: Amelie, Jake,
Elodie, Ralph and Bertie

CONTENTS

Preface *page* xi

INTRODUCTION 1

1 THERE IS NO TRANSITION 13

2 AN EXPLOSION OF ENERGY DEMAND 25

3 THE WRONG TARGET 45

4 THERE IS NO SUCH THING AS CLEAN ENERGY 62

5 THE BROKEN WINDOW FALLACY 81

6 RENEWABLES AND NUCLEAR AREN'T CHEAP 95

7 OFFSETS, BUYING INDULGENCES AND SEQUESTRATION 112

8 NO GET-OUT-OF-JAIL CARDS 127

9 THE COP-OUTS 141

10 UNILATERALISM, BOTTOM-UP AND NO REGRETS 163

11 WHAT HAPPENS IF WE DON'T ACT? 177

12 HOW NOT TO WASTE ANOTHER 25 YEARS 191

CONCLUSION 207

Acknowledgements 214
List of Abbreviations 218
Notes 220
Websites 243
Bibliography 244
Index 256

PREFACE

When I finished writing *Legacy: How to Build the Sustainable Economy*,[1] the gap between what the sustainable economy required of us and what we are actually doing haunted me. Our economies are profoundly unsustainable – almost everyone can see this – and yet we plough on regardless. It can only end badly. It is unsustainable and hence it will not be sustained.

Nowhere is this more apparent than in climate change. We have achieved so little, despite 35 years of effort. The facts are not in dispute: since 1990, China has gone from a minor bit-part polluter to the largest carbon emitter in the world, now burning more than half the world's coal; the US has, under all the presidents since 1990 – including notably Obama and Biden – driven hard to become the top world oil producer and put its foot on the gas; and Russia doesn't appear to care. The emerging major polluters, like India, are focused on economic growth and coal. None of the leaders of these countries took much part in the 30th Conference of the Parties (COP) in Brazil in late 2025.

The result is that the concentration of carbon in the atmosphere – the only number that counts – has exceeded 425 parts per million (ppm),[2] up from the 275 ppm before the Industrial Revolution. Ever since 1990 it has been going up by around 2 ppm every year. For all the talk about 'the transition' from fossil fuels, there isn't one. They remain over 80 per cent of world energy supply.[3] As the great new surge in energy demand gets going, driven by data centres, artificial intelligence (AI) and quantum computing, the starting point is that nuclear, hydro, biomass, solar and wind still remain bit-part players. The precise percentages are beside the point when fossil fuels remain the overwhelmingly dominant source of energy.

The more I have studied climate change policies, the more I have come to realise that the basic architecture is fatally flawed, and if we go on like this, we are well on course towards a very hot world, well beyond 2 °C. The reasons aren't hard to detect, but they are highly challenging to those in the climate community who go on and on about the transition to the sunny uplands of a world powered primarily by solar, wind and some nuclear.

The wrong targets have been set. The wrong targets mean wrong outcomes. There is no such thing as 'clean energy': the supply chains for the critical minerals including the rare earths,[4] and their refining, are dirty, as are those for fossil fuels. Renewables on a system-cost basis are not cheap.

It is quite extraordinary not only how persistent these mistakes are, but also the vehemence with which they are defended, and anyone raising doubts gets branded as a denier, and even cancelled. I have felt the full impact of this backlash. I would not mind if I'm wrong about all this. I sincerely hope I am. But the evidence is all around us. I don't see energy-intensive industries flocking to the 'clean-energy superpower' that the UK thinks it is becoming, as they have not to Germany with its *Energiewende* ('energy transition') and the European Union (EU) more generally. I see the US as the current energy winner, with its cheaper shale gas and oil and no longer needing oil or gas from the Gulf. I see China happily burning over half the world's coal, and cornering the market in critical minerals and solar panel manufacture (with all the massive environmental consequences), and intending to go on with roughly its current emissions for a long time to come. Looking to the future, I see India, Nigeria, Brazil and Indonesia, and many other fast-developing economies, as the main vectors of further economic growth and future emissions, and ever-greater damage to ecosystems and hence to carbon sequestration.

The most frequent question I am asked in lectures, presentations and podcasts is: 'Are you an optimist or a pessimist?' It's the wrong question. There is only one way to look at climate change and broader environmental destruction all around us. Look at the facts. Look at what is and is not working. Be realistic.

Yet the optimism/pessimism divide is very much alive in the climate community. There are those optimists who think that technology will crack the multiple problems. Bill Gates is one of these, as are most of the tech leaders. Elon Musk thinks we can go to Mars. They assume that there is a stack of get-out-of-jail cards. If salvation is just around the corner, and somehow we will be able to manipulate the composition of the atmosphere itself, then why bother now? And, anyway, you can buy indulgences ('carbon offsets') to ease your conscience. Gates tells us that he may have a private jet, but he buys carbon offsets, so that's OK.[5]

Many in the climate community have the best of intentions, but the road to hell is also paved with good intentions. The annual pilgrimages to the COPs go on, even though 30 of them so far have not dented the rise in the carbon concentration in the atmosphere.

The poster child of addressing climate change is the UK. Territorial emissions have fallen. But it is not an example of leadership. The leaders of China and Russia are not looking to the UK to find out how to do it, as Boris Johnson claimed in an official government document.[6] What world leader wants to emulate the highest industrial electricity prices among the reporting International Energy Association (IEA)/developed economies? What world leader wants to close down much of its energy-intensive industries and switch to imports so that their emissions figures look good? The UK is an object lesson in how not to do it.

What I try to do in this book is to set out these mistakes, to explain the failures. In doing so, I hope to show why carrying on along the current path is digging an ever-deeper hole that will not halt the disaster that is the coming climate change. Doing so has already led to the fracturing of what consensus there was on the importance of the problem.

Could it be different? Are we doomed to fail? This is the pessimists' forecast. Realism tells us to avoid doom-and-gloom because it leads to even greater inaction, making the problem worse. Realism focuses on the underlying causes of the problem and what would have to happen to head off climate change before it gets really out of hand.

The answer is remarkably simple and massively challenging to all those showing 'world leadership' and many in the climate community. It is central to my book *Legacy*. The simple fact is that we are living beyond our environmental means, and this is reflected in the fact that we are not paying for the environmental damage we are doing. We are really bad stewards of the world we inhabit and which we hope to pass on to future generations.

To change our ways is going to cost – a lot. Human advances can go on. We can gradually get better off. But this is a world far away from maximising gross domestic product (GDP) growth, as our 'world leaders' on climate change also want to do. The sustainable economy mandates a sustainable consumption path, and that includes the polluters (ultimately us) paying for the damage they (we) are causing. That would indeed be very painful. It is do-able, but it is not something most people want to hear. There are instead the mantras about 'cheap energy', that is also 'secure and sustainable', about 'clean-energy superpowers' with 'home-grown' energy, and slogans like 'Just Stop Oil'. These are at best naive, and all share the delusion that there are lots of 'win–win–win' opportunities out there, instead of hard choices.

Climate realism tells us that if we carry on in this vein, it is inevitable that the outcome will carry on being unsustainable.

And if it is unsustainable, it will not be sustained. That is in fact what is happening with climate change. It doesn't have to, but it won't be solved if we carry on with the current deeply flawed and often counterproductive climate policies. There is no escape from this basic realism.

INTRODUCTION

In May 2025, I gave the Battcock Lecture in Oxford.[1] My title was 'Climate Realism: time for a re-set' and my lecture infuriated lots of what might be called 'the climate change community'. The climate community can be defined as a very loose coalition of academics, politicians, activists and media commentators who share a number of concepts and basic assumptions, and see the evidence, new hypotheses and policies shaped through this lens. Because they see the world this way, apparent refutations and conflicting evidence get reinterpreted in ways that leave the basic framing intact.

It's a classic intellectual paradigm[2] with an added campaigning activism to stop the disaster they, perhaps rightly, see coming. Like all paradigms, this one comes in different shades, and the wider climate community which coalesces around this paradigm is inevitably a loose and often quarrelsome network, and a progressive one, convinced it is on the right side of history. Most, but certainly not all, are on the political left.

Some describe it as a religion, but it is not. Paradigms have considerable virtues, and this one has far more content. The theory of the greenhouse effect is grounded in core science. If the greenhouse gases (GHGs) in the atmosphere increase in concentration, then the climate warms. This is nineteenth-century science.[3] Different GHGs have different effects, but all go in the direction of global warming. Carbon dioxide (CO_2), as a core GHG, and as a proxy for the others,[4] has been increasing in concentration in the atmosphere, and looks like continuing to do so, and the temperature has risen, as it has in the geological past, when the concentration of carbon has gone up.

This is the scientific bedrock of the climate change paradigm. It is the claims that are added to this, and the policies, advocacy and activists that go with them, that make the climate change community more close-knit, more political and more closed to criticism and challenges. This is why my lecture and this book will prove challenging to them.

First up is the assumption that climate change is *the* problem of our age, to which all others are subsidiary. Second is the claim that existing technologies can solve the problem. Third, there is the claim that renewables are cheap and getting cheaper and are the route to cheap energy, and that fossil-fuel prices are going to be high and volatile, and hence getting out of fossil fuels is a good thing, independent of the carbon emissions. Staying with fossil fuels is claimed to be the route to economic decline: only the nations that embrace renewables have a competitive future. These claims are knitted together around the concept of 'the transition'.

A community defines itself not only on what it agrees about but also who are its enemies. This leads to a common vocabulary. The 'enemy' are climate 'deniers' and climate 'sceptics'. The root cause of our difficulties lies with the evil fossil-fuel companies and their directors and shareholders. We need to 'disinvest' and deal with these climate 'criminals'. Companies that do not adhere to strict net zero targets, compatible with the Paris Agreement 2015,[5] the outcome of COP21, are 'bad'. The task is to 'unlock' and 'unleash' 'green finance', which will produce 'green growth' and 'greater prosperity'.

Like any community, the climate change community has its heroes and its villains. The 'good guys' are leaders like Barack Obama, John Kerry and Joe Biden, academics like Nick Stern, and climate negotiators like Christiana Figueres and Pete Betts. The bad guys include George Bush Jr and Donald Trump, and all the far-right leaders that emerged in

Europe. It is almost entirely a Western league of the good and the bad. Vladimir Putin and Xi Jinping rarely get a mention, except to fawn over the cheap (subsidised) Chinese solar panels and electric vehicles (EVs), and ignore China's grip on the minerals and the rare earths and the pollution that goes with their mining and refining, and especially turn a blind eye to Chinese coal-burning – over half the world's total coal-burn and nearly 60 per cent of its electricity generation.[6] Autocrats like Xi Jinping in China are going to save the planet, whilst democratically elected Western leaders will take us on the road to hell. Hence, democracy is itself suspect: many climate activists want to impose their policies on the rest of us.

The antics of the 'activists' are often tacitly supported by the wider climate community, including scientists and academics. Greta Thunberg is treated as a kind of secular saint. The likes of Just Stop Oil pursue the very dangerous utopian idea that we could 'just stop oil', with little or no regard to what would happen if we did.

These factions all coalesce around two related ideas: that the United Nations (UN) COPs are a good way of solving the problem and that net zero carbon territorial production targets are the way to do this. Lots of climate activists can be found attending the COPs, part of around 50,000–90,000 attending, a communion of the believers, and most of them fly to these destinations.

There are many good people in this community, much very good research is done, and lots and lots of useful policy proposals are dreamt up. Climate modelling has made extraordinary advances. I know and admire many in the community.

Yet there is always a problem with 'groupthink'. Language gets debased, genuinely sceptical criticism is suppressed or shouted down, and the tendency is to talk to themselves rather than the rest of the world. The scientific process of trying to refute existing theories is not just put aside but often actively scorned.

Sadly, this is becoming all too obvious. Whilst the climate community gets ever more convinced of its righteousness, the politics is slipping away from them. The electorates in Europe and the US are not voting for the sorts of policies advocated by these activists. Quite the contrary: the far right across Europe shares an anti-net zero perspective, often second only to the focus on immigration. Trump has been elected twice in the US on a pro-fossil-fuel agenda. They all see net zero as a progressive left-wing idea, and lump it together with other agendas, like diversity, equality and inclusion (DE&I). Meanwhile, the key places where emissions are going up, and where the sequestration of the natural world is being devastated, take little or no notice. India is boosting its coal-burning to support its economic growth at over 6 per cent GDP per annum. Indonesia is burning lots of coal and doing great damage with its nickel mining, and China is building more coal power stations on its way to its future energy mix: coal, nuclear and renewables. In Sub-Saharan Africa, mining for cobalt, coltan and copper minerals adds to the expansion of oil and gas resources, and coal mining. The Congo, Amazon and Mekong are all suffering great damage in the name of extracting minerals for batteries, and hence for EVs. Lithium, copper, nickel and cobalt are all being extracted in the name of net zero.

'Zero emissions', 'carbon-free energy' and other fantasies do not exist in the reality of their great resource requirements and their mining and refining, nor in the materials for all the solar panels, wind turbines and batteries. Clean energy does not exist; there are just degrees of 'dirty energy'.

There are two other realities that the climate community needs to face up to. There is no slowdown in the increase in the carbon concentration in the atmosphere, the only number that really matters. By December 2025, it had reached 426 ppm, and it has been increasing at around 2 ppm every year since 1990. In 2024, it was over 3 ppm.[7] This is net of emissions and sequestration, and both are heading in the wrong direction. The temperature is rising: having in practice already tested 1.5 °C warming, busting through the Paris Agreement.

There is also no transition. In energy, there never has been a transition. Fossil fuels are still over 80 per cent of world energy supply,[8] and that is 80 per cent of a much bigger number, as GDP has expanded since 1990. The rest is large hydro, nuclear and conventional biomass, none of which has been built solely for climate reasons, but rather for energy supply, and wind and solar make up the rest.

There was no transition from wood to coal, from coal to oil, or from oil to gas. Every new technology helped to meet the *extra* demand for energy, whilst the existing technologies carried on expanding too. Each new technology has served to increase the demand for energy. More supply has created more demand. Digitalisation, AI, data centres and quantum computing are the new energy-intensive demands of our age. The idea that we are on a transition *from* fossil fuels *to* renewables and that this can be achieved by 2050 remains a fantasy, unless something truly remarkable happens. Even then, even nuclear fusion would take several decades to be built at a scale to meet the ever-increasing total energy demand.

For those in the paradigm, contrary evidence on the effectiveness of the policies they promote gets re-interpreted to make it fit the paradigm's basic assumptions. There are side explanations to reconcile the way the world is with that of the paradigm. Take the fact that the UK has emerged with the highest industrial energy prices in the industrial world. You might expect that this would at least prompt a questioning of why this is the case, and lead to the inconvenient conclusion that perhaps ever-lower costs of energy are not compatible with the 'transition' to wind and solar? Perhaps wind and solar are not cheap after all?

But no, those in the paradigm double down on the 'cheap' argument. It is not, they say, because renewables are expensive, but rather because gas prices are always going to be 'high and volatile'. They conflate a spike (like those caused by the Ukrainian invasion and the attacks on Iran) with trends. And, anyway, even if wind and solar are more expensive now, just around the corner their costs are going to crater, whilst the price of gas will keep going up. Those in the paradigm appeal to the 'S-curve',[9] which purports to give convincing evidence that the price of solar, in particular, is going to fall so that – as was once claimed for nuclear – it will be too cheap to measure. Even if the holy grail of cheaper energy gets repeatedly postponed, faith in its inevitability remains.[10]

To make the cheap energy argument stick, those in the paradigm need to pick a measure of costs that gives them the answer they want to get to. They point to the fact that the *marginal* costs of wind and solar are both close to zero. Indeed, these energy sources do not have marginal costs at all, whereas gas and coal (and oil) do. The wind and the sunshine are free. Yet a moment's reflection should signal that it is not the marginal cost of a solar panel or a wind turbine that determines the system cost.

In the UK, it already takes twice as much capacity to deliver the same energy when the technology comes in small units, is geographically diffuse, has low energy densities, and, critically, is *intermittent*. Intermittency requires batteries and storage, which gas does not, and being decentralised and small scale, it needs a lot more transmission and distribution infrastructure. The result is very different from relying on an S-curve in respect of solar panels and the marginal cost argument. Even the S-curve is questionable – it is an extrapolation of past cost changes to technologies that the paradigm takes as the answers to climate change. There is little explanation of why fossil-fuel prices might not fall a lot, not just because of technology but also because there are vast reserves which are at costs well below the current prices.

The climate community once believed in peak oil – that there are limited oil, gas and coal resources and we are in imminent danger of running out. As the supplies dwindled away, the prices would inevitably rise. It was nonsense, though a large number of otherwise sensible people did in fact advance this hypothesis. The amount of oil, gas and coal that we know about is the amount that it has been worth finding out about. It turns out that there is more than enough to fry the planet many times over, and new fossil-fuel technologies just keep coming: modern fracking and seabed platforms, to name just a couple. Worse, climate change may actually make even more resources accessible, notably the abundant resources of the Arctic, as the ice melts.

The default reaction to any criticism or countervailing view for a paradigm is to re-interpret the claims so that they are compatible with the paradigm.[11] Throughout this book, we will meet repeated examples: in criticisms of net zero territorial carbon production targets; criticisms of the COP processes and outcomes; criticisms of the pollution caused by mining for renewables and refining; criticisms of costs; criticisms about security; and criticisms about the impacts on economic growth.

As these criticisms are examined, I will no doubt condemn myself to the full force of the climate change community, for I am committing the ultimate heresy. My claims are that current policies are not working, that the main policy-related assumptions of the carbon paradigm are wrong, and that the policies advocated will not solve climate change.

The heresy is to suggest that what the carbon community is advocating will not solve the problem. Indeed, some of the policies put forward may actually make matters worse. And in doing so, the political hostility that has grown up will not be assuaged. Repeated claims that renewables can mostly meet energy demands and that they will be cheaper and that bills will consequentially fall towards the marginal or levelised costs of wind and solar make for good speeches and encourage 'progressives' in politics. They get the activists going. But as voters find out that they are not true, their reaction is perfectly predictable and understandable. That is why the net zero consensus, such as it was, has broken down, and not just led by the far right, but now increasingly by the political mainstream.[12]

All, however, is not lost. Having first demolished some of the main foundations and assumptions of the existing paradigm, the ground is cleared to put something better in its place. The starting point is to revisit the core problem – climate change and its causes – rather than take all this for granted. It requires a focus on the 'global' bit and the primary causes of the rises in emissions and the falling sequestration. It requires an understanding that it is not just the US and Europe that are causing climate change and always having in mind the simple fact that it does not matter where a tonne of carbon is emitted or sequestrated. Because it is a global problem, it will be solved (or not) in places like India, China, Indonesia, Brazil and Nigeria. Claiming 'world leadership', as UK and EU politicians do, only works if India, China, Indonesia, Brazil and Nigeria are listening. Why should they bow down to our claimed superior leadership, especially if it brings the highest prices for electricity and deindustrialisation?

Sorting out the causes leads to the next bit. Net zero targets, as constituted by the UN COPs and the national determined contributions (NDCs) and unilaterally by the EU and especially the UK, are the wrong targets. The target should be net zero carbon *consumption*, not net zero carbon production. Focusing on territorial emissions is not just insufficient but can be actually perverse. Remember, it does not matter where the emissions take place. Steel produced in China instead of in the UK or Germany still has emissions, and if it is imported rather than made at home, total emissions are probably higher. Deindustrialisation is not a strategy to address climate change; it does not lead to economic growth and prosperity, but it is very effective in reducing territorial carbon emissions.

As ever, the climate community has a ready-made answer. Net zero carbon territorial emission targets will work if everyone has them and everyone achieves them. Welcome to utopia, not the world we live in. Lots and lots of countries do indeed sign up to NDCs, but signing up is not the same as achieving them. Recall that fossil fuels are still over 80 per cent of total global energy supplies, and the demand for oil, gas and coal is still going up. Peaking of these fossil fuels, if it ever happens, is not a great achievement – it would still leave us with extraordinarily high fossil-fuel emissions. Peaking is still disastrous. If everyone was set the more appropriate carbon consumption target, the goal would also be achieved, but the distribution of burdens would be very different.

Getting the causes sorted out properly and setting a net zero carbon consumption target instead of a net zero carbon territorial production target would change the game. It would also turn the lens onto the carbon footprint of the renewables. Remember all that mining. Remember all the environmental damage being caused. Think of all the energy needed for the refining, and the associated pollution. Take a look at the aerial pictures of the damage to the rainforests from nickel mining in Indonesia. Look at the cobalt mines (and copper mines, which cobalt is associated with) in the Democratic Republic of Congo (DRC). Look at the great environmental horror that is the Bayan Obo mine in Inner Mongolia, and the mines in Yunnan Province in China.[13] Look at the coal mining and burning to make the Chinese solar panels (80 per cent of the world's supply[14]). Look at the disposal of the batteries.

It is hard to escape the conclusion that not only is the paradigm not presenting a very good picture of what is going on, and not providing a credible set of policies, but that working within this paradigm is not a very productive way forward. For those in the climate community who have reached the same conclusion as I have – that we are not cracking the problem and that we are well on the way to 2 °C and probably 3 °C warming this century – one answer is to double down on technology. If we cannot control the emissions, why not bury them? Why not do carbon capture and storage (CCS) and why not do direct air capture and storage (DACS)? Let's manipulate the atmosphere itself to geoengineer carbon concentrations in the atmosphere with a 4 rather than a 5 in front of it, extracting enough carbon and burying it so that we don't reach 500 ppm?

Contemplating geoengineering is a recognition that current policies are not working. The 30 COPs have not dented the rising ppm in the atmosphere and are unlikely to do so. At least it is a start on rethinking the paradigm. But here too it gets dangerous. The search for get-out-of-jail cards leads to some very worrying territories. Injecting sulfur and other chemicals into the upper atmosphere and using solar reflectors could be done unilaterally, and have obvious military purposes. Others get more extreme. SpaceX wants to go to Mars and found a colony there. Whilst there are many who might welcome Elon Musk's departure from this planet, it is an incredibly expensive way of achieving very little for us here on this planet.

There are lots and lots of ideas out there as to how technology might augment the dash for wind and solar. Some might work. It might turn out that solar is too cheap to measure. It might turn out that solar and batteries can be made 'clean'. But it probably won't be soon enough. Which brings us back to an alternative way of looking at the problem and a different, but sometimes overlapping, environmental paradigm. Perhaps the problem is us and our consumption? Perhaps we are living beyond our environmental means? Whilst we can go on advancing our knowledge and ideas and making new discoveries – and hence have a genuine advance in human potential – the conventional economic growth does not cut the mustard.

Carbon consumption as the primary target is a very different way of looking at climate change and it is very radical. The starting point is the polluter-pays principle, and it is us, the consumers, who are the ultimate polluters. The sustainable level of carbon consumption is that consistent with maintaining the climate, which in turn means an overarching target of the ppm in the atmosphere. One admittedly simplistic way to think about this is that, in order to meet this carbon consumption target, there would have to be a carbon tax set at a level necessary to hold to the ppm target, and it would rise and fall according to how well we are doing.

Of course – and it is obvious – a carbon tax is not the only instrument that would be deployed. Research and development (R&D) is a public good and needs subsidising and there are lots of regulatory tools in the box. The best combination emerges by trial and error, but the key point is that they all ultimately cost us – in taxes, in fuel costs, and in the prices we pay for the impact of the regulations. They are all different parts of the polluter – us – paying, and a carbon tax is a neat theoretical way of representing the sum total of these costs.

This approach is advocated in this book. It slices into the conventional carbon paradigm. It has a target for carbon consumption, it has a carbon price, and it impacts on our standard of living. It tempers our enthusiasm for GDP growth without being a no-growth or de-growth approach. Living within our environmental means is a wholly new world for us on this planet. It is something we have never done in the past, except perhaps in small communities where disease, hunger and constrained resources kept our numbers low and life generally short. It does not have to be a hairshirt world. We have great science, great medicines and great information highways.

But it would have its pain too. Ever-expanding cruises, long-distance and resource-intensive tourism, a consumption lifestyle with a trail of plastic and other wastes would be hard to justify, as would extreme wealth and the lifestyles that go with it. The antics of Musk, Mark Zuckerberg, Gates and Jeff Bezos, the new global tycoons, would sit uneasily with the sustainability of consumption.

There would be other payoffs. Climate change is not the only threat humans face. The loss of biodiversity, the pollution of the oceans and the great waterways, and the destruction of the rainforests are all incompatible with the sustainable economy. They would all have to stop too.

You may well say – as many did when I described the sustainable economy in my book *Legacy* – that all this is never going to happen. You may well be right. I fear you are. But the consequences of this are inescapable. It would most likely end very badly for many, perhaps most, of us humans.

1 THERE IS NO TRANSITION

The climate community talk a lot about the 'transition'. But what is this transition? From what to what? How is it going, whatever it is? Is there any prospect that it will be successful? How long will it take?

The sad fact is that so far there is no transition *from* fossil fuels *to* renewables and low-carbon technologies. Nor has there ever been a transition from one major energy source to another. So far, all that has been achieved is that there has been a relatively small contribution from wind and solar towards meeting a growing energy demand. Recall that over 80 per cent still comes from fossil fuels.[1] All the while the total demand for energy rises.

A massive achievement would be for renewables to take up some or even, at the outer edge of the possible, most of the increase in demand for energy by 2050. Meanwhile fossil fuels would still meet the current demand. The 80+ per cent is a share of the total, so as the demand for energy keeps going up, the 80 per cent might fall back whilst overall fossil-fuel burn goes up. This would be consistent with the world still burning at least as much coal, oil and gas in 2050 as today – that's almost 40 billion barrels of oil (over 102 million barrels a day, mbd), almost 9 billion tonnes of coal, and over 4,000 billion cubic metres (bcm) of gas in 2024.

Jean-Baptiste Fressoz, in his brilliant book *More and More and More*, provides the economic history.[2] Until I read his book, I used to think that our expanding utilisation of energy created a transition from manpower to animal (horse power) and then from horse power to coal power, and from coal to oil and then from oil to gas. Fressoz explains why this commonly held view is not correct.

The central role of energy remains. Marx's economic determinism, with technology determining the forms of production, and the forms of production determining classes, and the classes determining political organisation of societies gives a coherent, if simplistic, framework for thinking about how the great spurt in economic growth got us from the end of the eighteenth century to now. This central part played by technology is grounded in energy, not just labour, as Marx believed.

Treating Marx's labour theory of value as a special case of a more general energy theory of value (when labour was a core energy source) and technology as all about the different techniques to harness energy provides a perspective on the current 'energy transition'. Rather than a simple replacement of one technology by another, each is added to the existing ones. Economic history is about finding new and better additional ways of harnessing energy, building on the foundations of existing energy.

In Fressoz's account, the succession of technologies is from wood to coal and then oil. But it is more than this. There is more demand for physical labour now than there has ever been, there is more demand for animal (horse) power than ever, and on top of this, there is more demand for wood for fuel, and more coal demand, and more oil demand and more gas demand. The growth of energy demand, and the compounding of each supply to meet it, provides a lens on economic history and the story of how the human economies first gradually and then rapidly grew. The transformation is in economic growth and output, and it is powered by adding more and more and more energy supply, to borrow the great title of Fressoz's book. It is about to ratchet up yet another gear, as the new demands for energy from digitalisation, AI and eventually quantum computing usher in the age of electricity.

Those who advocate and activate for an energy transition are demanding something much more radical than anything previously witnessed in economic history, and in a remarkably short period of time, measured in decades not centuries or millennia.

What would it really take to get out of wood, coal, oil and gas? This isn't something that activists who support Just Stop Oil or Greta Thunberg appear to give much more than superficial thought to. It is just something they simply demand, and now. Their lack of focus on how this might actually work is understandable, for if they gave any serious thought to the proposition they want to immediately foist on all economies and societies, their demands would crumble in their hands. Almost all of the gas, oil and coal would have to be replaced, as would probably the biomass also, for the reasons set out below.

Getting Out of Wood, Peat and Burning Biomass

Let's take the easy bit: how to get out of wood, which was one of the major fuels of the eighteenth and into the nineteenth century. Imagine just stopping burning wood. This means stopping deliberately burning wood for energy, and also just stopping burning forests for land clearance and agriculture to produce food, with all the associated emissions.

Wood gets burnt for domestic heating as a key input in biomass fuelling of local heating systems, to produce charcoal and to generate electricity. Some of the net zero policies actively promote the burning of wood pellets, on the assumption that burning wood is 'renewable' because the trees re-grow. At the household level, wood is still a key energy for heating and for cooking.

Much of this is a byproduct of forestry, and biomass as a whole makes up around half of the classified renewables within the EU. It is how the EU managed to agree to and achieve its 20 per cent renewables target by 2020 (its simplistic 20-20-2020 targets).[3]

Some of the biomass is the use of plants and plant extracts to create fuels directly. The most absurd is the use of palm oil to create 'renewable' fuels for transport. The EU even went so far as to set targets for biofuels for transport, in the full knowledge that much of this was from palm oil. An added absurdity is that a lot of the palm oil is grown on cleared rainforests, some of it on peats and fragile soils. The emissions released from the peat and soils were conveniently not taken into account in the claimed status of 'renewable'.

Biomass more generally is widely advocated as a way of creating sustainable fuels. The most egregious is 'sustainable aviation fuel' (SAF). This takes 'waste products' like chip frying oils and adds biofuels, including on a large scale, corn and sugar cane ethanol to mix with fossil fuels. There is now a substantial scientific literature which questions whether any biofuels can be beneficial in reducing emissions.[4]

'Renewable' energy generated via anaerobic digesters (ADs) is just one of the questionable uses of biomass. Whilst the idea of using animal and other wastes to produce methane is a good one, growing crops to *create* waste for the AD plants requires fertilisers and machinery, and results in carbon loss from soils and indeed often loss of the soils themselves. Maize is grown intensively for this purpose.[5]

Taken together, modern solid biomass accounts for around 3.5 per cent of global energy,[6] whilst traditional biomass from wood charcoal, crop residues from cooking and heating makes up about 6 per cent, roughly matching the contributions from wind and solar.

Then there is peat, between biomass and conventional fossil fuels. Peat delivers household heat and is even used to generate electricity.[7] It is widely used in horticulture. The direct emissions from peat burning for heat and power are now a small contribution to global energy, but the emissions from exposed peat are not. Peat fires are also the consequence of land clearance in the name of renewables, as in the palm oil case above. Some of these fires, for example in Indonesia, are in effect in perpetuity. Though there is a decline in direct peat burning in Europe, the combined emissions from peat fires probably outweigh this. To claim a global transition from peat is at best only credible if a narrow measure is taken.

Getting Out of Coal – Still an Ambition

The argument that the key to the transition is to start by getting out of coal has received great attention, but proved much harder to deliver, as the global coal burn keeps going up, notably in India, but still marginally in China. Globally, there is no transition away from coal in absolute terms.

But haven't some countries – notably, the UK – achieved this?

There are two parts to this: the exit from coal generation of electricity in specific countries and the exit from coal in consumption, via its burning in other countries that then export finished goods to those countries that claim to have exited coal. The UK fulfils the first, but not the second.

The UK claims to have got out of coal for electricity generation, which it has indeed done, replacing the coal generation mainly with gas (and some wind and solar). But has the UK really got out of coal? Does it consume less coal than it once did?

Some coal is still burnt in industry in the UK, notably in steel production. This is an easy problem to solve: just close steel production using coal in the UK. It is indeed being solved: the last blast furnaces are on the verge of economic collapse and closure.

Does this mean that the UK is stopping consuming steel? No, of course not. In fact, the imports of steel have been rising sharply in recent years.[8] The imported steel is manufactured in EU countries, Turkey and China using coal, lots of it. Germany continues with steel production, relying increasingly on imported hard coal, whilst continuing in 2024 to use its brown and hard coal for generating over 20 per cent of its electricity.[9]

Now consider the coal incorporated in the production of materials, cement, chemicals, paper and textiles, components and machinery used in UK industry, and in the products produced overseas for sale in the UK. How much coal is embedded in products sold in the UK? More embarrassingly, how much coal is burnt to make a solar panel or a wind turbine in China, then installed in the UK as part of a 'zero-emissions' technology?

These questions are rarely raised and never answered. Yet the claim to 'have got out of coal' depends on the answers. To be clear, the UK has not got out of coal, though it has got out of using it for electricity generation in the UK.

Now think what it would take to 'Just Stop Coal'. Coal would no longer be used for electricity generation, and would no longer be used to make steel, cement, paper and textiles, aluminium and for heating. This is never going to happen in a decade or two – if ever. Coal's advantage is that it is cheap, widely dispersed and secure. These advantages are not going to disappear for decades. Hence, no transition from coal is on the horizon globally.

Just Stopping Oil

Oil is ubiquitous in our economy. Not only is it a core input in manufacturing and in transport, but it (and gas) provides the petrochemicals embedded in plastics, clothing and most consumer goods. It is embedded in agriculture too, via fertilisers, pesticides and machinery.

Those who wish to Just Stop Oil presumably mean that we should just stop plastics, most transport, lubricants, heating, asphalt, most agricultural pesticides, fertilisers, cosmetics and fuel additives. No doubt we could do without some of these, and could use gas and coal instead, but a world without plastics is a different matter.

Plastics now account for the main source of growth in demand for oil. This increase in demand widely exceeds the decrease in demand for oil for transport. Although transport is being electrified, this will not result in a terminal decline for oil. Indeed, gas is potentially a bigger threat to oil demand, since it can produce the electricity for transport and the petrochemicals. But, even here, it is important to bear in mind what a fabulous form of energy oil is.

Oil is high-density, easily transported and stored, and there is a global infrastructure to produce, transport and store it. There is lots and lots of oil, and the sources are multiplying, with Brazil and Canada having grand (and credible) plans to become fossil-fuel superpowers. We are never going to run out of oil, and notwithstanding temporary spikes, such as the disruption to exports of both oil and oil-based products through the Strait of Hormuz during the 2026 Iran war, the trend is towards oil getting cheaper.

Anyone serious about a transition would need a credible strategy to get out of plastics, or to switch to alternative low-carbon ways of making them. Yet there is no consensus at the global level to get out of oil, and attempts to negotiate a global treaty have failed, not surprisingly.[10] Hence, no transition from oil is on the horizon globally.

Getting into Nuclear

Nuclear was once going to be too cheap to measure. It was to be the new miracle energy, superabundant and able to power the world. So thought its pioneers. The military nuclear side would be contained, and civil nuclear would give very dense energy that was also superabundant. The age of coal and oil was going to give way to the new age of nuclear power.

It has never lived up to its billing. Nuclear comprises less than 10 per cent of world energy supplies (as at 2024).[11] It towers over renewables, but it does not even outdo hydroelectricity.

Why? The answer is mundane and incredibly important in challenging the various forms of the transition arguments. It is also simple; nuclear turns out to be expensive – indeed, very expensive, even before considering the public concerns about very low probabilities of bad accidents and the links to nuclear weapons.

The risks of accidents and the costs are correlated. Accidents tend to come every decade or so (at least those known about and not hushed up, as, for example, in the former Soviet Union). There was the Windscale disaster in the UK (1957), Three Mile Island in the US (1979), Chernobyl in Ukraine (1986) and Fukushima in Japan (2011). To these, known accidents also include Kyshtym (1957) in Russia, SL-1 (1961) in the US and Chalk River (1952 and 1958) in Canada. Each time the consequence has been to review safety and to re-double the investment required to reduce risks even further. It has been a one-way ratchet on safety and hence a one-way route to higher costs.[12]

The two countries that built nuclear power stations at scale – France and Japan – did not manage to break the cost barriers to a level sufficient to give a decisive competitive advantage. France built 52 similar reactors, at one time having six simultaneously under construction. Japan built over 50. Russia and now China are the other two major nuclear developers. It helps both that their environmental and safety standards are widely regarded as lower, and hence costs are lower.

It is not the risk of nuclear that halted a great expansion of it. It was not the leading environmental non-governmental organisations (NGOs) – like Greenpeace (which was anti-nuclear before it was green)[13] – that stopped nuclear. It was simply costs. Striving to be a clean-energy superpower,

UK new nuclear is about the most expensive in the world. A twin reactor costs around £40–£50 billion (in 2025 prices). That is a staggering £15 billion per gigawatt.

Even in countries like Germany, which exited nuclear, this was made easier because new nuclear was not cost competitive. The coming of cheap gas as the preferred fuel for electricity generation did for nuclear anyway – at least until now and the considerations about climate change.

Long before gas became the fuel of choice for electricity generation, and before it was even permitted to be used for this purpose in 1990 in the US and Europe, the oil price fell back, rather than rising, as anticipated by the architects of these great nuclear programmes in the 1970s. The argument for getting out of oil was that it was expected to get ever more expensive. In fact, in real terms (with two brief periods of exceptions), it got cheaper, whilst the costs of nuclear went up.

It is the same wishful thinking that now dominates the climate community and the advocates of net zero: assuming now that both gas and oil prices are going to be higher and volatile. Since the Russian invasion of Ukraine, gas prices in Europe have gradually fallen, and by the end of 2025, they were 90 per cent lower than when Russia invaded Ukraine, and in 2025 fell by 40 per cent in nominal terms. In real terms, they had fallen even further, back to or below the levels of the past decade up until the end of the Iran war. In the US, gas has become cheap as a result of the advances in fracking, and so plentiful as to enable the export of liquefied natural gas (LNG) to make up for the Russian shortfall in supplies as sanctions bit and the Nord Stream gas pipelines from Russia to Germany were blown up, and again with the Iran war, as the price rose, supply responded.

Will nuclear now finally deliver on its promise to take on the mantle of oil, gas and coal, at least in generating electricity? Will it facilitate a transition? To do this, it has to be seriously cost competitive, even after the intermittency of solar and wind are taken into account. There is significant new investment in China, India and South Korea, and possibly the US. But it takes time, and it has to first offset the retirements of old nuclear power stations. Currently, there are just over 400 reactors in the world with an average capacity of just under 1 GW. Over half of these are due to be retired by 2050.[14] Over 70 new reactors are under construction, at an average of just over 1 GW each, 37 of which are in China.[15] What this means is that the total global nuclear capacity may struggle to remain constant through to 2050.

Small modular reactors (SMRs) may come to the rescue, but they and conventional large reactors will take another couple of decades to make much impact. Fusion at scale is at best a long-term possibility.

There is no global transition from fossil fuels to nuclear.

Rolling These Arguments Over into the Claimed Transition to Renewables

As with nuclear, so with renewables when it comes to claims about their cost advantages. According to many in the climate community and especially the activists among them, renewables are going to be so much cheaper than gas that rolling them out is the route not only to 'energy independence' and getting out of the gas price rises and volatility, triggered by the Ukraine and Iran wars, but also to lower consumer bills and greater industrial competitiveness. The aspiring great clean-energy superpowers, like the UK, claim that they will be the destination of choice for energy-intensive industries of the future. Those stuck with fossil fuels, like the US, will lose out, and with relatively high energy costs will find themselves stuck with low economic growth and decline. All the new energy-intensive industries like AI and data centres will consequently want to get out of the assumed to be very expensive fossil fuels in the US.

It is nonsense, and extremely expensive nonsense. As will be explained in Chapter 4, the system costs of renewables are expensive, and their relative system-price position is declining rather than improving. Renewables, once properly analysed on a system-cost basis, and hence when firm power is taken into account, are not cheap in many developed countries, and that is why they need lots of system subsidies. Writing the obituaries for coal, oil and gas in favour of renewables, as with nuclear, is at best premature. Because nuclear and renewables are unlikely to be cheaper than fossil fuels, the incentive will be to go on using fossil fuels in the context of rising demand for energy, and specifically electricity. That, indeed, is what is happening.

More Renewables and Nuclear Push Down the Cost of Oil

Think through what would happen were a genuine transition away from fossil fuels to be on the horizon. Imagine if the shares of fossil fuels fell precipitously. There would be a fight to produce 'the last barrel', the last bcm of gas, and the last tonne of coal. Oil production would shift down the supply curve to concentrate on the cheapest oil in the Middle East, the price would fall, and eventually it would end up at, say, $10 a barrel or probably less in today's prices.

The implication is pretty obvious: the more successful the roll-out of renewables and nuclear, the greater the relative price advantage to the fossil fuels. The only way to stop this killing off any transition would be to impose a carbon tax on the remaining production, and a very high one. The greater the fall in output for oil (and gas and coal), the higher the carbon tax would have to be to compensate for the gain in fossil-fuel competitiveness.

How would this be enforced? And how would it work? We will return to carbon taxes in Chapter 10, but for now note that it would probably be effective only if most countries had gone hard for their own net zero carbon consumption targets, and could rely on their economies' independence from the goods and services from those remaining refuseniks.

How likely is this? Not very. It would have to include China, India, Indonesia, Russia, the US, Brazil, Saudi Arabia and the Gulf States, assuming that the EU was still going hard down its renewables pathway (by no means a certainty).

Our Current Predicament

There is as yet no transition. To Just Stop Oil, Just Stop Gas and Just Stop Coal by 2050 would be extremely radical. It is something way beyond human experience to date. Replacing even some of current oil, gas and coal in the energy mix – say from more than 80 per cent to 20 per cent – would be a massive shock to world economies. Look at what the change from even a temporary closure of the Strait of Hormuz in 2026 did to world economies. It would take a political earthquake to just stop oil, with dramatic impacts on standards of living.

Climate realism is not just about how we have failed so far to make a dent in the carbon concentration in the atmosphere, but also about what would have to happen for the ppm to even stop going up. And this is before the further element to climate realism: the great surge in demand for energy we are now confronting.

2 AN EXPLOSION OF ENERGY DEMAND

There is one other possible way a transition might materialise: that there is no great increase in the demand for energy, and in particular electricity, and that the world's economies decouple GDP growth from energy demand. That really would be a radical break from the last couple of centuries or more.

It is a possibility with a long pedigree of advocacy, propounded by those who mistook a 'decoupling' of energy demand and economic growth in the EU and especially the UK, post-1980, which reflected a relative shift in the composition of production (and deindustrialisation), for a global decoupling.[1] Whilst the demand for energy did fall back in the UK, globally it carried on going up. The error is compounded by assuming that energy efficiency reduces demand, whereas it lowers the relative cost of energy and hence increases demand. Two big mistakes: one born of hubris and the assumption that the UK and the EU lead the world, and that others would follow; and the second just an intellectual error.

Global energy demand currently rises at just over 2 per cent per annum, up from around 1.5 per cent per annum in the 2010s.[2] The uptick is driven by China, India, Indonesia and Vietnam – not the UK and the EU. It is about 1 per cent less than the growth in global GDP, at around 3 per cent. That energy is used for making virtually everything, and includes buildings, construction, steel, heating, petrochemicals and plastics, alongside the conventional transport, electricity and machinery powered by fossil fuels. This is where the 80+ per cent of the world's energy supplies from fossil fuels go.

Let's now take a look at what the main drivers of energy demand going forward might be, most or all of which would have to be met by renewables and nuclear even before the transition away from fossil fuels kicks in.

The Electrification of Almost Everything: A Wall of New Demands

The new game in energy is all about electricity. It is the demand for electricity that will drive the growth of energy demand over the coming decades and probably exceed the growth rate of global GDP. Global electricity demand is growing at 4 per cent per annum.[3] More electricity does not mean less fossil fuels. That's a common mistake the climate community makes, even where more electricity comes from renewables and nuclear. The growth of new demands for electricity will most likely be additional to the existing demands for energy, not substitutes for them. That is why there may not be a transition, even as the share of electricity rises. It is a rising share of a bigger, and potentially much bigger, number.

There are multiple ways in which the demands for electricity (and energy too) are likely to rise, and on a scale perhaps never seen in the past, as multiple energy-intensive technologies come to the fore, and ironically some of them because of climate change.

Three, largely new ones, stand out: advances in information technologies, and the associated demands of AI, data centres and in due course quantum computing; air conditioning and cooling; and desalination. The first is an underlying radical technological change of the twenty-first century and is a general-purpose set of technologies – technologies that change everything. The second is the result of increased wealth (richer people like to moderate heat in summer as well as increase it in winter) and climate change;

and the third is the result of the scarcity of fresh water, in part driven by climate change and in part by a desire to make the deserts bloom with new cities and irrigation. So far, the climate community has not come out with Just Stop AI, Just Stop Data Centres, Just Stop Air Conditioning, and Just Stop Desalination.

In addition to these new increases in energy demand via electricity, there are substitutions. Transport is an obvious example. There will be more EVs. There may be more heat pumps for heating. Yet these will not all be powered by renewables and nuclear electricity. There is a long tail in fossil fuels generating electricity for decades to come, notably in the countries with the highest GDP growth. There may be more gas-generated electricity and less coal burnt, though even here this is about absolute coal burn, not the relative share. It is also true for data centres, AI and for air conditioning and desalination. Using electricity does not mean decarbonising; that requires decarbonisation of electricity generation, and that is a long-term project, and it is why these new sources for increases in energy demand do not mean less aggregate emissions.

The New Sources of Electricity Demand

Data Centres, Digitalisation, AI and Quantum Computing

As you read this book, you may wonder whether these are actually my words, or whether they are generated by AI. It is worth thinking about this, just to get a handle on how big a technological revolution is under way and how advanced it already is, before considering where it might go. There are 'influencers' with hundreds of thousands of followers who are actually AI creations. Gradually almost everything is being replicated through AI, and you and I are increasingly unable to detect the AI from the real. Indeed, some would say that the real is AI.

As with the overall demand for energy, again you ain't seen nothing yet. The EU, the US, China, India, Japan and Taiwan are all competing to be the 'world's AI powerhouses'. AI is as big or bigger than the invention of the printing press. It transforms not just how we do what we do, but increasingly who and what we are. Marry it up with synthetic biology and the interface between the computer and our brains begins to blur and even merge. We can process information at an order-of-magnitude greater speed, we can have all the information at our fingertips, the stuff of life itself can be synthetically matched with AI, and, frighteningly, humans can be significantly improved upon. The common currency is data, and data is the valuable asset of the future which technology is focused upon.

There is, as always with great technical change, a lot of hype and excess valuations, fortunes made and stock market bubbles. Inevitably, there is irrational exuberance.[4] The bubbles may burst, as they did in the railway mania of the nineteenth century and the dotcom bubble at the end of the twentieth century, but that does not make the new technologies go away.

Now the energy bit. AI is fantastically energy intensive, because data processing is energy intensive. The cost of energy is a constraint on the development of data centres (and especially their location), but even as data processing becomes more energy efficient, demand for energy from data centres is likely to go up not down. Thus, when you read about data centres becoming more energy efficient, do not conclude, as much of the press (and many in the climate community) do, that their impact on climate change will be lowered. What lowers the impact is if they are supplied by large-scale firm-power energy. That isn't intermittent wind. It is gas and nuclear electricity. It could be solar, but only if located in solar-rich parts of the world, like North Africa, somewhere which, for other reasons, is not going to be the location of choice in the near future. It could be geothermal energy, and Iceland is an obvious candidate, but again the locations are not just about the energy source. AI is doing for electricity demand what steel did for the demand for coal in the nineteenth and twentieth centuries.

How big is the demand from data centres going to be? It is at about 1.5 per cent of global electricity demand now. The IEA says that it will be 3 per cent by 2030 in its Base Case (and 4.4 per cent in its Lift-Off Case), making an annual growth rate of around 10–15 per cent.[5] In the US, it is already around 4–6 per cent of electricity demand and may rise to around 11–12 per cent by 2030.[6] That is the direct estimate for the data centres. But they are not in isolation from the uses of the data, and hence the outputs of the data centres. Data centres enable lots and lots of extra demand for the services that AI provides, and these lead to you and me searching through AI apps and using lots of electricity in the process.

The AI developments are happening so fast that predictions, scenarios and forecasts are highly uncertain except in the very short run – and 2030 is very short term. Think of the planning permissions, the grid connections, the water supplies and the construction lead times. Most of the data centre additionality comes after 2030 not before, and many of the applications of AI (and hence their energy demands) are yet to be discovered, as the technology rolls out across all of industry and governments, and in our daily lives. And there are the military demands too.

What all this means is that the projected 3–4 per cent by 2030 is probably only the beginning, and that, in the 2030s, demand will most likely rise considerably. AI in the wider sense could require 10 per cent of electricity demand by then.

How is all this demand for electricity from data centres going to be met? At present, there is a scurrying around for electricity generation. Old nuclear plants (like Three Mile Island) are being refurbished,[7] old coal plants are being brought back on stream, and gas is the big generation source. Already in the US, rising demand for coal to meet electricity demands has contributed to the rising global coal burn. The search for grid infrastructure connections and the desire to avoid all the policy costs of the intermittent renewables lead some to try to tap into direct gas supplies and hence go down the on-site, own-generation routes. Further out there are link-ups with nuclear SMR developers, but these are mid- to late-2030s generation providers, if all goes well with the technology.

As with the wider argument about no transition from fossil fuels, strip back from the PR and the claimed green virtues of Big Tech, and see a continued increase in the demand for gas and, to a lesser extent, coal to power the data centres.

Think about this in the following way. Were all the data centres to be powered by solar and wind, with the necessary back-up to render the intermittency into firm power, how much more solar and wind and batteries and other storage would be required to add to the existing systems by, say, 2040 just to meet this *extra* source of demand? If it becomes 10 per cent of the total electricity demand, and if no coal or gas (or oil) is utilised, then that is more than three times the current global energy supplies that these renewables currently provide and before the other increases in demand have to be met by renewables, and even if there is some substitution away from oil, gas and coal as well. It is important not to confuse energy and electricity as being equivalent, but then much of the global economy is supposed to electrify over the period too.

This gives just a flavour of what AI and data centres mean for the demand side. Now add in quantum computing as the elephant in the room – a complete transformation of computing – and from what might seem in a couple of decades' time a primitive binary digital approach. Who knows what the demands might be? Indeed, that's the point: any strategy to be a 'world leader in AI', as well as a 'clean-energy superpower', has to have a strategy to rapidly expand electricity generation over and above current forecasts, *and* to do so with only renewables and nuclear *and* in a cost-competitive way. The challenges of doing this and having a genuine transition are immense, even before the cheap energy bit is addressed. So far, cheap US firm gas (and cheap coal) has a massive cost advantage over expensive intermittent wind and solar in the UK and the EU, both generally and to drive the US dominance in AI.

Robots and the Digitalisation of Production

AI will increase the attraction and efficiency of replacing labour with robots, and robots are digital, relying on electricity. The process of introducing robots is already well under way. The car industry is a good example. But there is a long way yet to go. Agriculture is ripe for robotics, as it intensifies production and vehicles become hands-free.

The big targets include those industries that remain labour intensive. The way to think about this process of digitalisation is to ask whether there are *any* currently labour-intensive industries where production cannot be switched from human labour to AI and robots. In addition to agriculture, globally lots of textiles, construction, hospitality, tourism, mining and food processing remain labour intensive. Developed countries with declining and ageing populations have the biggest incentives to digitalise, and that now includes China (which has the greatest take-up of robots). The domain of genuine personal services that require a face-to-face person are getting smaller and smaller, and avatars can impersonate in many circumstances.

These trends have massive social and political consequences. Our concern here is with what they mean for the demand for energy. There are two parts: the overall demand for energy and the dominance of electricity as the vector of that energy. Added to this, there is a third consideration: the extent to which these new demands can be flexible or require firm power and hence can't tolerate the handicap or otherwise that intermittency creates.

A core feature of digitalisation of economies is the greater importance of security of supplies, as the cost of interruptions goes up. A digital economy, reliant on fibre networks, is 'always on'. Banking, the internet, AI server engines and the media have become massively interdependent, and hence the priority, as with AI directly, is for continuous electricity supplies. Neither wind nor solar can meet this without large-scale storage, and even then only for short durations. Cyber networks are becoming the critical infrastructures upon which everything else depends. As witnessed with the power cut in Spain and Portugal in April 2025, interruptions bring almost everything in a modern economy to a sudden halt. The banking system seizes up, people have to resort to paper and coin-based cash, and, as the internet goes down, hospitals, schools and other essential activities cease to function. Mobile networks are vulnerable, making even the most basic communications difficult. Industry more generally is more reliant on robots and electric-powered production. Even for restaurants and food outlets, without a payment system these stop too. Gone are the days when power cuts represented temporary inconveniences. An always-on economy relies significantly on firm power to generate electricity – i.e. nuclear, gas and coal. Renewables are additional, but not stand-alone.

Some argue that AI-enabled robotics leads to greater energy efficiency and hence may reduce demand. As discussed above, this is a flawed logic. Yes, robotics has the potential to greatly increase energy efficiency, not just directly, but also in the ways in which smart grids and electricity systems operate. But, no, this does not reduce electricity demand; it increases it. By how much? It is near impossible to come up with a credible forecast. Much better to envisage high- and low-penetration scenarios, disaggregated for different industries.

It is a question of how long it takes, rather than whether it happens. In developing countries, imagine the impact on agriculture, and specifically the new intensive agricultures promoted by China and others. Consider the transformation from labour-intensive and costly peasant farming in Brazil, say, to vast monocultures of soya beans and sugar cane. The costs plummet, the yields rise. These in turn provide the inputs to intensive large-scale indoor farming of cattle (US) and pigs (China). This increases household incomes (because the costs of food fall) and this in turn increases consumption, which increases the demand for energy. It is a multiplier effect through economies.

Air Conditioning

Many of the dire predictions about the impacts of climate change are the result of applying assumed increases in temperature and the number of heatwaves against existing technologies to cope with heat. These predictions leave out the possibility that almost any part of the world can, in theory, be made habitable if it has air conditioning (and water, which we will come to shortly).

Let's take an example. Think about the Neom city project that Saudi Arabia is developing by the desert shores of the Red Sea.[8] This is not an obvious place for humans to live. But the intention is that they will. How? By essentially being indoors, in air-conditioned surroundings. How is this possible? Because of abundant energy.

We are used to a world where heating is needed to live in northern latitudes, at least in winter. We heat our cars, our houses, our offices and our shops (this last category often leaving the doors open). We even heat the outdoor spaces of restaurants and pubs, and in our gardens. Domestic heating alone uses far more energy in the UK than electricity. It takes up over 60 per cent of household energy use. More energy flows through the gas pipes than through the electricity network.

Now imagine a much hotter world, where, instead of heating, we use cooling. This is already a problem for the tropics. Now shift the latitudes north and increase the temperature through climate change. Imagine how much extra cooling will be needed, and whether the consequent reduction in heating offsets this.

This even extends to air-conditioned indoor agriculture, for example for dairy cows.[9]

Desalination

One of the highlighted news items for the climate community is the heatwaves and the spectre of droughts. The world's stretched freshwater supplies are already under ever-greater strain, and with climate change some will run out. As an example of geoengineering, Iran in 2025 was so desperate for water that it engaged in very large-scale cloud seeding. Yet this is the blue planet, with most of the surface covered in water. It is not lack of water, but rather the lack of the right sort of water in the right places.

There are several possible responses, including reducing water usage and storing more water. But one stands out offering the possibility of practically infinite supplies – desalination. It helps that the world's population increasingly lives in cities and many of these are on the coast. Large-scale desalination might become the water supply of choice for these cities. Indeed, it probably will, and already desalination provides for about 300 million people, most of whom are in the Middle East and North Africa.[10]

These numbers are pretty small so far, against what might be coming. Desalination is growing at around a rate of 10 per cent per annum globally, and in the Middle East it already accounts for around 10 per cent of electricity demand.[11] There are all sorts of environmental issues associated with desalination. From a climate perspective, it is all about energy demand, and specifically electricity demand to carry out reverse osmosis, the conventional technology. The process of desalination is basically salt water plus energy, lots of energy.

Desalination adds another factor to the overall growth in the demand for electricity and for energy, although it may have one advantage over data centres and AI: it might not need firm power. There is debate about how efficient intermittent desalination can be.[12] If it can be without serious cost implications, then it can utilise solar, and the places where desalination is most needed are areas where there is a lot of sunshine. Desalination could then be powered by large-scale solar panel farms. These need lots of land and come with the environmental pollution of the solar supply chains.

The Electrification of Existing Industries

Green Steel

All of the above are *additional* to the other areas of fast growth in the demand for electricity. Faced with policy pressures on climate change, many energy-intensive industries that have traditionally relied upon coal and gas are trying to use electricity instead. Steel is an obvious example. 'Green steel' cannot easily match some conventional steel products (such as high-strength alloys) and is very expensive relative to conventional steel. It mainly uses recycled inputs rather than primary iron ore. The electricity can come via electrolysis, as it does for making 'green hydrogen'. Not only is this energy intensive, but the losses from generation to the finished products tend to be very high. After all the enthusiasm that green hydrogen was going to be the way energy-intensive industries decarbonised, the bubble burst in 2025. Most hydrogen is not in any event 'green' but 'blue', made from natural gas.

Beyond steel lie the even more challenging territories of cement, petrochemicals, fertilisers and aluminium; all very hard to electrify. Yet, for a transition, they must.

Transport

Next up is transport and its demand for electricity. EVs are coming, primarily for cars, but gradually more widely, as battery-powered trucks and trains come on stream and even short-haul flights go electric. Having briefly been the technology of choice at the outset of the auto industry, and then wiped out by the internal combustion engine, EVs are a century later finally coming into their own. Most of the focus is on the scale, cost and availability of batteries and charging facilities.

The extra electricity required for transport is argued to be modest because it is assumed that the transport batteries will interact with the electricity grids and distribution systems, charging at night and even providing peaking services back to the grid in daytime. Where there are battery-swapping technologies, this might be possible, but for the rest, not only is a sophisticated smart-meter system needed, but also the drivers need to be willing to risk insufficient power at night and trust the operators to ensure that their cars are charged to go to work in the morning.[13]

So far, lack of trust in the charging systems has been a major obstacle to the take-up of EVs in developed countries, adding to the cost premium and running costs such as tyres (given the weight of the vehicles) and the difficulty of repairing damage as opposed to writing off vehicles, in turn leading to higher insurance premiums. Not surprisingly, the targets for banning non-EV car sales in the EU and also the UK have come under pressure and are being gradually rolled back.

That is in the developed world. EVs promise a great boost in the demand for cars in developing countries, and it is the growth of electric cars in Sub-Saharan Africa, Latin America, India and Indonesia which will in turn boost the demand for electricity. This boom in extra car demand adds to extra electricity demand. A transition requires that all this extra electricity comes from renewables and nuclear, and that the existing fossil-fuel-powered vehicles are also phased out globally. It would therefore be fair to assume that the electrification of transport will add to electricity demand.

Increasing GDP and Energy: Will the Demand for Energy Just Keep Going Up?

It was once fashionable to argue that GDP growth was being decoupled from growth in energy demand, and that GDP growth was being decoupled from carbon emissions, just as it was once very fashionable to argue that peak oil was just around the corner (and peak coal, but not peak gas yet).

These fashions had their origins in the great OPEC (Organization of the Petroleum Exporting Countries) oil shocks in the 1970s. These showed how vulnerable developed economies were to oil prices, and led politicians and policymakers (and academics, who should have known better) to see the future as ever-rising, fossil-fuel prices, inducing a sharp contraction of GDP growth. As late as 2014, peak oil was widely thought to be imminent, and the gas crisis in Europe following the Russian invasion of Ukraine (and the price spike with the Iran war) led politicians to predict high and volatile gas prices, and hence to claim that the route to cheaper relative (as well as absolute) energy lay in accelerating the 'getting out of gas'.

Associated with the peak oil and later the gas panics was a significant change in the structure of the UK and EU economies. The relatively high energy prices in the EU did significant damage to its economies and especially to its energy-intensive industries. For these – and other – reasons, the UK and the EU began the long road to deindustrialisation post the last hurrah of the OPEC price shocks, which came with the Iranian Revolution in 1979.

As EU economies switched from manufacturing to services, and especially as the UK made the most dramatic switches, it looked like GDP and energy demand had decoupled. This encouraged the fashion of the time – to believe that the two had decoupled. We could have more and more GDP with less extra energy. Lower demand for energy meant lower emissions, and hence that the territorial carbon emissions could come down. This was the origin of the claim that the UK was leading the world in decarbonisation. It was nonsense, disguised in the offshoring of manufacturing, but since it fitted the UK politicians' inflated views of the UK's place in the world, and because it fitted with the emerging climate community's preferences, it stuck around for a while and became a conventional wisdom. To some in the climate community, it still is.

It was an illusion on so many dimensions, and it was at times delusional. Recall it is global energy demand and its relationship with global GDP that matters for climate change. The 'break' in the established relationship between energy demand and GDP growth was a product of the times, especially in the UK and the EU – industrial decline, high fossil-fuel prices and the growth of services.

The UK was on the extreme of these impacts. Following the end of the Second World War, it had witnessed 30 years of GDP growth at around 3 per cent per annum with an associated 7 per cent annual increase in electricity demand. In the 1970s it was still building power stations to meet the 7 per cent pa growth in electricity demand expected in the 1980s.[14]

But then, eerily similar to today, the oil price fell back down again and stayed there through the late 1980s and the 1990s, with a brief blip around the first Gulf War in 1991. Suddenly, the UK had excess electricity-generating capacity for all that demand that did not materialise, as a deindustrialising economy exacerbating the surpluses. Whilst the believers kept claiming that peak oil was coming, what was in fact happening was the coming of shale oil and gas in the US, emerging after the turn of the century.

Whilst there would be a sharp rise in oil prices up to 2014, they fell back again, but into a world where the US is now the largest oil producer in the world and an exporter of gas, whereas once it had been assumed that Qatar's LNG would be needed for the US to import (and for which Qatar developed it). Now Qatar's LNG heads east to China, India and Southeast Asia.

Why does all this matter? For two reasons: the relationship between GDP and the demand for energy is most likely going to be 'normal' in the future, and hence closely correlated; and falling fossil-fuel prices, especially in the US, may be a source of increased demand for energy. The correlation may be re-established, but not necessarily on a one-to-one basis. It may return to the pre-1980 world of energy demand running ahead of GDP.

All of this brings us to a sobering possibility. GDP may be the ultimate driver of the demand for energy, and if GDP powers ahead, so will energy demand. We will be running uphill just to meet the increased GDP with renewables but won't be decarbonising the core GDP. We may be burning at least as much, or more, fossil fuels in 2050, as well as generating lots of low-carbon electricity to meet the additional demands, from data centres, AI, air conditioning and cooling, desalination and transport. Decarbonising GDP is a much taller order than decarbonising additional electricity demand to meet these new additional production activities.

How much might GDP grow in the rest of this century? The answer is determined by the power of compounding growth rates. If world GDP growth continues at the current rate of, say, 3 per cent per annum for the next 75 years, by 2100 world GDP will be nearly six times bigger. This means that there will be the equivalent of nearly five more global economies added to the existing one. If global GDP grows at 4 per cent, it will be 24 times larger than today.

Now ask yourself: what are the chances that an economy six or even 24 times bigger will use less than the 100 mbd oil used now, burn less gas than now and less coal than now? It is not impossible, but it needs massive and extremely rapid technological progress. If it is powered by renewables, it would take an extraordinarily large number of solar panels and wind farms. Nuclear might do it, but it would need to be on an enormous scale.

This GDP growth is not uniformly distributed. At present some of the fastest-growing economies are in Sub-Saharan Africa (over 4 per cent per annum), countries that also have the fastest-growing populations, India (at around 6.5 per cent), followed by Southeast Asian economies, like Indonesia (5.5 per cent), Vietnam (6.5 per cent) and the Philippines (5.5 per cent). At 7 per cent GDP, an economy doubles in ten years. All very possible for any or all of the above. That is what China did from 1980 to recently – its economy doubled four times.

If the demand for energy and the growth of GDP are correlated and not decoupled, then it begs a question: should the climate community start with GDP as the cause of the demand for energy and ask whether a global growth rate of GDP of, say, 3 per cent or more is compatible with mitigating climate change? Won't it lead to both more emissions and more destruction of sequestration capabilities? This leads to an awesome central challenge but also a way out, however unpalatable. It would mean that we would have to concentrate on sustainable economic growth, not GDP growth.

In the meantime, a host of politicians are trumpeting green growth as the route to GDP growth, and not least the UK as the 'world leader' on climate change and a country aiming to be a clean-energy superpower. That many in the climate community do not see the tension here – especially when that tension is denied by a left-of-centre government – is an indication of the paradigm overruling the evidence. Those on the right see net zero as an obstacle to GDP growth. They see net zero as increasing the cost of energy and, because they want GDP growth as their overriding objective, they want to end the dash for more wind and solar.

It is truly remarkable that the left and the right agree about the GDP objective, and yet radically diverge on the role of renewables as a cause or an obstacle to economic growth. At present, the right are correct in identifying the tension, and, in this, the fact that the UK has the highest electricity prices for industry in the developed world supports their position. Some on the right go much further, dismissing climate change as a 'hoax', as Trump does. They point to the emissions that are rising elsewhere and, if anything, the net zero targets for territorial emissions make matters worse by incentivising the outsourcing of energy-intensive manufacturing.

What is missing is any alternative strategy to address climate change. It will not go away. For both the left and the right, the problem starts with GDP growth, rather than sustainable economic growth. The outcomes for the climate under both left and right policies may end up being roughly the same, howbeit that the left's policies produce higher electricity prices and the right's lower prices.

Jevon's Law and the Energy Efficiency Argument

The underlying rationale for those who believed that energy demand could be decoupled from GDP growth is that new technologies with greater energy efficiency would lower energy demand. It was always nonsense, and it remains so. It takes only a little thought to recognise that an increase in energy efficiency is equivalent to a reduction in the relative price of energy. If it takes fewer units of energy to keep your house at 20 °C in winter, then unless the price of those units has gone up, demand for energy will rise. In economic terms, a fall in price leads to a positive substitution effect.

A fall in price makes energy relatively cheaper, and hence more is bought, and it makes income higher because there is money to spare that would have been spent on energy.

It may be that, at 20 °C, you might not want the house to be any hotter – although the average indoor household temperature has been rising from around 13°C in winter back in 1970 to almost 18°C now.[15] But if you spend the money saved, it is almost certainly going to involve energy in whatever produces the good or service the money is spent on. For example, it might be spent on air conditioning or to subscribe to another streaming service. Whatever it is, the income effect is likely to be in the same direction as the substitution effect – more demand for energy.

This is not a new idea. Jevon's Law (named after the nineteenth-century economist who came up with it) predicts that an increase in energy efficiency increases the demand for energy.[16] And so it has turned out. Since Jevons came up with his Law, there has been one invention after another that has increased energy efficiency, with more to come with AI and modern information and data systems. Every one so far has increased demand for electricity. If this is what the climate community rely upon, and if they think that smart meters and smart energy technologies will come to the rescue, and in reducing demand, will lower the demand for fossil fuels, they need to explain why Jevon's Law and the basic laws of demand in economics are wrong. On the contrary, to meet the climate community's assumed results of lower demand, there would need to be an increase in the price of energy (perhaps through a carbon tax) that was in excess of the increase in energy efficiency, and for it to keep rising.

Aggregate Electricity Demand Growth

Turning all these new, emerging and growing demands of electricity into an overall system capacity requirement is a tough call. There are two possible ways of thinking about this: to assume it can and will be done; and to assume it will be partially constrained off. The capacity in the generation and networks could be built close to the demands emerging. If it takes a matter of a couple of years to build a big gas power station, then the build-out could closely match short-term expected demand. It might be tough to build the electricity grid capacity to this sort of short-term projected demand, and hence it would need to be built over-scaled well ahead. That is already a challenge almost anywhere.

The other way of thinking about this is that the demand will be constrained by the supply. The new technologies are added only as and when the electricity generation and grid infrastructure become available. In the UK and the EU, whilst there are great plans to build out lots and lots of renewables and the supporting extra network, the latter is most likely. This has a geographical distributional impact. The UK and the EU have (very) expensive electricity, undermining their competitiveness.[17] Add to this capacity constraints and the lead that is already clear for the US will grow and grow, together with the leads of China and Southeast Asia. Demand for electricity grows much faster in these more competitive countries which are able to build out capacity and networks more quickly, though even here they may struggle. The UK is unlikely to match this, and hence it will not be a global clean-energy superpower.

Demand for Oil, Gas and Coal in an Electricity Age

All the above is about the derived demand for electricity. What about the demand for coal, oil and gas? The first point to make is that the demand for coal is derived from that for electricity and from heavy industries like steel. Just because the share of electricity grows rapidly does not mean that the share of fossil fuels correspondingly contracts. On the contrary, analogous to how the coming of coal led to an increase in the use of wood as an input to coal mining, so the growing demand for electricity is increasing the demand for coal and gas too. The electricity industry is a growing source of fossil-fuel demand.

Then there are the non-electricity demands for fossil fuels we met earlier. It is a long list, including heavy industry, like primary steel production, cement manufacture and refining of a host of minerals. For oil and gas specifically, there are also petrochemicals and, in particular, plastic polyethylene (for packaging, wire and cable insulation), polypropylene (carpets, tiles, furniture) and nylon (carpets, clothing, paints, wall coverings, vehicle fittings and finishes).[18]

There is, in consequence, no transition on the horizon, with renewables and nuclear not likely even to meet all the additional demands for energy. To start to curtail the carbon in the atmosphere as a result of all the consumption examined in this chapter would require much more radical policies, or a technology breakthrough. Neither look likely to happen any time soon. Better to assume a wall of extra demand, and then think how this extra demand could be met by renewables and nuclear, and then cut into the existing coal, oil and gas. Climate realism points to the challenge of decarbonising not just the existing world economy, but another one as well. Perhaps double the size of global GDP, and double the demand for energy in 2050?

3 THE WRONG TARGET

Since climate change is caused by changes in the concentration of carbon in the atmosphere, and since it is the concentration of carbon that we have been increasing through both our emissions and our destruction of the Earth's ability to sequestrate carbon, you might think that therefore the target we should aim at is the concentration of carbon in the atmosphere.

But we don't. Instead, we concentrate on two targets: the temperature increase and the national territorial emissions. It is worse: the concentration is a global one, not a national one, so as with the temperature target, the correct focus should be on the global concentration of carbon in the atmosphere. This should be a target first for slowing the rise, currently at over 2 ppm per annum, then stabilising and then eventually bringing it gradually back towards the pre-industrial level. National targets should be set so as best to contribute towards stabilisation and then reduction of the carbon in the atmosphere.

How Much Warmer Do We Want Global Temperatures to Be?

Why have the targets of 2 °C and then 1.5 °C warming been chosen? And why are these averages over periods of time such that the extent to which the 1.5 °C and 2 °C targets are exceeded will not be known for a decade or two after the event? The answer on the 2 °C is a mixture of expediency and the need to have a catchy number. Climate policy has an affinity with neat, round numbers. For example, the EU decided it would try to achieve a 20-20-2020 target – 20 per cent renewables, 20 per cent energy efficiency, all by 2020.[1]

Whatever the optimal answers are, there are almost certainly not neat, round numbers and the optimal temperature increase is not 2 °C or 1.5 °C. If the number has to be neat and round, at least it could be a good approximation. But what would that be?

You might think it is determined by some combination of science and economics: an understanding of the way a complex atmosphere works and its stability, set against the impacts on biodiversity and us humans as part of the diversity of life. In other words, it might be about the ability of the atmosphere and the ecosystems to cope with different overall temperatures and the ways in which variability would be determined by the aggregate total warming. You might also expect that the chosen temperature target would be one that reflected the costs and benefits of different global temperatures.

On the former, the overall consideration has been what might be feasibly achieved. For there is no optimal climate in the long run for the planet. Over geological history, temperatures have varied a lot, and these temperature changes have been a major engine for evolution. It is true that humans are adapted to the current temperatures, but even over the brief history of human life on Earth, there have been big variations, including ice ages.

However, this geological perspective is mainly about temperatures that have changed gradually and allowed evolution to unfold gradually. The characteristic of current climate change is that it is very fast, which makes evolution and adaptation much harder for biodiversity generally. Humans may be able to react more quickly to climate change, given the sum total of human knowledge and the sheer speed and scale of technical change. No other species has air conditioning, heating and large-scale buildings to create a gap between them and the climate. It is why humans can live in the Arctic and the tropics and in arid landscapes and flooded deltas. We humans are very good at dealing with a wide range of climates – the best species at this there is on the planet.

Speed matters, and it might be that we could have a target for global warming set against the speed of change. In a way we have: the 2 °C and the 1.5 °C targets are very short term, less than a blink of a geological eye.

The reason 2 °C was chosen had very little to do with the science of impacts, atmospheric stability and the speed of change. It was set at a level that scientists and politicians at the time thought not only might be feasible, but also which politicians could sign up to. It was sufficiently far ahead that most of the politicians who agreed the target would be dead by the time the 2050 deadline came, so they could sign up to something for which they and their governments would not be held accountable.

What about the economics, the costs and benefits? Here, the analytical problem with the targets is most stark. The conventional economic techniques of analysis are marginal ones. Cost–benefit analysis looks at discrete small changes, keeping the rest of the economy as an exogenous constant. There could be (and have been) endless debates about the marginal damage of an extra tonne of carbon emitted versus its marginal cost and marginal benefit, but these are largely spurious. It's the wrong technique to analyse the wrong sort of problems. Climate change is all about the atmospheric *system* as a whole and how it interacts with the territorial *ecosystems*. It is a *systems* problem. It is the antithesis of a marginal analysis.

Integrated assessment models (IAMs) are constructed to integrate the science and the economics into a single model output. This combines apples and pears, except that the pears crumble in the modellers' analyses. IAMs purport to provide an accuracy (albeit a spurious one) of forecasts against baselines, with the economics in the driving seat.[2]

The more questionable sort of modelling is that which was also amongst the most influential. Stern's *Economics of Climate Change* is a set of economic arguments rushed through, with an outcome that suited the politicians of the day and the emerging climate community, and gave them all a hymn sheet which persists to today.[3] Stern claimed that the economic hit of climate change would be around the same as the economic hit of the Great Depression of the 1930s. That would be the threat. Against this, he argued that it was not going to cost very much to fix the problem, and indeed addressing climate change might present major opportunities to accelerate economic growth. Yes, it would be terribly damaging, but it is avoidable and would not be expensive to cure. It is, as Nordhaus wrote, best read as a political exercise.[4]

How very convenient for the setting of the territorial emissions targets, which evolved into the NDCs at the Paris COP in 2015. It is not hard to see how this sort of analysis helped to get soft agreement at the global level and how it encouraged the mistaken idea that climate change could be addressed unilaterally by any country that chose to show 'climate leadership'.

Is it really true that climate change is likely to have the sorts of economic losses Stern identifies? The climate community has been very vocal on just how awful the damage will be. Every major flood, drought and heatwave is cited as evidence of the costs. The climate community has been silent on the benefits of climate change. Remember there is no optimal climate. As it gets warmer, some countries initially benefit. In the Northern Hemisphere, the growing seasons get longer as frosts are later and less intense. Warmer winters mean less heating, less damp in houses, and fewer deaths from cold-related causes like hypothermia and respiratory diseases caused by sealed-up houses and their combination of damp and cold. Few in the climate community point to the greater benefit from lives saved because it is not so cold, versus the lives lost from heatwaves.

This is of course true only in some locations, but inconveniently for the climate community it happens to coincide with the locations where most of the world's wealth resides. The US plus the EU plus China are all in the Northern Hemisphere and are subject to cold winters. As the planet warms up, Russia in the short run could be a major beneficiary, as could Canada.

The situation in the tropics is rather different. Heat is already a problem in the tropics. In some areas, like the fringes of the Sahara and in the Middle East, agriculture is a precarious activity already, and drought and hunger combinations are all too common. These people have very little now. Their economic output is not very significant. But they are humans and deserve human support and dignity, and their lives cannot be simply traded against the richer areas less exposed to global warming.

There are the tropical islands exposed to rising sea levels. They may well have to be abandoned to the sea. Their leaders are prominent at all the COPs, and rightly so. But against this, their populations are very small and given the already precarious state of their fragile islands, many with a growing dependency on tourism, their future is already in question. Young people leave for greater opportunities elsewhere, the pattern of most remote island communities over the last century. Depopulation is a threat anyway. It is not irrational to ask how much it would cost to provide for these people elsewhere against how much it would cost to stop global sea levels rising.

The point of these comments is not to shock, but rather to explain that the impacts of climate change are not uniformly bad. They are very bad for many people, but not necessarily so bad for others, and for some they are beneficial.

This leads to the balance of mitigation and adaptation. Perhaps humans will adapt to higher temperatures? As with the remote islands example, let's take an extreme case. Is it possible to live in climates where the temperatures often exceed 40 °C? The Saudi Arabians think so. Recall the example of the new linear city of Neom, now scaled back because of escalating costs, being built in what is a very hostile climatic context. How can this be sensible compared with building a city in, say, the thawing north of Canada?

The answer is that many of the things necessary to sustain life and to make a city work are increasingly independent of climate – but not of energy. Desalination provides abundant water. Air conditioning provides a liveable internal temperature. Factories and production can happen indoors – they usually do. So can indoor farming.

The vital ingredient is energy. In the Saudi Arabia example, the country not only has an enormous surplus of oil (and this is paying for the development of the new city), but also abundant solar and lots of potential wind. It can, in theory, have unlimited desalination. It can power air conditioning. Its energy resources are abundant, cheap and available.

Coping with higher temperatures is primarily an energy problem, and the theoretically available energy is only limited by the supply of the key minerals and solar radiation, whilst there are more than enough fossil fuels in Saudi Arabia, and indeed globally. Solar delivers a vast energy surplus to the Earth relative to our utilisation of it. Energy supply is not a problem – in theory.

The trouble comes in practice, and this loops back to the earlier point about the ability to meet a rising demand for energy and specifically electricity. This is a timing and a coordination problem, and a minerals problem. Solar energy, whether from current radiation or post-fossilised solar, has to be transformed into usable energy. The materials for solar panels and wind turbines, cabling for transmission, and, of course, all the oil and gas and coal to manufacture the equipment, notably in China, are required. The supply of these minerals comes with lots of environmental problems and also GHG emissions. That is why, as we shall see in Chapter 4, there is no such thing as clean energy. If the question is whether adaptive cities like Neom in Saudi Arabia can cope with climate change, it depends upon whether they can be sustained without further significant carbon emissions. That is a big ask. So, yes, humans can live in contexts with higher temperatures, but not necessarily without adding significantly to the pollution that is helping to cause the higher temperatures, and a lot of other environmental damage. But, no, there is no optimal temperature.

Carbon Concentration Not Degrees of Temperature

Which brings us back to the question of the overall target and whether this should be a temperature or a measure of the ppm of carbon in the atmosphere. In addition to the latter being a primary cause of climate change, its advantage is that it is pretty easy to measure in real time and it is not location specific, other than needing to be apart from immediate emissions before they disperse in the atmosphere. It is a stock, not a flow target. The flows contribute to or subtract from the stock. The current focus on emissions is on the flows, and less attention is therefore paid to the stocks. Recall that it does not matter where emissions and sequestration take place; what matters is their impact on the stocks wherever they occur.

Temperature is very different. It varies from year to year for reasons that have little to do with climate change. Indeed, it is the simplistic read-across from, say, a higher temperature in a particular year, or even a short-duration heatwave, to climate change that tempts the climate community to point to any significant hot weather event and claim that this is consistent with climate change, despite the fact that a temperature that is remarkably low can also be consistent with climate change.

There is no such ambiguity with the ppm. It is what it is, and the greenhouse effect results from changes in the ppm. Weather may vary, and indeed temperatures may vary, but the causal link between ppm and climate change is pretty unambiguous.

What would be a sustainable ppm target? It would be best if set on the basis of ppm of CO_2-equivalent gases, and hence it would be the composite of a basket of GHGs, weighted by their impacts and duration in the atmosphere.

The current concentration is around 425 ppm. Setting a short-term target below this level is in effect to set a practically impossible target. Why? Because not only are emissions going up, and sequestration is coming down with ecosystem destruction, but also the gases stay in the atmosphere for various and mostly long periods of time. It is a bit like trying to stop a ship: it takes time to slow the momentum, then stop it, before there is any prospect of reversing it.

At the rate of around 2 ppm added annually every year since 1990, it will be getting close to 500 ppm by 2050. This will be getting close to doubling the concentration in the atmosphere compared to before the Industrial Revolution. It is sobering to realise that holding the line at 500 ppm would be a great achievement, given the continuing coal, oil and gas burns, and the ancillary pollution from the non-fossil fuels. That would mean limiting additional ppm to less than 3 ppm per annum.

These sorts of numbers tell us that the 1.5 °C target is unattainable. At the Paris COP, the parties looked at numbers which suggested that the 2 °C target would be breached, and in consequence decided to adopt a 1.5 °C target and try to force countries and companies to adhere to that. It was never going to happen, and it hasn't, and although the formal breach will not be acknowledged for some years to come, in practice we are already through 1.5 °C.[5]

There is little point in setting a ppm target without first having some idea as to whether it might be achievable and how this might be done. We might like to get back to the pre-industrial 275 ppm, but we know that is all but impossible. The discussion in the previous chapter about the wall of additional demand for energy relative to this period to 2050 is pertinent here: any ppm target has to reckon with accommodating a big increase in electricity generation and supporting networks and continuing to produce all the other stuff, and to provide the energy necessary for all the mining and refining of critical minerals. Doubling the global demand for energy and doubling global GDP by 2050, whilst at the same time holding to the current increases in ppm, is already a stiff challenge.

Should There Be a Specific Date?

Whether the target is set for degrees or ppm, giving the target a date is fraught with its own problems. What happens in, say, 2040 when it is obvious that 2 °C will not be met by 2050? How will it be revised? Is it easier to set a flexible ppm target rather than a fixed temperature target? Indeed, why have a target at all?

The argument for a rigid target is that it is a 'sighting exercise'. A given target requires all the parties to make sure their numbers are consistent with it. The question becomes how to get to, say, a 2050 target rather than simply trying flexibly to reduce emissions and increase sequestration. It helps if the target date is given a longer-term context. When, for example, might stabilisation of ppm be achieved, not when it might begin to fall. All this points to a 2050 target being placed in the context of a 2100 target.

The added advantage of the ppm target is that it does not distinguish between emissions and sequestration. It requires both. An emissions target focuses overwhelmingly on fossil fuels. Yet sequestration is every bit as important. Agriculture is making the conventional sequestration carbon sinks now sources of emissions, as land and rainforests are cleared.

Worse, some policies to reduce emissions reduce sequestration. Think palm oil for 'renewable' fuel and biomass for electricity generation, and 'sustainable' aviation fuel (SAF). A ppm target puts sequestration centre stage, on an equal footing with emissions reductions. It has the added advantage of bringing ecosystems and biodiversity loss into the wider consideration of our destruction of not just the atmosphere but also the Earth's living systems.

Translating a Global Target into a National Set of Targets

Perhaps the greatest failure of the current targets comes when they are translated into the responsibilities of individual countries. Here, the focus on territorial carbon production targets leads to great distortions and great illusions of progress. Focusing on carbon produced and emitted in a specific country tells us very little about the carbon footprint of that country. That requires carbon consumption to be measured as well.

The best example of the dangers of looking to the territorial carbon production numbers, which are reported along the UN lines,[6] is the UK. Take a look at the recorded territorial emissions reductions and it looks dramatically good. The UK has reduced its emissions since the baseline in 1990 by an impressive 54 per cent.[7]

It looks too good to be true, and it is. The actual territorial emissions are not quite this good. The UN accounting system allows the UK to exclude its Drax power station from the numbers, on the grounds that trees are renewable and Drax is compensating for the emissions from the UK power stations by trees planted and growing abroad, and therefore that the emissions should be counted in the country of origin of the wood pellets. It's a statistical trick: the actual sequestration is highly questionable, given the ambiguity about the baseline against which the sequestration is measured. Much of the purported sequestration is probably not really additional; it takes many years; and there are emissions associated with the planting of the trees and no certainty that these will not be damaged by pests, disease and fire.

Drax is one of the largest emitters of carbon in the whole of the EU. Its emissions can be compared to those from a major coal-fired power station (which it was previously). Worse, it emits all sorts of other pollutants.[8] There are all the emissions associated with Drax's full supply chain, from cutting, pelletisation, drying and transport before the combustion takes place. To exclude its emissions is all the more questionable because the sequestration could have happened anyway.

In addition to the Drax problem, emissions from diffuse sources like agriculture are most likely under-represented. Yet these considerations pale into insignificance compared to the major reason why the UK has been the 'world leader' in cutting territorial carbon emissions – that it has largely exited coal as an energy source, switching quickly to gas. In electricity generation, this was largely complete by 2024. There has also been sharp contraction of the energy-intensive industries in the UK, with steel the stand-out example.

Sounds good, but it is too good to be true as a way of measuring the UK's contribution to causing climate change. The reason why it is smoke and mirrors is that carbon territorial emissions do not measure the UK's carbon footprint.[9] Once consumption is brought into the picture, the global pollution we cause in the UK rises a lot. From a consumption perspective we have not exited coal. It is just that the UK consumers buy stuff from abroad which is made with coal and coal-fired electricity and then import it rather than produce it at home in the UK.

Try the following thought process. Suppose the UK decided to be an entirely service-based economy. Suppose it did not manufacture anything. Suppose it did not produce any food at all. Suppose it tried to live on the basis of selling financial software and IT services and R&D only. Suppose it used only EVs for travel, and electric trains and electric trucks and this electricity was generated entirely from renewables and nuclear. The economy would have pretty close to zero carbon territorial emissions. But its carbon footprint would be very large: all the food and the manufactured goods would be imported, and these would be produced in countries that used coal, oil and gas. The minerals for the batteries and the back-up supplies would be imported, as would the solar panels and the wind turbines. Global carbon emissions would probably go up.

It is pretty obvious that the territorial emissions in this example have very little to do with the carbon footprint. They cannot be the right target in addressing climate change.

Now consider an economy that manufactured only energy-intensive goods and energy-intensive food, and used a lot of coal, oil and gas to do so. Let's call it China in the 1990s and early 2000s (though of course China produced a lot of other stuff too). Let's assume that it exported all this energy-intensive stuff to our hypothetical UK in the above example. Its territorial emissions would be terrible, in contrast to the UK's.

This is a stylised example, but enough of it maps what has actually been going on to debunk the UK's claimed great world leadership. What the UK has been doing is closing down much of its energy-intensive industries and switching to imports. This isn't just existing factories. It has also been attracting virtually no *new* energy-intensive industries. It may be that 'carbon leakage' has slowed down, as there is less and less industry to close down, but whereas other countries – like China and the US – have seen investment in lots of new factories, the UK has not.

In fact, the UK has closed down its aluminium industry, several of its major refineries, much of its steel industry, almost all of its fertiliser industry, its glass industry, and its car production collapsed back at one stage in 2025 to the level back in 1948. It even imports some 30 per cent of its cement.[10] It has not helped that, as a result of its territorial emissions policies, it has among the highest industrial energy prices in the developed world, as we shall see.

The UK is an outlier in deindustrialisation and the switch to imports, but it is not alone. Much of the EU has been following a similar, if less extreme, deindustrialisation pathway. Hence it is no surprise that the UN Kyoto pathway[11] and subsequently that of Paris have been associated with sharp reductions in recorded territorial emissions in the EU and the UK, whilst offset by sharp increases in China and India and a number of developing countries in Southeast Asia and the Middle East.[12]

This leads to an obvious conclusion: the overall target should be global ppm, and individual country targets should be based on carbon consumption and not carbon production.

That leaves one more step. What should the individual country carbon consumption targets be based upon? The answer must be on emissions *and* sequestration. This is not about just offsetting carbon emissions with sequestration, but rather about reducing emissions *and* addressing the damage to sequestration. We need both.

There is no right answer to the question of what contribution a country should make towards the global goal of halting and then eventually reversing the ppm in the atmosphere. There is a variety of possible targets. It could be that a country decides it no longer, unilaterally, wants to be causing climate change. It could aim for net zero carbon consumption, incorporating the damage it does in its consumption in terms of both emissions and sequestration. This would mean not only that the consumption emissions must be zero but also that full account is taken of the damage caused elsewhere to support that consumption. This includes, for example, the destruction of rainforests to mine nickel or cobalt for EV batteries, to raise beef or grow agricultural crops for imported food, to build roads to transport goods that are consumed in the country importing them, or to produce palm oil for SAF or to add 'biofuel' to petrol and diesel.

This would be a massive leap challenge for a country like the UK and for many EU member states – and for the US. It would almost certainly reduce living standards. But it could be argued that even something as radical as this is not a sufficient contribution, because past emissions from territorial production and imports are also an inherited responsibility. The climate change wreaked so far is not caused by many developing countries and yet they suffer the consequences. There would be a further adjustment to take into account these past emissions that remain in the atmosphere, until they eventually drop out. For methane, this would be a short period, for CO_2 much longer. For the UK and the US, this would be a painful extra burden. It would extend to China too. It has been claimed that around eight years of emissions in China is roughly equivalent to the extra UK emissions since the start of the Industrial Revolution.[13]

Such a current carbon consumption plus legacy addition would be the sort of target which, if adopted globally, could slow down and eventually stop the ppm rising. It would not be without consequences to those countries exporting to a country that adopted such a target. There would have to be a carbon border adjustment, and this cost would need to be reflected in a carbon price. More on this in Chapter 10.

The demand for imports would fall at the margin, and hence the exporting country would face a reduction in demand and this in turn would have an impact upon it. There is no escaping the fact that carbon is an externality which is not currently paid for, and as and when it is, then there will be a price effect and an income effect of the carbon border price. It is not only the country that goes down the full carbon consumption target route that is affected. It is also the exporters, for both have been living beyond their environmental means. The great global expansion of trade would now face its environmental consequences.

Take the example of China. Its great economic growth has also been an environmental disaster and has been driven by exports. In the early part of that growth, it was overwhelmingly dependent on energy-intensive exports. For things like steel, and cars, and solar panels, and wind turbines, and rare earths and refined minerals, it still is. Had the EU and the US addressed their consequent imports of the embedded carbon in China's exports with a carbon border adjustment, the demand for these exports would have been much lower. The effect would have been analogous to a tariff. But it is only analogous. For the carbon border adjustment would apply only to those imports for which a carbon price had not already been applied back in the exporting country. Instead of paying the carbon border price to the importing country, it could itself levy a carbon tax and hence keep the money. The relative price of carbon-intensive exports still goes up, but the impact of the carbon price can be roughly neutral. Later on in Chapter 10, the wider role of carbon border adjustments is discussed in the context of a bottom-up approach to creating a coalition of the willing.

There are other commitments that countries could make. An obvious one is to make such efforts as are consistent with the efforts made by other countries, recognising the free-rider problem. If a country does adopt a carbon consumption target, and others don't, they are free riding on its willingness to sacrifice the standard of living of its population. The US has repeatedly resisted taking decisive action because China has not. From Bill Clinton's failure to get votes for ratifying Kyoto (there were virtually none in the Senate, so he didn't put it to the test), through to Obama's unwillingness at the Copenhagen COP in 2009 to go down the UN COP route, through to Trump's twice opting out of the Paris

Agreement, it could be argued that the US has acted reasonably. Why damage its own economy to give an open goal to its emerging competitor?

Some go further, arguing that climate change is not going to get solved at all, or at least not until some new technologies, like nuclear fusion, come along. They argue that, instead of targets, they should concentrate on no-regret policies. If you believe, like some politicians and many in the climate community do, that low-carbon energy will be (or even already is) cheaper, then there is no need for targets at all. No target was needed for smartphones to take over from fixed telephones and lines. Simple economic competitiveness did this. If it is believed that renewables are, for example, nine times cheaper than gas, as the UK's Secretary of State for Energy Security and Net Zero has repeatedly claimed,[14] there is no major problem to be solved. It will solve itself. The reason we need targets is that this just isn't true.

The Right Targets

In summary, the current climate change targets are the wrong ones, and as a result it is not surprising that they are ineffectual or worse.

The better way to set a global target is to start with the physical cause of climate change: the concentration of carbon in the atmosphere. There should be an overarching global ppm target, with an associated profile for gradually reducing the rate of increase, then stabilising the ppm and then eventually starting to bring it down. This is what the Intergovernmental Panel on Climate Change (IPCC) should advise on, and this is what should be the main focus of the COP meetings. It should be a neutral exercise, free from global leaders doing global grandstanding.

For individual countries, the target should be carbon consumption, not territorial carbon production. It should be inclusive of damage done to the natural world's ability to absorb carbon. These national carbon consumption targets should be set in the context of the global ppm target framework.

To stop climate change, we have to stop the increase in ppm. You may well be thinking that there is little chance that any government would be brave enough to try to implement a net zero carbon consumption target. You would probably be right. But you would then have to recognise that, on the current net zero territorial carbon production targets, there is also little chance of stopping climate change and especially when carbon production is inadequately measured and sequestration is largely ignored.

4 THERE IS NO SUCH THING AS CLEAN ENERGY

Perhaps clean energy will come to the rescue so that the failure to set the right targets (or even to meet the current ones) might not be so bad? Perhaps the clean energy will replace the dirty energy? The language of the climate change community is distorted by this extraordinary simplicity, trampling over its great and inconvenient complexities. A prime example is the neat asymmetry between 'clean' and 'dirty' energy. Clean is 'good', dirty is 'bad'. Clean is 'zero emissions', dirty means emissions.

As with George Orwell's 'four legs good, two legs bad' in *Animal Farm*, reality is much messier. Nuclear, wind, solar, biomass and hydroelectricity turn out to be less than perfect, all with significant environmental footprints. The best that can be claimed for some of these is that they might be 'cleaner' than some fossil-fuel-based technologies, and even this claim deserves close inspection rather than endless and mindless repetition. Unfortunately, there is no clean-energy future Nirvana. Our energy future will be one of more environmental damage, howbeit there is the possibility that it could be less than it might otherwise have been.

There are several ways to consider the full environmental impact of 'clean' technologies. One way is to draw out the full supply chains, analogous to the coal, oil and gas ones that are often mapped. The second is to look at the minerals embedded in a typical solar panel, wind turbine, EV and storage battery. Best to do both to get a clearer picture of how clean 'clean' actually is. These can then be compared with those for gas and coal power stations, petrol and diesel vehicles, and fossil-fuel strategic reserves. Though every case is different, the point being made is that clean is a *relative* and not an absolute concept, and that there is no climate-neutral way of delivering energy. It is all dirty; the question is just how relatively dirty. As energy demand rises, and especially for electricity, the environmental damage will persist.

Sunshine is free and so is the wind that is ultimately driven by solar energy. So, too, are the vast deposits of coal, oil and gas. It is all natural capital. The Sun is a massive nuclear fusion reactor and is the ultimate source of the energy in fossil fuels, via photosynthesis, and without the carbon that results, there would be little life as we know it on Earth. Many, but not all minerals were born out of the Sun.

At the heart of all energy production is mining, digging up the solar legacy and minerals buried in the Earth's crust. A solar panel needs lots of minerals, and these need to be refined. Coal is the main power source for the refining of these in the overwhelmingly dominant supplier country, China. Coal also powers the manufacture of wind turbines. It, too, is mined, as are oil and gas. Steel comes from mining iron ore and refining, again primarily by coal. Batteries, solar panels and wind turbines all require a host of minerals. These include iron, copper, nickel, lithium and cobalt, as well as some rare earths, such as neodymium, to make magnets.

Before the word 'clean' is used, it is worth searching the web for pictures of mines for all of these. None is environmentally benign. All involve emissions – no zero emissions here. Add to this the great damage to ecosystems and their biodiversity that mining causes. Add the civil wars and gross abuses of human rights often associated with mining. It is not a pretty picture. There isn't a clean mine anywhere in the world. They are all dirty, some appallingly so. All solar panels, wind turbines and nuclear power stations incorporate some of this dirt.

The Pollution That Mining Causes

Human economic development is driven by mining non-renewable natural resources. Having hunted and fished for thousands of years within the boundaries of what nature can renewably reproduce, the step to farming was partially caused by and subsequently followed by a succession of mineral and refining technologies. Starting with copper and tin and then bronze (combining copper and tin to give us the Bronze Age), and then iron (the Iron Age), there has been a succession of mineral ages. Ours is a steel, cement, plastics, copper, nickel, lithium, uranium and fossil-fuels age.

Each built on the shoulders of its predecessors. There have been no significant transitions: we use more and more iron, copper, silver, gold, bauxite, uranium, oil, gas and coal, and now more lithium and nickel than ever before. As with the energy, no transition here, just cumulatively ever-greater production and consumption. Bronze still has many uses and more is made now than in the Bronze Age, even if it is relatively unimportant. Copper from which bronze is made has vastly increased in production, as indeed has tin. Iron is a fundamental for modern economies, as is cement (limestone).

Mines get economically rather than physically exhausted, as new ones are developed. The Earth's crust offers a cornucopia of mineral resources, and the next frontier is deep-sea mining. The scars left by mining are not just the craters and the underground tunnels, but the water pollution, as the mineral waste seeps into the aquifers and the rivers and seas, and failing dams burst.

Mines are heterogeneous. Each has its unique environmental footprint. Each starts with its own environmental baseline, and this is cleared to get the mining going. In a rainforest, as in the Congo, mining takes out critical bits of biodiversity-rich ecosystems. The clearing of the land is typically an energy-intensive business, almost always driven by diesel and other fossil fuels.

Surface excavation is very energy intensive. It may also require dynamite and sometimes chemical solvents too. Land has to be cleared for miners, and they bring their own pollution, almost always being from non-sustainable communities.

Once the stuff is excavated from open sites and from tunnels and underground seams, it has to be transported to the refineries and final points of use. Mining is a heavy activity. Rock weighs a lot. That means more energy-intensive transportation, and new highways.

At the refinery, more energy-intensive activity gets under way, and the refined product then goes on for fabrication and incorporation into products like EV batteries, solar panels and wind turbines. In the case of China and Indonesia, this is all very coal intensive and typically involves long distances and often shipping.

All along this supply chain, there is pollution. There are emissions (all of which go into the development of the solar panels and wind turbines) from the fossil fuels, nuclear and biomass as direct energy or via intermediaries. To this, add the cement in huge dams. The difference between renewables and hydro is that, once built, the pollution from hydro is much less, until decommissioning, and similarly for transmission and distribution.

Focusing on the mining, let's take three of the core minerals for renewables and EVs – nickel, copper and lithium – to get a picture of the scale of the environmental damage.

Nickel is used to make stainless steel, alloys, batteries (and especially to improve the energy-intensiveness of EVs). For renewables, it is useful for making strong, corrosive-resistant materials, as used in wind turbines, especially for offshore and in the components. For solar, its use is in the ancillary infrastructure around storage and wiring.

The world's main producer of nickel is Indonesia and, having determined to capture more of the value chain, it is also the main refiner, supported by Chinese investment. It has over half the world's total production and almost half the world's known resources.[1]

Digging up nickel has resulted in significant deforestation, including in biodiversity hotspots, water contamination and sedimentation, and air pollution. Soil and vegetation are cleared, water pollution (from sulfur) contaminates rivers, aquifers and coastal waters, tailing ponds leak or break. Sulfur dioxide and particulates add to acid rain and particulates harm air quality. Dust contains toxic metals.

When it comes to refining, Indonesia relies on coal,[2] with the associated air and water pollution, which is carbon intensive, especially for high-temperature smelting for batteries. The damage in Indonesia, and also in the Philippines and Russia, is awesome. No battery containing nickel is properly going to be 'zero emissions'.

Lithium is not rare. It comes in a variety of forms, one of which is in brines. The three main deposits are in the Salar de Atacama in Chile, and the Salar del Muerto and the Salar de Olaroz in Argentina (the 'lithium triangle').

The deposits in this triangle lie below thick crusts of salt and are in desert-type environments, yet they have massive environmental footprints. These arid areas are not devoid of biodiversity. Salt pans are major habitats and deserts have their own ecosystems. Only deep environmental ignorance can lead anyone in the climate community or more generally to think that salt pan and desert mining has little or no environmental footprint. Open-pit mining for lithium (in the form of spodumene) has all the main environmental pollution impacts. Like nickel mining, it is energy intensive. One ton of lithium carbonate might produce 15 tons of CO_2.[3]

To these location-specific impacts, there is the additional question of water and water resources. When mining involves the extraction of great quantities of underground salt brines, aquifers are drained, and trailing salts and chemicals are the byproducts.

Copper is central to decarbonisation. Indeed, its importance goes far beyond: we humans need it to survive and thrive. We literally can't do without it.[4] It came before the Bronze Age, and it is already a major mineral of the global economy, before decarbonisation is considered. The main current production is located in Chile. Copper is about to go through a further explosion in mining and refining. A typical electric car is made up of 60–80 kilograms (kg) of copper, more than a typical petrol or diesel vehicle (20–30 kg copper).

Copper mines can be vast. The Escondida mine in Chile is the largest by production, producing over 1 million tonnes per annum,[5] followed by the Grasberg mine in Indonesia, and then two other Chilean mines. Take a look at pictures of these, including from space, and see the vast environmental impact. Chances are these are the places the copper in your car comes from, all the greater if it is an EV. As with nickel and lithium, there is a range of associated air, water and land pollution, and again lots of carbon emissions associated with its mining and refining. There is lots of tailing waste and toxic byproducts. Copper smelting is a very dirty activity. Again, as with nickel refining, it is sulfur intensive and water polluting, with air pollution, dust and lots of carbon emissions too.

All of these have done collateral damage to biodiversity. It may be true that climate change can be harmful to biodiversity, but so can the supply chains for clean-energy technologies.

Rare earths – part of the 'critical minerals' – are not rare, but they are not concentrated. It takes a lot of rock to get small amounts out. They tend to be associated with other elements, including thorium and uranium. Refining of rare earths is typically very chemical intensive, and hence pollution from chemical wastes and heavy-metal contamination is added to 'all of the above' for the mining of lithium, nickel and copper. China takes a more relaxed view of environmental damage, but other countries would have to take more care. China, as a result, has a lead in these vital minerals, which is hard to overcome.

Waste Disposal and 'Recycling'

Never mind, the argument is made that mining will be replaced by recycling. The lithium, cobalt, nickel and copper in batteries can be recycled, as can the rare earth elements in solar panels and wind turbines, and the steel and other materials. Even waste nuclear fuel can be recycled. Nowhere is this more prevalent an idea in the climate community than when it comes to the green steel we met earlier. We will use scrap metal rather than raw iron ore.

The scrap-metal argument links up with the idea that steel production can be turned from iron-ore blast furnaces, typically using coal, to electric-arc furnaces – and that these can be powered by renewables. They could also be powered by hydrogen made through electrolysis from renewable energy, or from nuclear.

This all opens up the possibility that we could stop mining and refining iron ore and therefore avoid all the associated carbon and environmental pollution. We could in theory stop almost all the mining of the minerals essential to decarbonisation too.

Is this possible? Is it practical? Let's concentrate on green steel as an example, which bears upon the wider question of how much mining and refining and associated pollution is associated with the great electrification and renewables and nuclear. The first question is whether recycled scrap metal is in fact equivalent to steel made in blast furnaces. The answer is possibly in theory, but in practice recycled steel is typically of a lower strength and better used for reinforcing concrete and buildings rather than high-grade steel for making tanks and missiles and railway lines and wind energy masts.

The second question is whether there is enough scrap metal to make the required steel for an expanding global economy. The theoretical answer is probably again yes, given that the world has already produced a lot of steel over the last 200 years, but in practice supply and demand are not so easily matched.

The third question is whether recycled steel is really green. Think of the supply chain. There is the collection of steel from demolished buildings, factories and other past uses. It has to be sorted to strip out non-steel components, and that which is retained is of mixed quality. All this material and its sorting requires energy and much of this is going to be carbon based for a considerable period. There is the carbon and other pollutants associated with the production of the renewable energy and its losses through the electric-arc process, even if there is enough of it.

This illustrates an important caveat to the recycling get-out-of-jail card. Recycling is never a closed loop. There are typically hazardous recycling residues,[6] and these can have serious environmental consequences. All of the above applies to the recycling of batteries, solar panels and wind turbines. Recycling is not 'clean' in any of these cases. It is dirty and sometimes very dirty. It is almost always energy intensive. Again, it is a matter of degree of dirtiness. And sometimes it is environmentally better not to recycle.

Cabling and Additional Infrastructure

Renewable energy needs to get to the customer. It tends to be geographically dispersed, low energy density and intermittent. That means a lot of cables.

Transmission cables comprise conductors, insulation and sheathing, all with supporting structures. For conductors, copper is used for lower voltages and aluminium for higher voltages, the latter typically reinforced with steel (ACST[7]). For insulation, PVC, XLPE and EPR[8] are used, all requiring manufacture. For sheathing, it is PVC again, and for the support structures, steel pylons with reinforced concrete have to be installed across the landscape. For sub-sea cables, there may be additional armouring with steel wiring and PVC and other extra sheaths, and they, too, require substations and pylons once ashore.

The intermittency of renewables like wind and solar necessitates lots of extra transmission capacity over and above that required for conventional coal and nuclear electricity systems. The UK provides an example. As already noted, when the electricity was generated primarily by coal and nuclear, some 60–70 GW of installed capacity comfortably met total demand. The transmission system took electricity from large coal power stations located near or at coal fields and from large, coastal nuclear power stations to the centres of demand. Now already with renewables, well over 100 GW of capacity is required to meet a slightly lower total demand, and much of the electricity from renewables comes from offshore and peripheral areas of the UK. Correspondingly, a massive expansion of the transmission network is needed to meet this same demand, and with this comes the demand for all the minerals, PVC, steel and other materials needed to manufacture and install a much greater transmission system capacity. None of this is environmentally benign.

The Environmental Consequences of Intermittency: The Batteries

There are two reasons batteries are needed, and at scale. Batteries are the core of an EV, and they are a key way of addressing short-term intermittency. In the case of wind, the variability is determined by weather systems, and these in turn vary across geographies. Some geographies have lots of 'good' wind: not too strong, not too weak, and persistent rather than sporadic. Others have long periods of low wind, and short periods of variable wind speeds. Sailors have long known of the trade winds and also the doldrums, whilst autumn gales are familiar in Northern Europe. A good wind flow, such as in parts of the North Sea, has a load factor of around 45 per cent and sometimes higher.[9] Even here, for roughly half the time, wind does not generate, because there is not enough, too much, or the turbine has failed and needs maintenance and repair. The fact that the UK now needs over 100 GW to supply what 60 GW did in the past is partly explained by the half of the time when wind doesn't generate.

By contrast, solar is much more predictable. It does not work at night, and hence the higher the latitude, the longer the periods of no solar generation. In lower latitudes and areas with very low cloud cover (notably deserts), the duration and stability of solar generation are much better. This is why the prospects for solar panels are so much greater in North Africa, Sub-Saharan Africa, and in India and parts of the Far East. As with wind, it is a question of location, location, location.

There is continuing refinement in these technologies, to stretch out the wind speeds that can be captured, to increase the 'take' of the wind in conversion to electricity, and to address lower solar intensity at the fringes of capture. No doubt these will get even better, and probably more so for solar than for wind.

The obvious solution to intermittency is to make demand vary with supply – to use electricity when the wind is blowing and not when it isn't. For solar, there are some obvious 'fits' of supply to demand. Most economic activity can be targeted to daylight hours, and peak demand, like for air conditioning, may coincide with peak solar production, even though it may not be economic to do so, given the increased importances of firm power in our digital world. The application of AI and smart metering and related energy-demand management technologies can improve the match of demand and supply.

None of these improvements in the wind performance and demand-side flexibility negates the great need for energy storage and in particular for batteries, and it is here that the environmental footprint of 'clean' technologies gets dirtier.

Batteries are a core part of renewable energy. They are particularly good at spreading out solar production into the evenings and managing short-term wind fluctuations. Batteries solve short-term problems.

Batteries require lots of minerals, some rare earths, refining and lots of manufacture, and consequentially are the producers of lots and lots of pollution. This extends to their disposal and to the pollution associated with recycling some of their components. Again, there are advances in technology which may reduce the environmental footprints, but the great bulk of the associated pollution remains.

The Environmental Tragedy of the Great Dams and the Destruction of the Great Rivers

Arguably, the oldest source of renewable energy is water, first through water mills and now hydroelectricity, mainly from dams, but also directly from the flow of rivers and tides. Along with biomass and nuclear, hydro dominates currently designated low-carbon electricity generation.

Hydro has numerous additional benefits. It has storage potential for energy and hence can help with intermittency (though not entirely when there are droughts). Dams can also supply drinking water, water for industry, and even create lakes for leisure activities, such as swimming and sailing. Post-generation, the water can be re-used and even piped back uphill to the dam for re-use.

Hydro can produce a lot of electricity. Think of China's Three Gorges Dam, and the multiple dams of the Mekong, Congo and Amazon. The Medog Hydropower Station which China is building in Tibet has a capacity of 60 GW and is set to become the world's largest hydroelectric dam.[10] That is capacity for a single dam which equals the total capacity of the British system prior to renewables.

All these sources of hydroelectricity claim to be very 'clean'. But large-scale hydro dams are not quite the environmental paragons that some promote them as. First, there is the construction and the enormous amount of concrete and earth moving required. A lot of mining goes into the materials for dam construction. They use masses of cement. A lot of steel is used to reinforce the concrete and for the pipes to supply water to the generators, and the associated tunnelling. These are all in practice very carbon intensive.

Where the environmental footprint gets much bigger is the impact on biodiversity and, in particular, the ecology of rivers. Rivers have evolved over millennia to flow as they do. There are natural dams comprising the great natural lakes. The ecosystems evolve to cope with these, and most remain connected to the rivers and reliant on the connectivity of the rivers themselves. A huge dam wall makes connectivity all but impossible. A fish ladder up the Grand Coulee dam in the US state of Washington is unlikely to be practical, and connectivity is not just about fish. Ditto for the Three Gorges Dam in China.

Dams change the flow volumes, variance and rates downstream, often radically altering ecosystems. The Mekong is a stand-out example. The great dams, mainly financed and funded by China, have destroyed much of the biodiversity of its great rainforests. The annual floods have diminished and, in some cases, gone altogether. Species of fish and mammals can no longer exploit the resources of the whole river, and even the delta and its flooding and silting have changed. China's plans to build ever-bigger dams in Tibet will change the Brahmaputra River profoundly.

Biomass and Its Pollution

Biomass is perhaps best thought of as a very inefficient sort of fossil fuel. Instead of digging up coal, oil and gas, the product of millions of years of deposition and compression of plants produced by photosynthesis, biomass short-circuits the mineralisation and takes immediately captured sunlight through photosynthesis (very inefficiently) and either burns it directly or digests it to produce methane to then burn.

The advocates of biomass claim that it is a 'renewable' source of energy because it balances photosynthesis capture with burning release, to have 'net zero' emissions, and when it doesn't quite balance, claim that planting more trees than have been burnt makes up the difference.

Some biomass enthusiasts go even further. They claim that if the carbon from its burning is captured and stored through CCS, then it is better than net zero. This argument is not, however, the decisive one: fossil fuels can be burnt and the carbon captured and put into storage too (i.e., CCS). What biomass advocates claim is that its net emissions are lower than those from conventional biofuels, and hence if these emissions are captured, the total impacts are less.

The environmental footprint of biomass depends upon how the fuel is produced and how it is transported and burnt. There are multiple possibilities, from burning straw produced as a byproduct of cereal production, to direct biomass crops and onto trees and in particular the concept of 'waste wood'.

Biomass advocates too often do the calculations to suit their desired conclusion. In principle, it should be simple. First, there is the counterfactual: what would the carbon sequestrated be if the land was used in other ways, and not just if it was used as at present. Most claimed biomass fails to show additionality – more carbon sequestrated than would otherwise have been the case.[11] Second, there is the carbon involved in producing the biomass – cultivating the saplings and planting them, cultivating the fields for biomass crops, fertilisers, pesticides using equipment such as tractors and major forest-clearance machinery. There are the losses whilst the biomass grows (and especially for trees). There is the carbon involved in harvesting. Then comes the transport of low-energy-density biomass materials, and in the case of wood, pelletisation and especially drying to avoid spontaneous combustion, and all this before the burning and the associated emissions not just of carbon but also PM2.5, and finally ash disposal.

As with the great carbon offset debates (discussed more extensively in Chapter 7), the gap between what some advocates and some in the climate community choose to believe and the reality is considerable. As a result, whilst biomass does already contribute quite a lot of electricity generation, it is unclear whether it moves the dial on ppm, and even whether the net effects are to reduce the concentration of carbon in the atmosphere from what it would otherwise have been once account has been taken of the counterfactual carbon sequestration. Biomass is not clean; it is a shade of dirty.

The classic example is Drax, the largest biomass plant in Europe. Its exclusion from the UK territorial carbon emissions on UN accounting grounds is a travesty and undermines the claimed reduction of emissions in the UK. Worse, it isn't true that it reduces net emissions. It takes 'waste' wood from forests in Canada and the US (and in due course Poland too), pelletises that waste, dries the pellets, trucks them to the coast and then ships them to the Humber on the east coast of England, transfers them to a special train, stores them at the Drax power station, including cooling to prevent fire, before burning the pellets and then disposing of the ash.

Waste wood is easy to portray as a free resource. But wood is never 'wasted'. Dead wood is a critical part of the natural ecology of forests. And it may have uses other than sustaining and enhancing the soils and the invertebrate and fungi communities. It could be used for paper manufacture, for example. It is not hard to hypothesise that if someone else takes the waste wood, then a papermill might turn to virgin trees. Using someone else's waste wood supplies does not reduce net emissions.

Electric Vehicles

With the invention of the internal combustion engine (and at roughly the same time, the invention of the EV too), transport was transformed in the twentieth century, with aviation and the modern bulk carrier shipping (and crucially refrigeration) adding to the great transportation revolution. The result is a world with over 1.5 billion cars, over 300 million lorries, and more than 30,000 active passenger planes. Add the military dimensions and the true scale of the twentieth-century transformation, and with it globalisation, becomes apparent.

In the twenty-first century, the EV has moved from the margins towards the mainstream. The EV bit has so far largely shifted from direct use of fossil fuels for transport to their indirect use via electricity, and within the fossil fuels from oil to gas and coal. To make any claim to be much 'cleaner' necessitates non-carbon sources of electricity and a non-carbon source of energy to make the EVs and their batteries, with the mining and refining of their mineral components. There is as yet nothing remotely like the amount of 'clean' energy to power all the electric cars and lorries and planes. Recall that over 80 per cent of energy still comes from fossil fuels and that the demand for energy is projected to double by 2050.

An EV is basically a battery in a frame. It is heavier than its fossil-fuel counterpart, and hence the vehicle has to be designed around this weight. It needs heavier-duty tyres which wear down more quickly. The battery itself is fragile. It has limited ability to withstand a crash, and hence crashes tend to lead to the vehicle being written off rather than repaired. Taking all the dimensions of EVs together, there is no such thing as a zero-emissions EV. There is no clean transport – just varying degrees of dirty.

Aircraft, Sustainable Aviation Fuel and Chip Fat, and Shipping

Perhaps one of the most questionable claims about 'clean' transport comes from the aviation industry. Many of the climate community are addicted to flying (including to COPs) and they kid themselves that this is not that bad because aircraft are using SAF and buying offsets. We deal with the offsets argument later in Chapter 7, but here let's first reflect on what SAF is supposed to be.

This is fuel for a conventional jet engine, made from 'sustainable' sources. But it isn't and it is unlikely to generally ever be. Why? Because it is a mix of ethanol (i.e., biofuel) and wastes, like chip fat. The former is not net-neutral; it causes net emissions and especially compared with the counterfactual of what the land would be used for. The latter is in very limited supply and the preparation of waste fats itself is a carbon-emitting process. There is no 'sustainable' aviation fuel.

When it comes to 'clean' shipping, it is hard to know where to start. The great globalisation of the last 50 years has brought a sizeable expansion of shipping. The total number of large container ships is nearly 7,000. There are nearly 400 large cruise ships. These are massive in size, and each has a big carbon footprint. Almost all their energy comes from fossil fuels (heavy fuel oil, HFO), and although there is limited use of short-term biofuels and some hydrogen, as the number of ships keeps going up, so does the pollution. When it comes to cruise ships, that pollution is not just the carbon emissions on board from their engines, but also from the lighting, food, pools and all the activities in the race to the ultimate tourist experience. Then there is the waste, rubbish and the impacts on delicate ecosystems. 'Sustainable' cruising is a contradiction in terms which will probably never be reconciled. Cruises are much worse than aviation and cars per person. And, generally, there is no such thing as sustainable, clean large-scale shipping.

Nuclear Power Stations

Once upon a time, the energy future was going to be all about nuclear. It would be too cheap to measure, it would be secure and would displace coal. Military nuclear technology would be turned into ploughshares, and civil nuclear power would provide limitless supplies of high-density energy in the second half of the twentieth century.

Environmental concerns have traditionally been the Achilles heel of nuclear, as waste was dumped and stockpiles of spent fuel piled up at power stations and at 'special' sites. Nuclear radiation is widely feared, and these fears have been exacerbated by the steady march of nuclear accidents that were not supposed to happen. Recall that, in the West, we know about the Windscale fire (1957), Three Mile Island (1979) and Fukushima (2011). In the Soviet East and in China, much less is known, though the impact of Ukraine's Chernobyl in 1986 was well recorded across Western Europe. There are also the unreported disposals of old nuclear submarines and other military nuclear installations and weapons.

It was quite a volte-face to move from environmental pariah to climate saviour. As nuclear moves back to a central role in mitigating climate change, the sorts of cavalier treatments of environmental risks in the past are now not so easy to hide. Whereas the UK government could suggest in 1959 in its first White Paper on nuclear waste that there were lots of old mine shafts to dump the stuff in, that is no longer feasible. It is only the fear of climate change that has led many environmentalists to drop their objections to nuclear, whereas not so long ago anti-nuclear and green were spliced together.

There are other reasons, too, for the renewed enthusiasm for civil nuclear power. These include the defence and security of supply concerns, especially with the Russian invasion of Ukraine in February 2022 and the interruptions and threats to gas supplies to the UK and the EU. Many countries now want their own nuclear weapons, and to do this they need uranium and uranium enrichment, together with the know-how and technologies that cross over the military and the civilian. Iran is the latest example.

The question is whether nuclear is 'clean' separate from questions of security. Can nuclear be 'clean' energy? The answer is no: again, it is a question of relative dirtiness. Uranium mining, uranium processing, and nuclear waste management and disposal are always going to involve a lot of carbon emissions, as is building new reactors.

Shades of Dirty

An obvious rejoinder is to claim that fossil fuels are worse. In many cases this will be true. But not always. Some types of biomass might even be worse than burning coal to generate electricity. EVs may be worse than small petrol cars, especially if the battery is charged partly or completely using fossil-fuel-generated electricity. The back-up for wind and solar can add more emissions than would have been the case if gas had been directly used to generate electricity. The full extent of the mining and refining of the minerals may be worse than natural gas extraction.

None of this is to suggest that renewables and nuclear are *necessarily* worse. But it is to point out that none of the 'clean' energies is actually clean. Switching from fossil fuels may reduce the overall carbon emissions, but it will not curtail them. If the demand for energy (especially electricity) carries on increasing at a rate that doubles every 25 years, then a smaller proportion produced by fossil fuels may not add up to a much smaller aggregate amount of emissions.

Renewables and nuclear may be less dirty in operation, but they need all the mining and refining, producing lots of emissions, and they can do lots and lots of environmental damage to ecosystems and biodiversity. So let's end the simplistic game of 'clean energy' versus 'dirty energy' and recognise that it is a matter of how dirty each of the options is. It is a relative not an absolute comparison.

5 THE BROKEN WINDOW FALLACY

To the climate community, decarbonisation is not just a good thing to deal with climate change, but it is also going to usher in a new era of green growth: win–win. Better climate, more economic prosperity. Building lots of solar farms, wind farms and nuclear power stations is, to them, investment, and investment that leads to more GDP. This new investment will not only cause economic growth but will also reduce the costs of energy: win–win–win.

In the next chapter we will see that the system costs of a primarily renewables-driven energy system are very unlikely to be cheap. But, for now, let's look at the economic growth bit of the argument. There are two flaws. The first is that more economic growth, as measured by GDP, is not necessarily an unmitigated benefit. It may be convenient to link renewables and nuclear to what almost all politicians set as their main measure of success – more GDP – but GDP is not sustainable economic growth and tends to lead to excess consumption, with all the consequences to the environment that follow. GDP growth increases the demand for energy and can involve a lot of environmental vandalism. However, objecting to GDP growth is not the same thing as objecting to sustainable economic growth, and having no growth is unlikely to be a good way forward.

Environmentalists tie themselves up in all sorts of knots over economic growth, but this is a sideshow to the main flaw in the green growth argument. The core flaw is that almost all of the renewables and nuclear build-out and the extra transmission and distribution required is not investment at all. It is *capital maintenance*. The result of switching from fossil fuels to renewables is a change in technology to produce the *same* output (actually, in some respects a slightly lower-quality output). The aim is to keep the lights on, and the lights from coal- and gas-fired electricity generation are just as good as the lights from wind and solar.

What the climate community does is confuse investment and capital maintenance and then gets all excited about the 'investment opportunities'. This in turn leads them into the finance fallacy. Capital maintenance is not about finance at all. It is all about current spending and current funding. Finance and funding are not the same, a mistake often made. Tacking on 'green finance' and 'green growth' to tackling climate change is a category mistake with profound consequences.

A Very Simple Idea

The broken window fallacy is pretty obvious to non-economists but passes most economists by. You won't find it in economics textbooks, and in macroeconomics it is repeatedly violated. Almost all discussions of net zero directly contradict the fallacy's obvious wisdom.

The fallacy was popularised by Frédéric Bastiat, a nineteenth-century French economist, in his 1850 essay 'That Which is Seen, and That Which is Not Seen'.[1] Bastiat considers a shopkeeper confronting the breaking of his shop-front window. That which is seen is all the activity this event generates. New glass has to be ordered, made, delivered and installed, creating work for the glaziers. That which is not seen is the diversion of monies from what the shopkeeper would otherwise have spent them on, or if he saved these monies what they might otherwise have been invested in. What Bastiat was articulating was analysis by counterfactual: compare the effects of an action with what would have happened had the action not taken place.

Breaking glass is an example of a destruction, and Bastiat rightly sees destruction as economically negative, whatever the immediate gains are from repairing the damage. Wars break a lot of things. Gaza has been levelled. Much of Eastern Ukraine has been ruined. Ditto for Iran. Hurricanes and floods deluge cities and destroy houses and buildings. Storm Katrina in 2005 destroyed much of New Orleans. Fires are great destroyers of vegetation and buildings and livestock. Accidents are part of life, as are car crashes, personal injuries and collapsing bridges and scaffolding.

What Bastiat was pointing out is that none of these is 'good news'. We are worse off as a result. Pretty obvious, except to economists. What economists do is add up all the additional demand and the resulting economic activity from repairing the damage and add this to GDP. All of the above examples create lots of economic activity. Even the prospect of war leads to rearmament, and it can be expected that the great UK and EU increases in defence spending as a result of the threat from Russia will be a significant boost to economic growth, even though the weapons are being built to be destroyed. They produce nothing intrinsically good. Climate change will cause lots of damage.

Economists of a Keynesian persuasion reinforce this mistake by adding in their 'multiplier'.[2] It is not just that the window repair business gets a boost from the shopkeeper's broken window in Bastiat's example, but this multiplies out. The glazier takes on more labour, the new workers have more money to spend, they buy other stuff, and the demand for this other stuff goes up, with the makers of the other stuff employing yet more workers. Demand is increased, and demand creates its own supply. Higher aggregate demand leads to higher aggregate supply, as measured in GDP. It causes investment which causes saving, not the classical model of savings causing investment. There is no balance-sheet adjustment for what has been destroyed, one set of assets replaced by another, because Keynesians (and GDP) are all about flows not stocks.

Keynes was not so gullible as many of his later followers. For him, this multiplier worked when there was excess labour. The unemployed would have otherwise remained unemployed, not been diverted from other employment. It is the slack in an economy producing below its potential that makes breaking a window so that it can be repaired multiply through the economy. Digging holes in the road and filling them up again – Keynes' famous example – is a sensible thing to do;[3] or, in the Bastiat example, encouraging people to go around breaking windows to create the economic activity of repairing them.

Breaking windows and digging holes in the road are relatively harmless (except to the shopkeeper and the driver and the cyclist), but when it comes to the climate change community, the broken window fallacy is committed on steroids. What is claimed is that all the wind farms and solar panels and solar farms and even nuclear power stations, and the batteries and grid infrastructure being installed are *investments*. They are claimed to be *additional* to the energy systems, not replacements of existing assets.

Once claimed to be investments, they can then be enlisted as great examples of economic growth projects, and as such they can be financed by borrowing, rather than paid for out of current incomes. It allows dubious fiscal rules to entertain more borrowing for investment, and hence national debt to be increased alongside private debt.[4] As investments, they are assumed to have positive net present value. So, better still, they will be paid for out of the profits from the completed projects and by the future recipients of the benefits.

Almost everything that could be wrong about this line of argument is indeed wrong. Let's start with the fundamentals. The purpose of wind farms and nuclear power stations and solar farms and batteries and the grid is to deliver electricity to industry and consumers. This electricity needs to be firm power: when the light is switched on, it must work.

The 'transition' is about replacing one set of assets to produce this firm-power result with another: replacing coal, gas and oil with renewables and nuclear. The old windows are broken (closing the oil-, gas- and coal-fired stations). The replacement windows are the renewables and nuclear. One set of assets is replaced by another. The output remains the same, although because the renewables are intermittent, low-density, geographically dispersed and small scale, the quality of the output may in fact be lower. The difference between before and after this transition is that the former requires much less capacity and storage and transmission than the latter. The new system is inherently more expensive, as we shall see in subsequent chapters. The broken glass has been replaced with more glass, which is of lesser quality.

The rejoinder is that the replacement energy is 'cleaner'. It does not emit so much GHGs. Where this is the case (and, as per the last chapter, this is not always straightforward), what is being argued is not that the capacity is an investment, but rather that the difference between before and after is that the price of carbon has been internalised. Polluters should pay, and, in the fossil-fuel world, the polluters are not paying, nor indeed are the polluters in the 'clean' energy supply chains.

Again, this is not investment. This is a change in relative prices caused by internalising the pollution. The output – firm-power electricity – remains the same. Recognising this transforms the way in which net zero should be accounted for, and therefore how the transition should be paid for, and how it should be funded. It undermines much of the nonsense proclaimed about 'green finance', 'green growth' and the fashion for ESG-directed (environment, social and governance) 'investments'.

In Bastiat's terms, what is seen is all the activity of building wind farms, solar farms, nuclear power stations and the extra transmission, batteries and storage. What is not seen is the diversion of resources to these ends which could have been used elsewhere and all to produce the same output.

Capital Maintenance versus Investment: Why the Accounting Matters

It is hard to underestimate how radical the implication of the broken window fallacy is for net zero and the climate change paradigm. If what is going on is the replacement of one set of assets by another to produce the same output, then the net effect is not economic growth. Deliberately closing down and scrapping existing assets (analogous to breaking the window) is not a growth-enhancing activity. It is not investment. The capital stock necessary to meet the demand for electricity is being maintained, just as the replacement of an old bridge by a new one maintains the ability to cross a river.

We are always repairing and replacing worn-out assets. Old assets typically 'depreciate', and depreciated assets make us worse off than we would be had we properly maintained them. In principle, most assets do not depreciate; they can always be maintained. My Oxford college has been maintained for centuries – since 1379. Stone erodes and floorboards wear out. They are patched up and mended. My college is probably now in a better condition than when it was built.[5] The college does not invest in replacement stones and floorboards; it maintains these assets for the benefit of current and future generations.

Where the bridge is better than the old one – for example, carrying more and heavier traffic – there is some enhancement. That enhancement improves the asset side of the balance sheet, and it is investment. But applied to electricity generation, renewables do not improve the electricity. They might reduce the associated pollution, but they do not make better electricity.

Now the radical bit. Capital maintenance is a claim on *current* income; it is *current* spending, not investment. It should not be paid for by borrowing. Each generation should do the maintenance to ensure the asset continues to be capable of delivering the services, just as each generation of the Fellows of my college in Oxford should set aside sufficient monies out of current income to maintain the buildings intact.

Imagine what would happen if renewables and nuclear were treated as capital maintenance. The electricity bills to customers now would include the capital maintenance, which would, in effect, be the payment for ensuring that there is no capital depreciation. Current customers would pay-as-you-go the maintenance expenditure of the energy companies, and the energy companies would borrow only for genuine enhancements, producing more and better electricity outputs – firmer power, for example, with greater reliability to ensure that the supplies are not only firm but secure.

Let's consider whether this is remotely feasible. The answer is that it was pretty much what happened in the past, and notably in the great expansion of electricity demand in the years after the Second World War through to the end of the 1970s. In the UK (and replicated in the US and most of Europe), GDP economic growth of around 3 per cent per annum was accompanied by a 7 per cent annual increase in electricity demand. This is roughly the demand growth expected over the next 25 years to meet the needs of digitalisation and AI, and all the data centres and associated communication infrastructure.

From the heavily damaged electricity generating and grid capacity that emerged from the Second World War, new coal and nuclear power stations matched the demand growth for 30 years. It was largely paid for by current customers through their bills, with borrowing mainly confined to smoothing out the cash flows of the state-owned Central Electricity Generating Board (CEGB), and with some taxpayer support.[6]

The service that the CEGB provided – to secure electricity supplies – was treated as an obligation, and ensuring that this continued to be met over time as demand rose was necessary to ensure the service in perpetuity. Each generation bequeathed to the next a set of energy assets sufficient to meet this obligation over time.

There are two ways of looking at this maintenance. One is maintenance of the physical assets – like my Oxford college. The other is maintenance of the services – for electricity supplies in the above example. For many assets there is no technical change. Natural capital is like this, and the aim is to preserve intact the key ecosystems. In the case of electricity supplies, the configuration of assets changes over time, whilst the service remains the same. There are different ways to generate the electricity to keep the lights on, just as digital technologies are replacing the postal services for letters.

If demand rises, as in both these examples, is this capital maintenance or investment? That depends on the intergenerational bargain and the ethics behind it. In the CEGB case above, meeting the extra demand was paid for by current customers. Now it is paid for through borrowing and hence by future customers. In the current context, where there has been little growth in electricity demand for several decades in the UK as it deindustrialised, there has been no additional need to add extra new capacity, other than to replace assets that wear out. In future, paying for this extra demand will come into play. But only for the extra demand, not the extra capacity needed for the same demand because the renewables are intermittent. In the CEGB case, even the extra capacity to meet extra demand was treated as a current cost, not as investment.

The contrast between treating capital maintenance as current spending and how it is treated now could not be starker. Almost everything is financed through borrowing, all to be funded and paid for by *future* consumers. We have abrogated our responsibilities to the next generation. We do not pay our generational dues. That further underpins the fiction that net zero is cheap, because bills do not fully reflect capital maintenance. Indeed, it is the main consequence of privatisation combined with financial liberalisation. The net zero debt is a legacy we leave for the next generation,[7] whilst also leaving them with the environmental consequences of failing to stop the rise in ppm of carbon concentrated in the atmosphere because the target is so badly defined and anyway not being met, and at best the same services of firm electricity are being supplied.

Green Finance

The broken window fallacy knocks the stuffing out of 'green' finance. The idea is that financial institutions should direct their funds to investing in projects and assets that meet certain 'green' criteria. Amongst these, the most prominent is net zero and the compatibility of their activities with the Paris Agreement 1.5 °C target.

By prioritising the directing of capital (rather than through current funding) in this way, some in the climate community claim that the cost of capital is lower. The reason for this is at best confused. Some argue the cost of capital for 'green' investments includes a non-monetary green premium to investors. Investors want to 'do good', whatever this means, and hence accept a lower return because they also get the 'return' from the warm reputational glow of being environmentally good. Yet others claim that green investments are less risky, and hence the lower cost of capital reflects that lower risk.

It helped those making these claims that the companies that qualified for the green label tended to be new tech companies, and these companies did very well anyway as their technologies took off. You could be 'green' and make lots of money because the share prices of these tech companies were booming. Hold a portfolio of the top seven US tech stocks over the last decade and you would become rich.

On returns to actual investments, it turned out to be otherwise for green investors. After some initial, sometimes spectacular, gains for wind and solar companies in the US, the UK and other European countries, they have taken big hits in recent years – the reasons have been multiple. Chinese manufacturers wiped out European and US solar panel manufacturers and Chinese competition has gradually eroded related green energy activities, and now is severely impacting on EVs. Interestingly, too, the Chinese companies have benefited from large-scale subsidies, and have made significant losses.

By contrast, the US Big Tech companies continued to prosper through 2025, but the gloss has come off their 'green' credentials. As the cause of major increases in energy demand, they, like the rest of the world, remain heavily dependent on fossil fuels. It turns out that, contrary to the ESG classifications, there is nothing particularly green about US Big Tech companies.

That leaves non-monetary reputational effects and altruism. Proclaiming a company to be green may be good marketing, provided its potential consumers are actually swayed by green considerations. The customers need to be willing to pay more for 'sustainable' products. Some companies which made a big play as being green made some spectacular gains in the early 2020s. Companies going 'beyond meat', for example, gained big inflows of investors' money. But as economic growth weakened – or simply did not recover from Covid – the evidence is that the number of consumers willing to pay green premiums has fallen, and this green bubble has burst.

Those that proclaimed their green virtues included oil and gas companies like BP and Shell, and consumer products companies like Unilever. Their shareholders paid a price rather than reaped sub-normal profits, and each of these three provides an example of shareholder-driven strategy reversals.

The retreat from green products has been exacerbated by the realisation that many of the claims to be sustainable relied on direct emissions only. The more service-based an economy, the more manufactured products and minerals are imported, the harder it is to present a green image. This is where the scope 1, 2 and 3 classifications of emissions come into play.[8] A company can have lower emissions from sources it owns or controls directly (scope 1), but still have higher emissions from the generation of purchased electricity, steam, heating or cooking used (scope 2); and even higher emissions still from all the other indirect emissions arising from its supply chain, up- and downstream (scope 3).

This indeed is what is happening in renewables generation: the wind turbine and the solar panel, once installed, produce few emissions (scope 1). But the supply chain, as we have seen, from mining through to refining and fabrication can be very dirty (scope 3).[9] This is true for countries too. Scope 1 territorial carbon emissions for the UK are low and have fallen a lot, but the country's scope 3 emissions are very much higher, as per the previous chapter.[10]

ESG applies to green finance, where the activity is treated as investment. But most of what investors do is not really investment anyway. Buying shares in a company is not investment, but rather the purchase of a second-hand asset. It is only when the money goes into retained earnings and rights issues – capital-raising actions to finance new enhancements – and debt is lent that enhancement investment is really taking place. And here, as we have seen, enhancements are noticeable largely by their absence when it comes to net zero. It is mostly borrowing for capital maintenance.

Adding on More Confusion to ESG

But why seek out investments for green finance which are just about net zero and the Paris Agreement target, however badly measured? If investors want 'to do good', then they should have in mind that 'good' has multiple dimensions. Investors might care about the social impact of a company's activities, and whether the governance of the company meets criteria in relation to DE&I. They might worry, too, about other environmental damage, not least to ecosystems from mining and refining, and not equate the 'environment' solely with carbon emissions.

In part, this is all an attempt to get investors as owners of companies to more closely supervise what their managers get up to, to close the gap between ownership and control. It is an attempt to move away from the idea that the primary purpose of a business is to make profits and extend its motivation to doing good in ESG terms.

The trouble with this approach is that the concept of 'good' is a highly contested one, and especially where the company faces competition, both nationally and globally. It better suits government-controlled businesses and organisations, where the costs fall ultimately on taxpayers, and large companies with market power, which can impose the additional costs on customers.

In terms of net zero, climate does not exhaust the environmental element of ESG, and there are trade-offs to be made. Not all net zero measures and activities are benign to ecosystems, as discussed, for example, in respect of large dams. Chinese mining and the environmental damage from its great dash for growth should rule out almost all products made in China from qualifying for ESG compliance status, whether purchased directly or as part of the supply chains of other businesses.

Who is to make these trade-offs? Is it for investors to do this via financial markets, or governments to make democratic choices? If it is the latter, it should come in terms of pollution taxes and environmental regulation, anti-slavery and workers' rights rules and corporate governance law, as well as government subsidies and levies. The government sets the rules, and the companies then profit-maximise in the context of the rules. This is what Milton Friedman had in mind in making profit-maximising the central aim of companies – always, he stressed, subject to the rules of the game.[11] The rules of the game are for democratically elected governments to set, not individual corporate executives and their shareholders.

Failure to address climate change and the great damage to ecosystems is primarily covered by failures in laws and regulations and their enforcement. Expecting companies to 'do good' and voluntarily forgo profitable opportunities is unlikely to be sufficient to deliver good climate or environmental outcomes.

Activists want to go further. They are not satisfied with the rules that democratic governments impose. They want to add their own. Oil and gas companies may contribute to the more than 80 per cent of global energy supplied, but activists don't think they should – or at least not Western oil and gas companies. They want to Just Stop Oil, and they are not content to be activists in their political campaigns to get parliaments to legislate. They want to directly undermine these businesses' social licence to operate.

Even if the switch to renewables did include investments as enhancements over and above the capital maintenance and replacement of assets to meet the same output, green finance is not the answer. It produced a booming industry of consultants and auditors, and a huge amount of greenwash, but it did not produce many genuine enhancements, and it came at the expense of the fiduciary duty of fund managers and trustees. As finance theory would suggest, if investors truncate the options to diversify their portfolios to a reduced subset, they will lose the full benefits of diversification. And they have.

The proof can be seen in the only target that really matters – the ppm. ESG and DE&I have not dented the growth in the ppm to over 425 ppm, and to the extent that these criteria have dented enthusiasm in the companies in the Western democracies to continue to underpin the fossil-fuel industries, the take-up of reduced outputs has been in the autocracies, and now in countries like Brazil. Oil, gas and even coal outputs have not fallen.

The Basic Arithmetic

The basic arithmetic of net zero is simple. For a given output – electricity – one set of assets is swapped for another. The first set of assets – coal, gas and nuclear power stations – is replaced by wind farms, solar (and possibly nuclear) – to produce the same output. The broken window is replaced by a new window.

In Bastiat's example, the windowpane is the same – like for like. In the climate change example, the assets being exchanged are not like for like. To achieve the same output, already as much as twice the capacity is needed, as well as much more transmission and lots of batteries and additional storage. A lot more assets are needed to replace the original assets to deliver the same output. As the share of renewables rises, so too will the multiple of capacity for the same output. True, the emissions will probably be lower, but once the carbon polluter charge is introduced, it is highly unlikely to outweigh the much greater capacity and networks and storage required.

The basic arithmetic is worse than in the Bastiat case. Even the net zero carbon argument is questionable, because what is also unseen is the negative impact on potential inward investment from energy-intensive industries that is deterred, as well as all the exit of energy-intensive production replaced by imports. These are part of what is unseen, but nevertheless all very real effects of the policies. This neatly brings us to the full costs of the renewables, and the system in which they are embedded.

6 RENEWABLES AND NUCLEAR AREN'T CHEAP

A central tenet of the climate community is that the renewables assumed to replace fossil fuels will be cheaper than fossil fuels. Many in the climate community believe and loudly assert that they already are. This is the win (mitigating climate change)–win (promoting economic growth)–win (lower cost). Like the mobile smartphones replacing the fixed phone lines and the laptop replacing the typewriter, wind and solar will take over from gas and coal and are both better and cheaper. Which begs an obvious question: why won't it happen in any event? Why is there a need for interventions and in particular subsidies? Smartphones and laptops did not need subsidies to take market share, so why is it necessary for renewables? If they have a competitive edge, there is no need to give them an even bigger one.

The easy reply is that these claims can be tested in the energy markets. Anyone can build a wind or solar farm. All that is needed is planning permission and a grid connection. Admittedly, this permission faces hurdles, but the reality is that few are applying for permission to bring merchant generation to the marketplace. On the contrary, most government-backed, fixed-price contracts require buyers to fulfil renewables quotas and ask for tax and other supports. No bidders offer to pay for the supporting infrastructure, nor do they want to pay for the costs of the intermittency their generation will cause. And when their power is not needed, they demand payment anyway. It's a million miles away from a subsidy-free competitive market.[1]

The reason for the need (necessity) for a subsidy (which is what the various supports add up to) is that once all the costs to the system are taken into account, renewables are not cost competitive in many locations (but crucially not all). In northern latitudes, offshore wind is widely unable to match gas (or coal) generation costs. Solar costs depend upon subsidised kit from mainly China and its competitiveness depends greatly on latitude. Onshore wind stands a better chance, but only if it does not pay for the costs of its intermittency.

The counterargument is that competition is rigged in favour of gas and coal, because these generators do not pay for the pollution they cause. A carbon tax would even up the playing field. This is indeed a major consideration, but coal generation in particular does already pay for emissions permits in the EU (the EU Emissions Trading System, EU ETS), and gas is subject to taxation. Not perfect anywhere, could be better, but still mostly less than the system costs of intermittency.

How then do the carbon community and its supporting politicians in the UK keep trotting out the line that renewables are cheaper than gas? The answer is the obvious one: by choosing a basis for comparison that gives this 'right' answer. Unfortunately, the chosen comparator is not the right one. Wrong measure for comparisons, wrong answer.

The Marginal Cost of a Solar Panel or a Wind Turbine

If you want to win the argument, the obvious place to start is with the marginal costs of generation from a wind turbine, a solar panel and a gas turbine. It is easy, because the marginal costs of wind and solar are roughly zero. The marginal cost of gas is the market price of gas, and this is certainly not zero. Wind and sunshine are free, gas is not, QED.

Make this comparison as the basis for claims about renewables being much cheaper, and the argument is overwhelmingly successful. Even nuclear wins on this basis: the marginal cost of nuclear generation is also close to zero.

This zero-marginal-cost measurement is important, not least for dispatch and the merit order which dictates how generation is brought onto the system as demand rises, but of itself it would not spur anyone into investing in these technologies. Why? Because the investor needs to pay for the capital project. Just because the marginal cost of generation is zero does not mean that the cost of renewables is zero. In the case of nuclear, if it was just about the marginal cost of generation, the world would be covered in nuclear power stations. Similarly, the marginal cost of rainfall is mostly zero, but the provision of water supplies is not. Ditto broadband and fibre.

The Levelised Cost

Turning to the costs of building and installing renewables (and nuclear), the comparator chosen is typically the levelised cost of generation. This has the merit of incorporating the capital costs and spreads them over the lifetime of the generation, all adjusted for by a discount rate.

Levelised cost is better than pure marginal cost, but it is still not very helpful. Levelised costs still play up the advantages of renewables, but do not incorporate the costs of intermittency. It is as if the new asset is just plugged in free of charge and the system is built up to include it. All the costs of the transmission and distribution, and the long-duration storage and batteries are excluded. It is still therefore a marginal concept: the cost of the asset over its lifetime *given* the system, to which it contributes intermittently.

The levelised cost can be made to look even better for renewables if it is assumed that the costs of solar panels (from China) and wind turbines keep falling, but the costs of gas turbines do not. This is indeed what has happened. It was once claimed that wind turbines would get ever cheaper – but no more. In the case of solar, the costs of the panels do keep coming down.[2] But falling costs of the kit does not equate to falling costs to the system. These may well go up as more renewables are bolted onto the system.

The one component of the levelised cost which matters even if it is much neglected is the cost of capital. Wind, solar and nuclear are all dominated by the cost of capital – the corollary of the zero marginal cost. In the great monetary laxity of 1990–2020, the cost of capital kept coming down widely across developed countries, ending up at around minus 2 per cent real before the monetary conditions began to normalise after 2020. At minus 2 per cent real, capital is effectively free, and hence any technology that is capital intensive must get cheaper, other things being equal. After 2020, the real and nominal interest rates rose. Offshore wind in the North Sea, the leading location in the world, is reflecting these higher costs, and the subsidy required in the contracts for differences (CfDs) is going up not down.[3] Despite all the efforts by government officials to massage the headline numbers (for example, by lengthening the contract period-guaranteed prices), this cannot be disguised. Whilst it is possible to argue that the higher cost of capital is temporary, the scale of the debt overhangs in public and private markets generally suggests otherwise.

Were the renewables to be treated as capital maintenance rather than investment, as argued in the previous chapter, the cost of capital element would be somewhat moderated, as pay-as-you-go passed through the construction costs. Ironically, by opting for pay-when-delivered, and renewables as investments, the cost of capital element bites much harder on renewables.[4]

Renewables Worsen the Economics of Gas and Nuclear

With fixed-price contracts and getting paid whether the electricity generated is used or not, the renewables are free to bid their marginal costs into the wholesale markets without impacting on their revenues from their fixed-price contracts. Recall, these marginal costs are zero. It mattered little in a world in which there was only a bit of renewables on the electricity system. But now it does: renewables generation can exceed the total market demand for periods of time. When this happens, the wholesale price is determined by the marginal renewable generator.[5] This is zero.

Whilst the fixed-price contracts shield the renewables, they don't shield the gas plants needed to cope with the intermittency. The result is that the intermittency of the renewables renders the gas plants intermittent too. They cannot earn a return when the wholesale price is below their own marginal (positive) cost. The consequence is significant: a gas plant can now be economic to build only if it can occasionally score a jackpot of a very high wholesale price when there are not enough zero-marginal-cost renewables to cover total demand. This is not a good basis for building new gas plants and can rapidly force off existing gas power stations. Add to this the need to contract for gas supplies on an on-demand, intermittent basis but without knowing the quantity needed. Not surprisingly, the economics of gas are undermined by renewables.

It is not just gas. Renewables have the potential to render nuclear intermittent too. There will be times when there is more wind and solar generated than total demand, and this means that nuclear might have to be constrained off too – or the renewables will be constrained off. Something has to give. The economics of running an intermittent nuclear power station are very difficult; in practice, it would probably have to keep running since it cannot easily be ramped up and down, but to no market purpose.

In this respect, renewables do not mix well with any base-load firm-power technology and the economics points to intermittent renewables being used only when they deliver sufficiently low electricity to the transmission to leave room for nuclear, assuming it is more costly to turn nuclear on and off. The 'wasted' electricity is an additional cost, as is the higher cost of running gas power stations in intermittent mode.

There are potential ways out of this system problem. The excess renewables output could be stored, but there is as yet no technology at a large enough scale to handle this except at the margin. Nor is any imminent. Alternatively, the excess renewables (or the otherwise intermittent nuclear) could be used for something else, like making hydrogen. That requires a coordinated investment programme and not only is this likely to be slow and later, but it also assumes that hydrogen production would be intermittent too. It does not help that hydrogen itself is costly. A similar argument would apply to utilising the excess renewable energy for desalination.

The Cost of Intermittency

The above are consequential costs caused by the impact of excess wind and excess solar power. It could be managed if the renewables could guarantee to supply the market at all and any times; in other words, if wind power could be more firm and less intermittent. But it isn't and it won't be for a considerable time, if ever. Intermittency is endemic to renewables and it has significant system costs. These all need to be taken into account to establish the correct approach to comparing the costs of renewables with the costs of other ways of generating electricity.

I shall use the UK system as the basis for the discussion below, for two reasons beyond its intrinsic interest to UK citizens and UK businesses. The UK aims to be net zero in electricity generation by 2030 and the UK has deindustrialised more than most. It offers salutary lessons to everyone else.

An electricity system needs firm power – available on demand. Renewables can't deliver this. They are de-rated, operating mostly less than 50 per cent of the time. When the wind does not blow and the sun does not shine, something else has to deliver the firm power to the system.

This means that a renewables-based system has to have much more capacity than a firm-power system, and that brings a major extra cost to the system because of the renewables. As noted earlier, in the case of the UK, the 'old' system required around 60 GW of installed capacity to meet the expected peak electricity demand, including a bit of margin (say 20 per cent) to allow for shocks. Now the system requires well over 100 GW to meet a slightly lower demand.

Let this sink in. The UK needs around *twice* the capacity to meet the same demand. Following Bastiat's broken window fallacy, the windows (the coal and nuclear capacity) have been broken. Both are largely closed down (though there will be some more nuclear added to the system after 2030, whilst almost all existing nuclear will be closed, except Sizewell B). The replacement windows are not as good (as firm), and hence there need to be a lot more of them to get the same firm-power electricity for the system. The cost of the extra, say, 60 GW is an *extra* cost to the system compared with the alternative firm-power options. It gets worse. NESO estimates that if peak capacity doubles by 2050, across its scenarios which meet the net zero 2050 target, capacity rises to between 384 and 450 GW.[6]

Much of the new renewables capacity will spend perhaps half or more of its generating life standing idle. That is when the wind is not blowing enough (or blowing too much) and the sun is not shining. When they are delivering to the system, there will be times when they force some other renewables to stand idle because the total demand will be well below the potential total renewables supply.

Mitigating the Intermittency: Standby Capacity

The sheer scale of the intermittency problem encourages the search for ways to mitigate its impacts. One option is to have lots of gas power stations ready to run at short notice, but mostly idle. These can be 'peakers' and small scale, or they can just be big gas power stations on standby.

For the UK, NESO estimates that by 2030 there will need to be around 35 GW of gas running perhaps 5 per cent of the time.[7] It is analogous to having lots of fire stations with fire engines ready to go in the event of an emergency.

Much of this would not be necessary at all with conventional power systems. It is an *extra* cost to the system of renewables. It is part of the cost of having twice the capacity to meet the same demand – now around three times the total capacity for twice the demand in 2050 – an extra broken windows cost.

Standby can also be very small scale and site specific. A system with lots of renewables is inherently more difficult to operate, and it is to be expected that there will be a large number and variety of challenges over a conventional one. Gas (and coal) power stations offer 'idling' services to manage frequency on transmission and distribution networks. When these are absent, the risk of power cuts rises. Whatever the eventually established causes (if they are ever established) of the power cut in Spain and Portugal in April 2025,[8] idling is one factor in the sudden loss of the required frequency, which then triggered the cascade of disconnections. More generally, power cuts and related incidents have been rising on many European power systems.

The problem with this is not just the usual costs of power cuts over recent decades, but the much greater costs to the new and emerging technologies that need 24/7 supplies. These include data centres, robotics and a host of cyber technologies. Since the water, transport and banking systems are now all cyber-dependent (as is energy), the value of security of supply – guaranteed 24/7 firm power – has gone up a lot. In Spain and Portugal when the great power cut hit, it was notable that only cash could enable transactions – and hence the economy – to function at all.

The consequence is obvious. Lots of businesses and public services will start to install their own standby generators, and these are likely to be mainly gas. This extra standby capacity could be considerable, and it is all an extra cost of renewables. In the UK in the 1970s when businesses faced the risks of miners' strikes causing power cuts (and a three-day working week was imposed on industry to husband remaining coal stocks for electricity generation), a significant amount of installed capacity was small scale, mainly diesel standby generators.[9]

It is not just banks and water treatment works that may require new standby capacity. The power cut at Heathrow Airport in 2025, which brought the whole airport to a standstill for a day, raises the question of whether it should now invest in its own power station.[10] Hospitals and emergency services face the same question.

These costs mount up. The cost of renewables to the system includes all this extra capacity to meet the same demand for the same service – firm power to the system. None of this shows up in the marginal cost of wind or solar, or in the levelised cost of these technologies. Coal, gas and nuclear do not need this great capacity overhang. This should enter the comparison of the cost of the technologies. If included, it is highly likely that the claim about renewables being nine times cheaper than gas would be seen as nonsense. To claim otherwise, as included in NESO's Future Energy Scenarios 2050, requires these system costs to be ignored. That is why its claim that costs and prices might begin to fall by 2045 in the 2050 net zero scenarios relies heavily on levelised costs for its comparisons between electricity generation technologies, and questionable assumptions about future gas prices.[11]

Managing Intermittency: Active Demand

The next option for handling intermittency is to force demand to be flexible. Instead of bringing on the back-up generation at moments of peak demand, perhaps the customers could be kind enough to turn off their electricity? If the lights are turned off, no power is needed. This is what might be called the 'voluntary power cuts' approach, as it is over and above what customers otherwise would have done.

Flexible demand has always been a part of modern electricity systems and largely confined to very large energy-intensive industries. Electricity systems have always had to plan for possible power shortages and the system operators work out how to flex the demand side. The UK's three-day week in the 1970s was an extreme version. Many options were successfully explored during the UK miners' strike in 1984–85. The flexibility is itself an additional cost.

Some of this flexibility had to do with plant maintenance and the management of the coal and nuclear power station fleet. The traditional 'August works holiday', when much production shut down, not only in the UK but in France too, enabled power stations to be taken off the system and the considerable maintenance in particular needed to handle the boilers in coal power stations, subject to the abrasive coal that was thrown into them, to be carried out. But much flexibility was a wheeze to give industry cheaper prices since the CEGB maintained a considerable excess supply margin, on the grounds that this was cheaper than constraining off demand. It was right. The costs of excess supply are spread over the whole system and less than the costs of interruptions. It was a good insurance policy. Long-term interruptible contracts were signed but rarely called upon. The option was there, and this is how the CEGB would plan to handle a major problem in its system.

Now it is more important to be able to shed demand, and especially industrial demand, quickly. But it is also just the moment when always-on firm power is required for the new cyber-dependent systems and technologies. The cost of an interruption has gone up not down. Demand is less and less able to be varied just when more and more intermittent renewables make it most needed to do so.

There are fortunately other options. Domestic households could be incentivised to switch off at short notice. Better still, smart technology could manage their demand for them. Yet again, the question arises as to whether households are more willing to do so now than in the past. Households are also 'always on' in the digital age. As people get richer, so their willingness to tolerate interruptions gets less. They are not even willing to put on more clothing and lower the thermostats for household heating and now demand air conditioning too. Again, the value of firm power has gone up not down. GDP growth means more firm-power demand.

As discussed in Chapter 2, perhaps EVs could help to solve this problem by flexing the time for charging to nighttime and again perhaps automatically via smart metering and associated software? Whilst it is true that there are opportunities to exploit potentially excess renewable supplies, notably for wind (not solar) at night (and nuclear), it is not a solution to a deficient daytime supply, unless EV drivers are prepared to export from their charged batteries. The always-charged preference for commuters might mitigate this. In any event, transport demand for electricity is additional to and not a substitute for the system as a whole.

It is relatively easy to demonstrate how these smart demand-side technologies might work in a modern home with smart technology and savvy consumers if they want to take up the flexibility. The reality is very different. Most houses are not new. Smart metering is still not universal in the UK, quite a lot of it works badly and some even not at all, and the plethora of companies, technologies and organisations involved makes the coordination far from perfect. All the while, the value of 24/7-demand electricity is going up and that is before heat pumps and air conditioning seriously add to demand for electricity.

Managing Intermittency: Batteries and Storage

The obvious answer to intermittency is storage, and primarily this is via batteries. But the equally obvious point is that this is an *additional cost* caused by the intermittency of renewables. It needs to be added to the other costs of intermittency to the system identified above – an increasingly heavy cost overhang driving the wedge between the system costs of renewables and the marginal and levelised costs typically highlighted by the climate community.

Batteries are their own environmental nightmare. As we have seen, the mining of the minerals and their refining, the manufacture of the batteries, and their disposal and recycling are not very green, to put it mildly. They bring big environmental costs to renewables and EVs and they undermine the label 'clean' typically unthinkingly attached to anything in the renewables box.

They are also expensive. All the mining and refining and the battery gigafactories are *additional costs* to the electricity system.

Batteries don't solve the long-duration storage problem. Although they have efficiency losses, their forte is short-duration storage. A solar panel plus a battery opens up the time envelope beyond the hours of daylight sunshine. It can, for example, be charged from daytime solar to be discharged at night. Larger-scale batteries can do a few days when connected to the electricity transmission and distribution systems.

But batteries cannot yet solve longer-duration periods of low wind and low solar (*dunkelflaute* periods, when little or no energy can be generated from these renewable sources). In the Northern Hemisphere, as the latitude increases, so do the winter periods when cloudy skies by day compound longer night times. Solar is not so good a power generator in northern winters.

Now add high-pressure cold weather systems to the dark winter skies, so typical of Northern Europe. The sun doesn't shine much, and the wind may not blow much for days (or even weeks), just when it is coldest and darkest, and hence the demand for electricity goes up, and especially if electricity is increasingly used for heating via heat pumps rather than gas boilers. This latter point is particularly important – the gas for heating in the UK is the biggest energy flow in the UK, so switching from gas to electricity is a really big electricity demand increase, especially in these winter periods.

What then happens? This is where the 35 GW of gas on standby comes in. In these periods, gas may be needed to cover almost all the demand for electricity, and with data centres also added to the system, it is not clear that even 35 GW will be enough. This is a very big *additional* cost to the system as a result of the intermittency of renewables – again not included in the marginal or levelised cost calculations.

Other options are available. Longer-duration storage is largely all about water. Hydroelectricity can be drawn from Norway to both the UK and the EU (especially Germany), via interconnector cables. Pumped storage may give a limited extra boost to supply in these *dunkelflaute* periods. The problem with Norwegian hydro is that many connected countries might want the power at the same time. The problem with pumped storage is that it is a very expensive option to build lots more facilities. Both are *additional costs* to the system of having lots of intermittent renewables on the system.[12]

Managing Intermittency: Interconnectors

Interconnectors are relatively low cost to install. Cabling is a well-established technology. It does need copper and steel and PVC and therefore does have environmental and notably carbon consequences. Onshore transmission and distribution need to be added.

Interconnectors have considerable advantages for the managing of electricity systems. Trade is generally 'good'. It brings competitive pricing. The downside to a renewables-dominated system is that it breaks the link between costs and prices. In a competitive market it is the least-cost supply price that wins. Much of the UK generation is expensive, with much offshore wind at guaranteed prices of well over £100/MWh. Hence at the margin, power supplies from other – cheaper – sources may expose these higher costs, recovered only by forcing customers to pay for them.

Putting the competitive bit aside, the main issues with interconnectors arise from the reliance upon them to manage the intermittency. In the UK example, NESO suggests that, as well as 35 GW of gas capacity, some 10 GW plus of interconnectors may be needed in 2030 to keep the lights on.[13] Electricity flows both ways, but the assumption for the renewables-dominated UK system is that the main flows into the UK will be concentrated in these darker colder winter days. This is precisely the time in high-pressure Northern European weather systems that Germany and other Northern European countries with big renewables generation will need the electricity too. The result will be higher prices. This is an *additional* cost of renewables.[14]

Higher electricity imports matter not just because of the extra direct costs to the system, but also their implications for the balance of payments. Energy forms a big part of global trade and is a big factor for the UK. Oil and gas exporters, like the UK until recently, with its North Sea resources, Norway and now the US, gain from strong benefits to their current accounts on their balance of payments and some currency support that enables interest rates to be lower than they otherwise would be. These impacts can now be seen in reverse in the UK. Switching from significant high energy surpluses as a result of North Sea oil and gas to imports of oil and gas and now electricity weakens the current account, and hence the value of the pound. It also results in higher interest rates, for example, to maintain any given euro–sterling exchange rate. Halting further licences for more North Sea oil and gas can only make this position worse. Now add in greater electricity imports too, which are a consequence of the intermittency of higher shares of renewables.

Finally, there are the costs of defending these cables. Recent events in the Baltic Sea underline the vulnerability of communications and energy cables and pipes. The blowing-up of the Nord Stream gas pipelines is a stark example. In the context of a greater need to be 'war-ready' to tackle possible Russian attacks, a credible defence strategy requires not only more protection of the cables and pipes but also plans to handle the consequences of widespread attacks and hence interruptions in supplies.

For the UK there are big costs here. The gas supplies to provide the back-up generation to the renewables are heavily dependent on pipelines. The Norwegian Continental Shelf provided around 35 per cent of UK annual gas supplies in 2020–24, most of it through the Langeled pipeline.[15] The electricity cables supply electricity and if the system needs 10 GW of interconnector supplies to support the renewables, then the loss of any of the interconnectors could be serious. No doubt a Russian attack could be timed for a *dunkelflaute* event to cause maximum chaos and damage. All of this contingency precaution comes with *additional* costs, and these costs are largely (but not exclusively) caused by the intermittency of renewables.

The Full Cost of a Renewables System versus the Full Costs of Gas plus Nuclear

The various *additional* system costs of renewables identified above are not exhaustive. Managing an electricity system with a frequent zero marginal cost undermines wholesale markets and creates both winners and losers. The scale of the subsidies is in many cases in excess of what is needed, and the debts that are mounting up to support what is really a case of capital maintenance for the broken windows will all have considerable economy-wide consequences. The net zero renewables-based strategy is a massive programme with inevitably major macroeconomic consequences.

Just by sticking to the easily identifiable and more direct costs of renewables, it is apparent that they are not cheap, and nothing like as cheap as the activists and some politicians and many in the climate community too often claim.

This should not be at all surprising, even if it appears so to the climate community. Not only is the reality of the need for large-scale customer and taxpayer subsidies apparent, when they would be redundant if renewables were nine times cheaper, but the fundamental need to pay the cost of the pollution that GHGs cause points towards a gap between what we pay for energy and what its full environmentally inclusive costs are. It is inevitably going to be expensive. Sadly, there is no win–win here.

If modelling suggests a high carbon price to represent the damage, and ultimately we as consumers – and hence as the ultimate polluters – are not paying it, it would be surprising if we could pay for the pollution and still end up with cheaper energy. The gas needed to keep the lights on and the fossil fuels embedded in our imports do not go away just because the UK has lots of intermittent renewables, and all is a cost of energy.

The climate reality is that we are living beyond our environmental (and climate) means, and that to get to a position of lower emissions and at the same time increasingly firm power requires higher prices because of higher costs. Otherwise, just as in the example of the fixed phone versus the smartphone and the typewriter versus the laptop, it would happen anyway. The fact that renewables are more expensive than their lobbyists claim does not mean that we should not build out renewables. But it does mean that we should be told that we will have to pay more not less, and we should not be sold stories about how the gas alternative is necessarily going to be one of ever higher and more volatile prices.

Whether renewables are, as some claim, the solution to climate change would be best tested against other technologies by being realistic about the full system costs and doing so in the context of a carbon price. Whether any major economy can be run on predominantly wind and solar is being tested in the UK, and so far it is being found wanting, especially as the UK deindustrialises in the face of the resultant highest industrial energy prices in the developed world. This adds a final cost of renewables – the subsidies that the UK government is paying to bail out large petrochemical and steel industries. Industrial subsidies are needed because of the high cost of energy, which is the result of the high costs of renewables.

7 OFFSETS, BUYING INDULGENCES AND SEQUESTRATION

Carbon offsets purport to be what is said on the tin: they offset the carbon we emit. Don't worry about flying, just tick the box on the air ticket app and pay a bit more and some organisation will plant enough trees to make up for the damage you are causing. There is no additional pollution, and hence it is consistent with living within our environmental means and stabilising the climate by not impacting on the concentration of carbon in the atmosphere. Fly to COP30 in Brazil, go on a holiday cruise, or let your emails and browsing sap up lots of carbon-based energy. It is all just fine, as long as you buy these offsets. In theory, it should all end very well. Some in the carbon community actually seem to believe all this.

Similarly, where renewable natural capital is damaged – say, by building a highway through the Amazon rainforest to get delegates to COP30 in Brazil, cutting down oak trees to make way for a data centre, clearing land for minerals for batteries, or erecting wind farms on peat soils – if natural capital is improved elsewhere to compensate, there should be no net loss of biodiversity. In both the carbon and the biodiversity cases, it could be better still, by taking a risk-averse approach and over-compensating for the damage and emissions. Net gain rather than net zero.

This all looks like a perfect get-out-of-jail card. Sadly, it is too good to be true. Offsetting will not bring the damage to an end. On the contrary, it will often make it worse.

A Neat, Seductive Idea

The climate change problem is typically viewed through the lens of emissions and their reduction. Reduce the flow of carbon into the atmosphere, and the concentration should stop rising. But this is a half-baked approach – half-baked, because the concentration of carbon in the atmosphere is a stock, and the result of two flows, not one. It is net of emissions *and* sequestration. To fix the climate change problem, we need to reduce emissions *and* increase sequestration, whereas what we are doing is increasing emissions *and* reducing sequestration, and this is where the climate change and the biodiversity problems meet. Almost everything that reduces natural sequestration reduces biodiversity. It is a question of emissions *and* nature, not a siloed carbon problem. It is simply naive to say that, by mitigating climate change, this is a positive biodiversity project. It all depends on how it is done.

On the sequestration side, the reality is that it has been inverted. Instead of sequestrating carbon, many of the natural ecosystems are now emitting it – indeed, quite a lot of natural systems are now net emitters. Think of the burning rainforests, think of the exposure of peat bogs, think of the intensification of agriculture stripping carbon from the soils.[1] Think of all the additional mining for the net zero technologies.

The first port of call for policies on sequestration is to stop these emissions from natural ecosystems. On this, offsetting should have no obvious role. The damage to sequestration and these extra emissions should be treated just like emissions from coal-fired power stations. Polluters should pay, and it would be a very odd climate policy that paid coal-fired power stations to reduce their emissions. Yet this is exactly what is going on in respect of natural sequestration, and it does much to explain why offsetting is a generally dubious policy.

In theory, an offset is just the payment for someone else to reduce their emissions, and in theory it does not matter whether this is a reduction of emissions that otherwise would have happened, or an increase in sequestration that otherwise would not have happened. Yet, in practice, these two are very different. The first is what might be called 'general offsetting' and the second is 'sequestration offsetting'. In this latter category, there are two types: natural sequestration and industrial sequestration. Natural means what it says and uses natural carbon take-up, for example, through photosynthesis, to extract carbon from the atmosphere and lock it up; whilst the industrial side takes carbon from polluting factories, vehicles and power stations, separates it out and injects it back underground, in, for example, depleted oil and gas wells, saline aquifers, solidified in rocks, or directly extracts carbon from the atmosphere and buries it. Industrial sequestration from point sources of pollution and the extraction of carbon directly from the atmosphere are both dealt with later on as examples of geoengineering; here we concentrate on natural sequestration.

These distinctions really matter. General offsetting – paying some government or organisation not to burn rainforests – is very different from paying it to add new trees and plants. The former has the following form: carry on polluting, and pay someone else to stop polluting. The alternative is, since they are both polluters, to make both pay. That would be a symmetrical application of the polluter-pays principle, a core component of the sustainable economy.

Worse still, the incentive problems are awful and might well increase net pollution. Why? Because any government or organisation owning or controlling a rainforest knows that the best strategy would be to threaten to burn it down, in the happy expectation that some polluters will pay them not to do so. Better still, burn a bit down just to show the threat is credible. If the owner of the rainforest decides to protect it, then the emissions from burning and cultivation will not happen, and hence there are no additional emissions reductions to offset the emissions of the purchase of the offset.

The case for paying someone to sequestrate carbon to offset your emissions – sequestration offsetting – is based upon some elementary economics: select the cheapest options first, and the marginal cost of sequestration may be lower than the marginal cost of emissions reduction. It is a simple idea, but it has an obvious flaw. It assumes there is a choice between the two. But if the concentration of emissions has to stop going up, and eventually come down, then *both* are required. They are all within the envelope of the total required to reduce the rise in the stock and then reduce its level. Reducing the flows in (emissions) and the flows out (sequestration) are both necessary; they are complements not substitutes.

To capture this idea, imagine if we *started* with natural sequestration first, and gave it all the attention we currently give to emissions. Could we raise sequestration enough to halt the rise in ppm in the atmosphere? Only then, on this reversal of our approach, would we turn to paying someone to reduce their emissions to 'offset' the failure to increase sequestration enough.

Back to the conventional emissions-first approach. What of the extreme cases where emissions cannot be reduced and the produced goods are essential to economies? Shouldn't the polluter be able to buy an offset instead of closing down?[2] The answer is generally no, even if the polluting activity which is hard to abate continues and therefore continues to emit carbon.

The reason why offsetting has gained such attraction comes back to the money. Developed countries won't transfer much money to developing countries – for example, to help them develop without destroying their rainforests, so they fall back on the idea that the private sector can step in.

The way it should work is that the government should tax the emissions with a carbon tax and then use this money to help developing countries. The money should be collected from polluters, bearing down on their pollution, and it should be spent as part of economic development, including the protection of natural capital. The carbon tax has incentives to go for the cheapest options first. In cases where it is hard to abate emissions, the carbon tax raises the prices so we the polluters who buy these products bear these costs.

An oil company, for example, should pay a full carbon tax, and then the money should be directed by governments to the protection and enhancement of sequestration. It would be a tax on non-renewable natural capital (in this case oil), funding renewable natural capital. The added advantage of government-to-government transfers is that they are much more enforceable than purely private transfers. Polluting companies have limited leverage over the recipient of offset monies; governments have much more. Such a carbon tax would also apply to the emissions associated with other minerals – notably, copper, nickel, lithium and cobalt.

Offsetting appeals to polluters because they avoid carbon taxes and regulations and are able to claim that they are going towards net zero. If the offsets count against the territorial carbon targets under the UN accounting framework, both the government and the polluters share an interest in these company-level transfers.

Whether it is general offsetting or sequestration offsetting, the assumption is that the offsets are transparent, and that the gains from offsetting are permanent reductions in carbon in the atmosphere. Even if the neat idea was a good theoretical approach (which it is not), it is in practice much worse. It is extremely difficult to prove that the general or sequestration offsetting turns out to be what has been promised, and even harder to make sure that carbon is permanently removed from the atmosphere.

The Conditions That Need to Be Met

Suppose for a moment that a sequestration offset is a good idea and suppose it is to be delivered through planting trees. How would anyone know how much carbon is being sequestrated? It is a simple question that must be answered before proceeding, for obvious reasons. Unfortunately, it almost always isn't. The answer is very complicated.

Let's say the project is to plant sufficient trees to offset 1 tonne of carbon emissions. Having found a site, the project developers need to ascertain the baseline: how much carbon is being sequestrated already, so the additional carbon to be sequestrated can be set against this baseline. There might be grass, trees, scrub or other vegetation already on the site, and the soils might be taking up carbon. The baseline is not that which is in place after the site has been cleared and prepared, before the trees are planted. Clearance and preparation will almost certainly make matters worse, before the planting starts.

It is not possible to be precise, especially about what is going on in the soils. It is bound to be an estimate, not a fact, and the incentives of those doing the baseline carbon assessment matter. Environmental and carbon consultants are usually paid by the parties to the offset. Each has an interest in the outcome. Neither presumably wants an answer that negates the offset.

Suppose that these obstacles are overcome. Suppose there is an agreed baseline, minus the carbon emissions from, for example, using herbicides to remove vegetation to enable clear ground around the saplings, minus the fuel expended and soil damage done in the planting, minus any emissions associated with raising the saplings from seeds, and minus any loss of sequestration that the previous vegetation might have delivered. The project is now set, having taken a significant step backwards with the site works. Offsets typically make sequestration worse before they try to sequestrate more. Lots of carbon can be emitted in getting an offset project going.

The baseline is just what is on site now. It is almost certainly not ideal. The state of many of the ecosystems is already degraded by all the damage done since 1990 and before. Ending up with maintaining the status quo would not be a great achievement. The promoters of offsets do not typically ask what the best possible outcomes could be, only whether the proposed project can be referenced against the (debased) baseline and then improved upon. The result is entrenching the current carbon- and nature-depleted state of affairs as the baseline.

The baseline is most likely just about carbon and is unlikely to take proper account of the biodiversity, water and other natural capital services that the site currently provides and subsequently might have carried on providing had the offset project not gone ahead. To take a simple example, planting eucalyptus trees would be a good way to sequestrate carbon fast (indeed, one of the best),[3] but it would almost certainly be very bad for biodiversity. Trees might dry out the soils and acidify water. Tampering with the natural environment has all sorts of consequences, intended and unintended. A carbon offset would need to be at least biodiversity-neutral to qualify. 'Do no harm' is the minimum rule required.

Trees don't just grow and deliver the carbon goods without help. As any forester knows, trees are vulnerable to disease, they might be destroyed by fire, and there are all sorts of animals that might harm them, from squirrels to deer and a host of insects and fungi. If the project is for a single species, then the chances of disease are higher, and if the trees are packed together, fire and wind will be greater threats.

To prevent any of these happening, a lot of economic activity is required, in addition to the costs of monitoring what is going on. The trees may need to be fenced in against animals with lots of wires and timber posts and using heavy machinery almost certainly powered by diesel engines. Biosecurity measures may be required. There may need to be fire breaks. Drainage may have to be adjusted. All of these have associated carbon emissions. All these additional emissions need to be subtracted from the project.

These costs and emissions are upfront at the start of the project. To reap the claimed extra tonnes of carbon sequestrated over and above what would have happened otherwise requires one more step. This is the counterfactual of the other possible uses of the site. Planting eucalyptus is probably not the only option for the land use. Other options may yield more natural capital benefits, and it is the net of carbon *and* biodiversity that matters, not just carbon.

Having crossed all these hurdles, the project developer then has to wait a long time. With the fast-growing eucalyptus, this might be 25 years. If it is oaks that are planted (much better for biodiversity), then perhaps the wait is 100 years or more? Not only does this do havoc to the economics – the money has to be invested without return for all this time – but the purchasers of the offsets also have a long wait for the full carbon sequestration while the emissions being offset by the project are happening now. The companies buying the offsets may go out of business or move their businesses to other countries. Over half a century or more, many – perhaps most – will.

From a climate change perspective, it is not obviously a good bargain – increasing emissions in the short term hoping to reduce emissions in the long term. The urgency is to reduce emissions *now*, and if the offset is really needed to make the numbers add up in, say, 25 years' time, then the climate change battle may already be largely over. Next time you buy an offset and go on a flight, remember that much of the damage you do may (or may not) be rectified in a quarter of a century or later. Compare this to just not flying now.

The trees will be sequestrating as they grow, so not all is postponed for so long. Sequestration is very much about the growing period, and not when the trees are mature. At the end of their useful carbon-sequestrating lives, they can be left to stand, or they can be felled. The choices include whether to burn them (returning the carbon temporarily sequestrated to the atmosphere), to turn them into timber, to create pulp for paper, and to leave them to rot back into the ground. The first is already done at scale: biomass burning for power generation using wood pellets returns the carbon to the atmosphere. The offsetting tree planting is a *temporary ex post* sequestration of carbon. If the offset is for a hedgerow, when the hedge is cut it is common practice to burn the hedge trimmings.

Turning the wood into timber has the merit of a semi-permanent locking-up of the carbon sequestrated (less the carbon in the manufacture, building and installation processes). But trees for fast carbon sequestration – like eucalyptus – are not known as a good source of timber. Larches and other pines may be better and fast, but they are prone to disease and wind damage. Paper and cardboard can be recycled, but not all is, and recycling can be water and energy intensive.

What all this illustrates is that the simple offsetting idea is anything but simple in practice. It is not clear how much additional carbon could be captured, how quickly and for how long, and the net effect could be more rather than less carbon in the atmosphere.

There is one further complication to those who see sequestration as a credible and significant way to tackle climate change. Photosynthesis is not very efficient, and as a result the totals of additional sequestration through photosynthesis are not that great.[4] It would not make much difference to the ppm in the atmosphere for a considerable time. It would, at best, be a bit-part player. That leaves industrial sequestration and DACS, and these are dealt with later in Chapter 8 as part of broader geoengineering options.

The Wild West of Offsetting

With these considerations and concerns in mind, the scope for greenwash has not gone unnoticed. There have been several attempts to try to regulate offsets and to certify them so that investors can have confidence that what they are buying does what it says on the tin. None has been successful so far.

Broadly these fall under two headings: the international carbon crediting mechanism under Article 6.4 of the Paris Agreement,[5] led by the United Nations Framework Convention on Climate Change (UNFCCC) Secretariat, and national government schemes (such as in California, Australia and South Korea), and the voluntary accreditation schemes run by NGOs and other private organisations, notably the American Carbon Registry, Climate Action Reserve, the Gold Standard, Plan Vivo and VERRA.[6]

The UN side is all about letting countries offset emissions made in their territorial domains against emissions reduced elsewhere. Under the Paris Agreement, this offsetting is voluntary, but from the UN's perspective it has the advantage of providing a mechanism for money to flow from those with more stretching NDCs (typically developed countries) to developing countries via specific projects. For developed countries, it allows them to slow up emissions reductions from what would otherwise have been necessary to meet their NDCs. Even this is less than it seems, for the options under Article 6.4 influence the NDC the country will propose and adopt.[7] From a presentational perspective, the hope has been that these NDCs would be more ambitious as a result of this get-out clause.

All these governmental and non-governmental parties try to develop standards and principles, and then to assess projects and to run lists and registries of them. Put simply, if the standards are not robust and credible – in the sense that they clearly require a net carbon saving that can be measured and verified – the offset is at best dubious. Sadly this has turned out to be the case in lots of examples, some of which are high-profile. Few projects can demonstrate that they sequestrate more carbon than would otherwise happen – that they are genuinely net additional once proper account has been taken of baselines, counterfactuals, project maintenance and end-of-life treatments. Few projects last very long and the voluntary side has been riddled with scandals and criticisms.

The VERRA case in 2024 is an example.[8] It did much both to highlight the problems and to undermine confidence in the outcomes. The case was all about 'avoided deforestation'. It raises all the issues noted above about baselines, and business-as-usual assumptions. Avoiding deforestation is a negative, whereas planting trees is an attempt at positive carbon sequestration. If tree cover is already 100 per cent, these sorts of carbon credits are about paying people not to cut down trees. As discussed above, the perverse incentives are considerable: just threaten to make the counterfactual even worse by making business-as-usual more destructive, increasing the gap between the 100 per cent and what VERRA and others assume would otherwise have happened. As ever, the counterfactual is not observable. The point of the project is to prevent it happening and there are no direct observations of what would otherwise have happened.

It is easy to see that, by manipulating the counterfactual (in theory at least), almost any number can be achieved, up to the point of complete destruction of any and all sequestration – in other words, turning the existing forests into a bomb site.

None of this suggests that there should not be urgent measures taken to try to protect forests and particularly rainforests, and as ecosystems not discrete bits. In many ways, the resort to carbon offsets is an admission that the broader options are just too difficult. It rests on the assumption that adding up lots of carbon offsets can build a patchwork quilt of protection, whereas, under the COP15 biodiversity framework,[9] the idea is that governments will do the protecting on the basis of land use and land-use planning, and under the climate change COPs, climate funds will transfer money to support developing countries' efforts at decarbonising.

An additional perverse incentive comes from the impact of VERRA-type schemes on the governments and their incentives to act. If it is possible to point to private routes to protect forests, then the pressure is less on governments to step into the breach.

In all these considerations, it is important to always bear in mind that, for the purchaser, the point of offsets is to avoid reducing its emissions directly and claim that someone else is doing this for them. This incentive is greatly increased when the price of carbon credits is taken into account. These vary greatly, but can be as low as US$1–$2 a tonne, whereas in carbon pricing for emissions in those areas where they are enforced, the price can be between $50 and $100 a tonne. From a profit-maximising perspective, it is a no-brainer to buy the credits, and take the credit. No wonder so many companies find offsetting so attractive. It is a very cheap get-out-of-jail card.

When it comes to the biodiversity offsets, the schemes are even weaker. In the case of carbon offsets, it is only carbon that has to be accounted for. There is no agreed definition of biodiversity, and no credible standards that can be universally applied (the aspiration of carbon-offsetting schemes). This is because each location is different and each occurs in an ecosystem, where the value of an offset is dependent on how these ecosystems as a whole function.[10]

The extraordinary gap between the simplicity of the standards and methodologies actually applied, on the one hand, against the complexity of ecosystems, on the other, is huge, making the biodiversity outcomes at best usually very dubious.[11]

Offsets Markets

Undeterred by all the practical difficulties, the offsetting concept has been taken to a whole new level – the creation of offsetting markets, where buyers and sellers can trade.

In the case of carbon, it is at least true that the units are defined (a tonne of carbon) and location does not matter from a carbon perspective. None of these conditions is met for biodiversity, and all carbon offsets have location-dependent biodiversity implications.

The carbon independence from location is, however, of little comfort. The sequestrated carbon is still conditional on the baselines, maintenance costs, time periods and counterfactuals. These obviously differ from project to project. Therefore, there is no neat fungibility. Each carbon offset has its own characteristics and each adds different risks and uncertainties to the parties. The consequences of the liabilities to the seller differ between projects.

A market needs fungibility, transparency and liquidity. These can be achieved for carbon offsets only if the accreditation agencies reduce all the heterogeneity to a neat homogeneity. This is what they claim to do, creating project registers and facilitating exchanges. But what is exchanged is not a carbon offset, but rather a *carbon contract*, which is related to, but does not match what is actually happening on the ground. Worse, the pressure to pursue homogeneity incentivises the sorts of greenwashing behaviours that have been widely observed.

A particular difficulty in creating a market in carbon offsets is the time dimension mentioned above. Each tonne of carbon that is claimed to be sequestrated needs to have a date. A carbon offset market is in effect a set of dated futures contracts. The specific problem is that valuing – and hence pricing – the time-value dimension depends upon the future expected carbon policies of specific governments and the price of carbon for emissions. On the one hand, once governments are able to count offsets towards their NDCs, they have an interest in encouraging offsets, and this in turn affects expected future prices. On the other hand, the prospect of future governments weakening or abandoning carbon targets may render carbon offsets worthless. As evidenced at

COP30 in Brazil, there is every reason to worry about future Trump-like approaches.

Taken across to biodiversity offsets, not only do all these problems arise too, but there are additional challenges to the homogeneity requirements. One biodiversity offset is *never* the same as another. The best the market advocates can then claim is that the specific biodiversity contract can be bought or sold from a register, and hence there can be a market in individual bilateral contracts.

Not only is the offsets market concept dubious, but it comes with all sorts of costs. The market is not 'free'. Rather, it is a bonanza for environmental consultants, lawyers and economists, and for accountants adjusting the purchasing company's accounts and reporting. These costs further reduce the overall benefits.

More Indulgences than Carbon Mitigation

What all the above leads to is a serious and depressing conclusion: offsets do not usually offset very much. More and more case studies have reached this conclusion.[12] Offsets act as a mechanism to delay actions and to allow more harmful emissions to perpetuate, leading to more destruction of biodiversity. They show how un-serious governments and the UN are about actually stopping the increase of concentration of carbon in the atmosphere and actually halting the decline of biodiversity. At worst, offsetting can lead to higher emissions by the buyers, on the one hand, and more destruction of forests by the sellers, on the other hand.

The word 'offset' is the key to understanding what is going on. What is offset is *additional* emissions and *additional* biodiversity damage. Hence the broader conclusion: if offsetting is the means towards addressing our great environmental challenges, the result is not going to be delivered. We will have to look elsewhere to make progress, or it will end up very badly.

Back to your offset for flying. Instead, what should be done is both more extreme and more painful. Airlines should focus on cutting their emissions, and you should focus on flying less. Whether 'sustainable aviation fuel' is really sustainable is at best debatable. But if it isn't (and it almost certainly isn't), then it is less flying that is necessitated if we want to stop aviation increasing the ppm of carbon in the atmosphere. And that is the opposite of what all governments are actively pursuing.

8 NO GET-OUT-OF-JAIL CARDS

Perhaps we do not need to worry too much about the costs of the existing low-carbon technologies, because we will be rescued by technology? The costs of the existing technologies could fall sharply, and new technologies could make the costs of a renewables electricity system tumble, ushering in a new era of cheap and clean energy. Maybe there could be a big positive technology tipping point just around the corner. A subset of the climate community think this is what will happen and they are supported by the tech billionaires, from Gates to Musk.

Perhaps the existing wind and solar technologies and conventional nuclear will be blown away by fusion, by smart ways of sequestrating carbon, and by revolutionary better batteries that not only cost a lot less but can provide longer-duration storage? Perhaps we can get solar from space and master geoengineering, and hence halt the rise in the concentration of carbon in the atmosphere?

Perhaps, but perhaps not, and perhaps even if these technological advances came along – some of which almost certainly will – they will not be in time nor enough to offset the advancing technologies for the fossil fuels, which may get much cheaper and perhaps could be much more efficiently used? And none of these addresses the sequestration disaster which may well continue to unfold.

Before we get to describing some of these possibilities, let's start by noting the deep ambiguity in the climate change community about technological progress. Some are techno-optimists, but not all, not even the majority.

Science and Environmental Degradation

For many environmentalists, technology is more a threat than an opportunity. They see two challenges. First, the general march of technology may lead to more rather than less pollution, more conventional economic growth, more destruction of ecosystems and hence the promotion of ever-more-damaging consumption. Second, they see the technology promise as a way for politicians and businesses to ease back on conventional low-carbon options. Why spend billions on wind turbines if fusion is around the corner? Better, it might be argued, to invest in R&D and trust the scientists to come up with better and less costly alternatives. In the meantime, relax, stop worrying about climate change as it is about to get solved.

These environmentalists are right to be worried. Scientific progress is correlated with ever-greater environmental damage. Every major technological advance has led to more ecosystem destruction and greater pollution. The great expansion of human population and economic growth in the twentieth century relied upon new technologies to exploit fossil fuels and new ways of extracting them and resulted in the great explosion of mining and the clearance of rainforests and natural habitats. Think of the Haber–Bosch process and mass use of artificial fertilisers. There would have been no population explosion without this, no eight billion people now. Think of the diesel engine, and in particular think what the tractor has done to the land cover and the soils. Think of the extraction of copper and iron ore, as well as oil, gas and coal. Think of rubber from rainforests and now the mass plantations for palm oil.

The twentieth century was one long environmental disaster, culminating at the end of the century in China. China's great economic expansion has used up a lot of coal, made the country the main emitter of carbon and much of this has been facilitated by trade, backed up by the technological advances in shipping. The modern container ships and the bulk carriers are the handmaidens of this trade. Gone are much of the downriver ecosystems of the Mekong; dead are China's three main rivers. The South China Sea has been heavily polluted and China's desert regions are expanding.

Looking ahead, the new AI and quantum computing technologies promise a massive increase in energy demand, and specifically electricity. They also promise a new era of greater economic growth and ever more consumption. In just 30 years, global-dominating companies like Google, Apple, Microsoft, Meta, Amazon, and Nvidia have become amongst the world's largest, creating multi-billionaires, dominating global stock markets and underpinning large-scale borrowing, and with it ever-greater consumption. By late 2025, Nvidia realised a value equal to twice the UK's annual GDP.

There are of course multiple benefits, not least the sharp falls in global poverty. The internet and modern communications have already transformed the lives of many. But for some environmentalists, the costs are just too great. One reaction is the age-old promoting of a much simpler life. In agriculture, farmers are encouraged to forsake the benefit of pesticides, to use fewer antibiotics, and to stop big machinery ploughing the lands. These environmentalists see the appeal of more self-reliance, and, where possible, more self-sufficiency and more 'home-grown' energy. These are all compounded together in the idea of de-growth.

De-growth is grounded upon the argument that we are already living well beyond our environmental means and that our planetary environmental footprint exceeds the capacity of the planet's renewable natural capital to support it. Though de-growth muddles up different kinds of growth and effectively rules out the sustainable economic growth described in *Legacy*, quite a lot of this can be lost in the noise. The scale of the over-consumption is so great that only a significant retreat can prevent a catastrophe.

This simple-life mentality has traditionally been the territory of mystics and religious sects. The hermit in the desert is stripping back consumption to its bare minimum, treading as lightly as possible on the planet.[1]

Getting back to Nature, living in eco-communities, has always had its attractions. The trouble is that this appeal quickly hits the brick wall of human nature. Most humans want more and more, not less and less, and increasing consumption is the prime objective of almost all politicians in reflecting our wishes. How many resist the opportunities to fly around the world, to go on exotic holidays, to buy more clothes and shoes and cars? We tend to seek ever more stuff. It is reflected, for example, in the obesity epidemic that has replaced starvation and famine as nations get richer. The World Health Organization (WHO) estimates that, globally, 16 per cent of adults over the age of 18 are obese; that's almost 1 in 8 of the world's population. In the US, it is over 40 per cent.[2]

Technology might help in all these examples. We can have weight-loss drugs, hydrogen and other ways of powering cruise ships, and EVs rather than petrol and diesel SUVs (sport utility vehicles). We are bombarded with advertising promising goods and services that are 'more sustainable'. We are offered 'sustainable aviation' and 'sustainable tourism' – both pretty much contradictions in terms. Indeed, the great new technology companies thrive on revenues from selling us advertising that is aimed at increasing our consumption – for food, tourism, fast fashion – promoting through social media 'influencers' who epitomise this, and create the fear that if we don't conform to the lifestyles promoted on TikTok, for example, we will be missing out. It even has an acronym: FOMO (fear of missing out).

Ironically, some of those responsible for the advancement of the science behind all this consumption share the conclusion that ever more consumption will overwhelm our natural environment. They start to think of moving to another planet, as an escape route from this planet that we have wrecked. At the extreme end is Elon Musk. Rather than join his tech peers in buying up refuges and building bunkers to shelter from the disasters they fear,[3] he thinks we should go to Mars and establish a new colony. The atmosphere of Mars will be warmed up and made more breathable by exploding nuclear bombs at each of Mars's poles. It's all on SpaceX's website to read about.[4]

It sounds very much like science fiction. There is nothing new in the idea of getting out of this jail and escaping into the universe. It is a staple of science fiction. What is different now is that space exploration is taking off. It is also one way the modern jet set (the 'space set') can do conspicuous consumption that everyone else can't afford. An example is the Blue Origin's New Shephard space tourism programme.

For environmentalists, this is not only wrongheaded (it won't work except perhaps for a chosen few), but dangerous. It diverts money and resources to purposes other than the ones that urgently need attention here, and it encourages a fatalism about trying to stop the rot back here on Earth. After all, if we take all the resources going into space travel and devote them to the climate change and biodiversity problems back here on Earth, wouldn't we be better off? Space tourism is even worse than cruise liner tourism, in which celebrity Katy Perry participated in a 10–11-minute flight in April 2025.

Science and Concentrating on New Technologies

Those in the climate community who focus on future technological possibilities face the accusation that it is a terrible distraction from the need to address climate change here and now. It might actually encourage us to slow up on deploying renewables and nuclear, spending the money on R&D

instead, and wait for new and better solutions in the second half of this decade. Forget net zero 2050 and mid-century targets. Instead, rely on being able to tackle the consequences later with new technologies.

Of these, the ones that play into this debate most strongly are forms of geoengineering. The idea is that we can do engineering on a planetary scale. We could engineer the atmosphere, by either changing its composition or reflecting off sunlight so as to reduce the solar radiation that gets trapped in the greenhouse. What if we could suck out the carbon and bury it back under the ground, create solar reflectors and shields, and seed the upper atmosphere and the ocean surfaces by spraying seawater to create low, bright clouds over the oceans (called 'marine cloud brightening') to reflect back the sunshine? The really scary thing is that these are all very possible. All the supporting technologies already exist.

This is the ultimate get-out-of-jail card, and the ultimate masters-of-the-universe scientific control by us humans over our planet. We can not only modify the entire surface of the planet, and build our megacities and factories, but also turn the atmosphere into a kind of giant air-conditioning system. We could control the air we breathe as well as control the land we inhabit. In the process, we could control the chemical composition and temperatures of the oceans. These are what Musk thinks can be done on Mars, and there is no theoretical reason why these technologies could not be done here.

In a moment we will take a look at what some of them entail and how they might be developed and controlled, and by whom. But first let's just consider the implications for the current climate policies. For developing countries like India and Indonesia, for Sub-Saharan Africa, for much of the Middle East and for Latin America, their overwhelming priority is economic growth *now*, so that they raise their standards of living to those already enjoyed in Europe, the US, Japan, Australia and enclaves in Southeast Asia.

This has two rationales: that the developed world has achieved its high consumption on the back of emitting lots of GHGs already and that in terms of priority, the needs of the present override those of the future. On the first, the facts are pretty clear. It is indeed the industrialisation of the great European powers and the US that put the carbon up there in the atmosphere and since it is the stock of carbon – the ppm – that counts, it is these developed countries that have caused the climate change witnessed so far. Why should Indians forgo the advantages of higher living standards when Europeans and Americans have not?

China is now in the European and America camp. It is already responsible for a big chunk of the carbon in the atmosphere, as well as being the world's greatest emitter. To put its emissions into perspective, recall that it is claimed that it now takes about eight years for China to emit roughly the same as the UK did over 150 years since the Industrial Revolution got going. On this argument, China should also now bear a proportionally large share of the total global costs of decarbonisation. It can no longer claim to be a developing country but has joined the ranks of the great polluters. Indeed, it is now the greatest polluter.

The essence of the argument is that developing countries should be allowed to do as much damage as developed countries already have, and then they can start to address the problem – just not yet. Let them do as much damage as us first. It of course greatly helps if the argument can be extended: let's all be allowed to do lots of damage now to the climate, because in any event we will all have the solutions in geoengineering later in this century. Grow with pollution, and then we can sort out the pollution later on, and we will have the technologies then to deal with the outcomes. If you really want to scare yourself, think what would happen if India replicated China's great GDP expansion with associated pollution on a Chinese scale through to 2050 and beyond, or, perhaps on a more limited but still terrifying scale, Indonesia, Nigeria, Sub-Saharan Africa, Brazil and lots in the Middle East follow a similar pathway?

Direct Air Carbon Capture and Storage, and Sequestration

The pure science of manipulating the composition of the atmosphere is pretty straightforward. It is largely about extracting carbon from the atmosphere so that the carbon concentration stops going up and then falls back.

How to do it? There are several options. One is to suck the carbon directly out of the atmosphere, and, once captured, store it back in the Earth's crust. A second is to stop the carbon getting into the atmosphere as a result of burning fossil fuels – and hence capturing the carbon before it escapes. It is then stored, as above. The third is to get nature to do the sequestration for us.

DACS is the most simple of the new technologies to understand.[5] DACS machines filter the carbon out of the atmosphere. This is straightforward science. It needs a lot of energy to do the extraction and separation – the capture – and this extra energy has to be zero carbon. The captured gas has to stored. The possibilities include locking it into rocks in deep depositories, putting it in depleted oil and gas wells, and locking it into saline aquifers.

All of this can be done – and indeed is being done in Iceland by Climeworks.[6] Iceland has lots of geothermal energy to power the process and there are lots of basalt rocks into which to fix the captured carbon.

It is a huge step forward and encourages the idea that perhaps we could carry on polluting and then mop up the consequences. Burning fossil fuels or biomass could be offset by carbon extraction. Net zero could be attained, or better net negative if more was extracted than emitted. In theory, we could even target the 275 ppm before the Industrial Revolution got going.

The problems are in scaling up this technology and in its costs. To simply keep pace with emissions, around 20 gigatonnes (Gt) of carbon would have to be extracted annually. The Mammoth DACS plant, built by Climeworks in Iceland, is deemed to be capable of capturing 36,000 tonnes per annum.[7] It is not very 'mammoth': that is 0.0018 per cent of the global emissions of carbon. To meet this challenge would involve a huge industrialisation with a massive number of DACS plants and at a vastly greater scale per plant. They would be everywhere. At scale, perhaps whole countries like Iceland would have to be industrialised with DACS? They need the right rock structures. There would be a very great increase in the demand for energy to run such large-scale DACS plants. Few places have abundant – and accessible – geothermal energy, which makes the Icelandic example so exceptional.[8]

Even if this was theoretically possible – with enough land for the industrial structures, enough low-carbon energy and enough of the right sorts of rocks – there is the question of the costs. The cost per tonne of carbon sequestrated in the rocks in Iceland by Climeworks is currently a mammoth $1,000.[9] Even if this halves (and most sites probably aren't as good as the Iceland one), the price would still be huge. It is one of the few technologies that makes wind, solar and nuclear look cheap. The funding and finance would be extreme relative to the current production costs of most of the world's existing industries. At Climeworks, the future costs are such that it has been cutting its workforce, as the existing DACS plants have captured far less carbon than hoped, way below the forecast 36,000 tonnes. Climeworks had projected that the costs of DACS would come down to $100 per tonne by 2030, but now this is projected to be in the range of $250–$350 per tonne.

This begs a second question. Why not deploy the same resources to replace the emitting fossil-fuel technologies with lower-carbon ones? Even when the full carbon emissions of the supply chains for wind and solar are taken into account, it still might be better to build out these technologies instead of building out large-scale DACS technologies.

Better still perhaps, why not use Iceland's geothermal energy directly for generating electricity, rather than deflecting it through the DACS machines? This could then be transmitted to Europe through long-distance direct-current cables, or if the transmission costs and losses are too great, why not shift energy-intensive industries to Iceland close to the geothermal energy? Imagine Iceland (and other geothermal-rich locations) hosting the data centres of the world, and then cabling the data to the markets, as well as acting as steel and aluminium industrial hubs, and so on.[10] The Industrial Revolution started in the UK because it had abundant cheap coal. Why not Iceland with geothermal, or North Africa, with its abundant solar potential?

Carbon Capture and Storage

DACS is almost certainly not going to solve the climate problems soon. It could be a useful addition and it does hold out the distant possibility of directly manipulating the atmosphere in the future. As R&D, it may be of marginal benefit, but it is not a get-out-of-jail card. The alternative option is instead of extracting the carbon once it is in the atmosphere, the carbon is captured before it gets into the atmosphere. Step forward carbon capture and storage (CCS). If the carbon that is captured is then used, we have carbon capture, utilisation and storage (CCUS). For now, let's stick to CCS.

As with DACS, we already know how to do it – indeed, in the CCS case, we have been doing it for a considerable period of time. Captured carbon has been used to enhance oil recovery (the irony is palpable). As oil wells deplete, the pressure falls and hence most oil wells are abandoned before 50 per cent is extracted. By pumping CO_2 into the wells, their lives can be extended.

The carbon can be extracted before or after combustion and then piped to a repository. As with DACS, this can, for example, be an old oil or gas well, or a saline aquifer. Once the store is full, it can be plugged and monitored. A bit might escape, but that probably will not matter much at the margin. It also is an energy-intensive process, so it is not perfect, but arguably better than simply venting carbon into the atmosphere.

To some, and to the horror of many in the climate community, this means that, in effect, a 'rocks-to-rocks' pathway is established. It is an idea that Myles Allen has doggedly developed both in its science, and also in thinking up policy rules to implement it.[11] He adds to 'rocks-to-rocks' his 'take-back' rule. The fossil fuels are taken out of the ground, used and their carbon is put back. Imagine if this worked at scale and imagine if it was economic to do so – say against a general carbon price for emissions. Burning fossil fuels would no longer be a problem. We would not need to stop burning them. We just need to insist that any that are burnt have their carbon reinjected. The fossil-fuels industry transforms itself into a fossil-fuels + CCS industry. You can see why environmentalists campaigning against the 'evil' fossil-fuels companies are horrified. Suddenly these fossil fuels are not bad at all, provided they are accompanied by CCS. No need to 'just stop oil' (or gas or coal), just enforce Allen's take-back rule.

All of this would come at a cost. The price of oil, gas and coal would have to rise by the increased CCS costs. Ultimately, we consumers would have to pay, as we are the ultimate polluters buying the stuff made from fossil fuels – that is over 80 per cent of global energy. This insight tells us that the take-back rule is, in effect, a version of a carbon tax, albeit a draconian one. Whatever the value of the fossil fuels in even very special circumstances, every tonne of oil, gas and coal has to be sequestrated.

Yet, even with these higher CCS costs, would they be greater than the costs of wind and solar discussed in Chapter 6? Unlike DACS, possibly not once the full system costs are taken into account.

Natural Carbon Sequestration

A third option is to get nature to do the sequestration for us, as it always has done. It is the natural geoengineer.

The trouble is that natural sequestration has been going backwards. Cutting down the rainforests, stripping the soils for modern agriculture, building roads and cities and industrial complexes, and damaging the vegetation more generally have reduced the capacity to absorb carbon on land, and the gross pollution and acidification of the oceans have damaged the absorption capacity of the greatest of our carbon sinks. To tackle climate change, we need to both reduce emissions and increase natural sequestration, unless we go for massive-scale DACS and CCS.

Recall that the payback from natural carbon sequestration has considerable merit beyond the carbon. Natural carbon sequestration helps to protect and enhance biodiversity. It reduces the damage that would otherwise be done, and by adding carbon to the soils, it adds to this, the greatest reservoir of biodiversity.

Enhancing large-scale natural capital sequestration is one of the few win–win opportunities: a win for climate change, a win for biodiversity. But it takes time. Its benefits will largely come later in this century and the next. It takes too long to be a get-out-of-jail card. To upgrade the natural sequestration by 20 Gt per annum (to neutralise the emissions) after first halting the decline in natural sequestration is a very tall order. Currently we are going backwards on natural carbon sequestration. By how much? This is very hard to estimate given the diffuse ways natural sequestration works. Some estimates suggest this might be as high as –5 Gt per annum.[12] Even if it is much lower, the scale of the overall challenge is amplified by the negative direction of travel.

Solar Reflectors and Seeding the Atmosphere

Whilst the DACS and CCS are all about capturing the carbon and so reducing its concentration in the atmosphere, there are a number of options for reducing the amount of sunlight hitting the Earth, for increasing the bounce backs from the Earth, and thus limiting the heating impacts of solar radiation.

The most ambitious of these is the placing of solar shields in space to reflect back sunlight before it gets to the Earth. In principle, this is a simple and straightforward idea, and a lot is already known about how to put devices into orbit around the Earth. It is a bit like the impacts of an eclipse, but targeted and continuous.

In addition to the question of costs, the dangerous drawback of this option is that it could have unintended consequences, or worse, intended consequences if viewed as a weapon. Individual states could control the solar reflectors and angle them to impact on specific land and sea areas. That might interfere with crops, daylight hours and ultimately with the weather and local climates. It could have the benefits of cooling specific areas, and that might be an advantage in hot places, but not so in cold areas.

Whereas DACS and CCS are local, and can safely be deployed by countries, companies and other organisations, solar reflectors have considerable international dimensions. There is as yet no global control mechanism, and it may be that, if used in hostile ways, the only resort would be to shoot them down.

Seeding the atmosphere is a particular version of solar reflection. The upper atmosphere can be sprayed with sulfur, and hence made a less penetrable layer, reducing the penetration of sunlight. It is not a particularly novel idea and cloud seeding at lower levels is already part of the ammunition of arid countries to try to make rain; for example, as noted in Chapter 2, Iran, when faced with severe and prolonged drought in 2025, engaged in cloud seeding at scale.

At a grand scale necessary to impact on global warming, there are again serious challenges with potential unintended consequences, and cloud seeding is a technology that individual countries could deploy at relatively low cost, though it would have to be repeated again and again. Could we trust countries not to use seeding the atmosphere as a weapon to alter monsoons and other weather events upon which agricultural systems and economies may depend?

Yet another geoengineering option is marine cloud brightening. This technology increases the solar reflections by spraying salt particulates above the ocean, which form water droplets, so that there is a greater albedo effect, cooling the surface temperatures.[13] As with cloud seeding in the upper atmosphere, it should work, but in the marine case there are lots of potential unintended consequences to salinity, biodiversity in the oceans, and the impacts of changing temperatures on currents and on wind patterns.

No Quick Technology Fixes

The problem with all of the above technology possibilities is that they deflect from the immediate priority of reducing emissions. Even natural sequestration is a potential incentive to slow down on emissions reductions, providing 'offsets' as an alternative to emissions reductions. In practice, we need both sequestration and emissions reduction, and of the technologies considered here, CCS and natural sequestration are the most practical and appropriate. The problem is that neither can really work at the scale required in a short time period.

The other geoengineering options are much more dangerous. They should all carry a health warning: 'beware of dictators and military uses'.

The sad conclusion is that, whilst research on geoengineering options has some value, and CCS is worth developing, at least at a demonstration level,[14] none gets us out of jail. They won't stop us frying the planet. To prevent that, the more conventional strategies of emissions reductions and sequestration by natural ecosystems are the most fruitful options – and both are needed anyway. Both are about trying to stop doing yet more damage.

9 THE COP-OUTS

The COPs are the annual ritual gatherings of the carbon community. They are where like-minded people gather to push for targets for territorial carbon emissions reductions, and where they meet resistance from those concerned with sovereignty and with fossil-fuel interests and with the overall costs of decarbonisation. The holy grail has been to have legally binding agreements to build on what the UNFCCC agreed back in 1992.

These gatherings have their own cycles, processes and procedures, and the various stakeholders play their parts in orchestrating negotiations each year, often reaching an 'agreement' in the final hour and minutes, after the clock has been stopped. There are set-piece speeches, draft texts, moments of crisis, last-minute concessions and then the final agreement. They are typically followed by recriminations, disappointments and a recommitment of the carbon community to push harder next time. It is high drama and performance politics, with maximum media coverage.

In advance, there is work for the UN's climate division, with its annual budget of around \$80m.[1] It is a bureaucratic process, with lots of bureaucratic jobs. Studies are commissioned, and the NGOs get in on the act, publishing scary forecasts of doom, on the one hand, and sunny optimistic projections of the tumbling costs of their chosen technologies, on the other.

At the COPs, lots and lots of like-minded people fly in. It can be as many as 90,000. No doubt lots of them buy carbon offsets, and others reassure themselves that flying with SAF is OK. Amongst the many, there are those who turn up to demonstrate, to raise their organisation's profile, and to raise its membership and money. Some come just to brandish their carbon credentials. Some present their research, typically paid for by government funding and private donations.

COPs are lobbyists' paradises, with much in common with other global gatherings of the elites. Davos comes to mind. Corporate leaders get to mix with politicians, and politicians get to have lots of side meetings. Lobbyists have a lot at stake. There are those in search of subsidies and tariff supports. The renewables lobbyists want to showcase their sustainability to beef up their corporate images. Financial institutions want to get in on the ESG act. On the other side, the fossil-fuel industries want to put the brake on the threat to their business models, and especially to hold back on explicit, enforceable commitments to phase out fossil fuels, and to try to limit or prevent changes in energy taxation, including carbon taxes. When countries have explicit objectives to increase fossil-fuel production, they too will want to put the brakes on any such commitments.

Developing countries want to exact economic compensation from developed countries. They want to be paid for damages and thereby get reparations, singing the same sort of hymn as the demand for compensation for the slavery in the eighteenth and first half of the nineteenth century. Small islands get special airplay, setting out the plight of their small populations as a result of rising sea levels. For them – and for the corporates – it is understandably almost always about the money.

If all goes well – i.e. the outcome meets or exceeds the carefully choreographed expectations – the leaders can then make the great speeches about how they are 'saving the world'. The key players tend to fly in at the last minute to ink in agreements that they have already privately agreed to, to create a sense of drama and emphasise their own importance. They have been doing so since the Kyoto Protocol negotiations in 1997. Kyoto was described as a 'breakthrough', setting the path to solving climate change. Even Copenhagen in 2009, when Obama and Wen Jiabao, the premier of China, signed up to the voluntary Copenhagen Accord outside the framework of the COP, was described as a 'triumph'. Paris in 2015 was a 'landmark', Glasgow in 2021 a 'watershed'. Since then, it has been gradually downhill, until we got to COP29 in 2024, when most world leaders simply stayed away. Brazil's COP in 2025 is best described as an embarrassment. The Chinese, Indian and US leaders stayed away at the crucial stages, and those leaders who did show up dropped in at the beginning and promptly left.

After 30 COPs, very little has been achieved. Remember always that the one number that matters – the concentration of carbon in the atmosphere – has relentlessly been going up by around 2 ppm per annum since 1990. The much-hyped 1.5 °C target adopted at Paris is past its sell-by date, having been breached by 2024. Whilst the COPs have been going on, emissions have relentlessly gone up, sequestration has relentlessly gone down, and fossil fuels have held their own at over 80 per cent of an ever-rising demand for energy. More COPs and more oil, more gas and more coal, and the search for a legally binding, enforceable agreement remains as elusive as ever. China and India resisted from the outset, and the US has never been willing to concede sovereignty.

The Context of the COPs – Climate Change Is Global Not National or Local

The one bit of the climate change problem that the COPs get right is that the problem is global. It cannot – and will not – be solved at the national level. A tonne of carbon released anywhere has the same effects – whether in Oxford or in Manila. The damage is global whatever the source of the emissions, and so too are the benefits from reducing emissions and increasing sequestration.

It is a fiendishly difficult global problem, because, for any country, town or individual, the selfish outcome is to get others to reduce their emissions, others to increase their sequestration, and hence others to bear the costs of actions to address climate change, whilst doing very little themselves. They can free ride on others' efforts and the costs that others bear.

The free-rider problem is, and always has been, an unavoidable feature of climate change, and it won't go away. It is obvious but mostly forgotten. Politicians and activists tell us we must build wind farms and close coal power stations to avoid the worse consequences of the global warming that will take place if we do not take these actions, failing to tell the truth that our own actions will not make any real difference and at the same time will increase our costs. Indeed, our actions might make matters worse if industry moves elsewhere to cheaper fossil-fuel-based energy. The 'fight' against climate change will not be won in Oxford if no one else does much about it.

It is a separate question of individual ethics as to whether each of us wants to no longer be personally responsible for causing climate change, even if our actions do not make any difference to the outcome. This is something we will come back to – our personal responsibilities – but it is not what motivates the COPs, much as some of the tens of thousands who attend would want to have us believe. Indeed, the very act of up to 90,000 people flying across the world to discuss climate change points up the scale of the disconnect between 'do as I say' and 'do as I do'.

The COPs have all been aimed at getting a global agreement to stop climate change, and to parcel out the required actions amongst the nations of the world. It is a top-down UN-style exercise, imagining that agreement at the 'parliament of man', as Paul Kennedy called it,[2] could be enforced through a global treaty between the nations of the world.

To some this is a noble ambition, analogous to the noble ambition of the League of Nations in the 1920s and 1930s of overcoming narrower national interests. The world would have world climate governance. To others, it is a fateful conceit that the nation state can be superseded, and ultimately that various peoples will give up their sovereignty to a greater entity in agreement with other peoples of whom they know little or nothing.

It is remarkable that the UN has lasted so long, but it has done so by not really being a supra-national entity, except when the major powers can agree. Hence, the Security Council and the vetoes of its five permanent members. Nothing of substance can happen at the UN unless all five agree or at least are prepared to live with the proposed steps. Small countries can be bullied in a way that China, Russia and the US cannot. Indeed, even small crises prove hard to grapple with. The Serbian, Croat and Bosnian wars of the 1990s proved hard to even peace-keep, and the UN could do almost nothing about the wars and associated carnage in Vietnam, Korea, Gaza and the Middle East, Sudan, and between Iran and Iraq. It is unimportant when it comes to the tragedy in Ukraine and in Iran. Its peacekeepers can only keep peace if the bigger players will tolerate their activities.

This is not to belittle the many humanitarian activities of the UN, nor the food aid. Rather, it is to point out that the idea that the UN can sort out climate change is both a bold one and very problematic. It is quite understandable that the UN should try, and indeed climate change has given the overall organisation a new rationale and bigger budgets. But trying and succeeding are two different things.

Think back to the origins of the UNFCCC in 1992 and how it came about.[3] The central report that grounds the UN approach is the Brundtland Report on the north–south divide.[4] This focuses on a core role of the UN, as a body through which the poorer Global South can demand money from the richer Global North to help it develop. It is all about the money, and understandably so.

When Margaret Thatcher stood up in 1989 and made a speech[5] at the UN about the new peril – climate change – it fell neatly into the broader context of Brundtland. The obvious and smart step for the UN to get on top of this new challenge was to set up a scientific endeavour, to do the research and modelling of climate change. It was hard to object to the earlier creation of the IPCC, which had already been set up in 1988.[6]

From the get-go, the IPCC was never going to be a purely objective scientific endeavour, because its results would always have a big political impact. 'Listen to the science' is a clarion call to those who already know the answers and want the IPCC to endorse them. It recruited mainly those who were convinced of the problem and gave these scientists the lead. Great work was done, but it is a huge mistake to think the science is above the politics, and that its results – especially when given a policy and political spin – would be neutral. The IPCC has always been about warning the world of the dangers of climate change and coming up with scenarios that point to the need for immediate action. It is just implausible to imagine that it could have said: 'The problem is not that immediately serious, and we can take a century to address it.' When it ventured into the policy fields, its advocacy was inevitably selective.

The IPCC claimed otherwise. It involved lots and lots of scientists, as if counting the number of scientists who agree with a scientific prediction increases its validity. It was never seriously interested in falsification, in seeking out work that pointed otherwise. These scientists were branded as 'deniers' by the wider climate community. The IPCC claims that everything is peer-reviewed, but any academic knows that peer review depends upon who is the chosen peer, and who is left out.

There is no doubt that the IPCC encouraged a burgeoning of climate research, and in particular of climate modelling. This is all to the good, as long as there is no attempt to capture the processes and eliminate critics. Climate modelling based upon the predictions and scenarios about the atmosphere is only one dimension. Turning atmospheric modelling into predictions of global warming is another much more tenuous activity, but this has a lot more credibility than trying to marry up such physical science with economics in IAMs.

Given that economists struggle to predict GDP, inflation and employment, even six months ahead, trying to ground scenarios on IAMs throughout the rest of this century gives a veneer of spurious accuracy and worse, spurious accuracy that the activities and advocates can cherry-pick in support of their policy preferences. It is just the sort of thing that unscrupulous politicians and lobbyists find too easy to appropriate, and too often the normal way of doing business for activists.

The UNFCCC was adopted in 1992 and carried the Brundtland Report approach plus the IPCC 'evidence' through to a grand declaration of purpose, entering into force in March 1994. It is a noble document, and one that everyone could sign up to, safe in the knowledge that they would not actually have to do anything they didn't want to as a consequence. They could all rest assured that free riding remains central. It was also well timed, after the fall of the Berlin Wall and the Soviet Union in 1989, and after the first Gulf War, which ended in 1991.

The Kyoto Compromise

It took until 1997 to get from the UNFCCC to the Kyoto Protocol, and until 2005 for the Protocol to come into force. It was at Kyoto that the central features of what followed for the next two decades were crystallised. Kyoto divided the world into developed and developing countries. The former would accept targets for emissions reductions, defined territorially on carbon emitted, not carbon consumed. The latter would take measures, but not formal targets, in the hope that eventually they would step up to formal targets.

The developed/developing countries distinction was very much in the spirit of Brundtland. What it meant in practice was determined by the position of the US. Clinton had been a key supporter of Kyoto, but in the build-up at the Marrakesh COP in 2001, it dawned on him that he would never get the Protocol ratified by the US Senate, and it was not even worth trying. Why? Because the senators took one look at the position of China as the rapidly emerging emitter and the challenger to the US in energy-intensive industries and realised that, with China treated as a developing country, the US would end up damaging its relative economic position, and at the same time that China's rising emissions would offset its own efforts. It had to be either both the US and China, or neither. From a US perspective it was bad enough that China could free ride, but worse that it could thereby steal a competitive march on US heavy industry. Both of these turned out to be true: China emerged in less than two decades as the world's greatest polluter; and much of that pollution was in heavy energy-intensive industries like steel, in which it undermined the US companies. In the meantime, the US shale revolution encouraged it to exit coal, for gas, while China doubled down on coal.

The US–China problem devilled everything that followed, and still does, now weaponised around critical minerals and dominance in the manufacture of solar panels and increasingly batteries and EVs. Obama and Biden both tried, and failed, to bring the US fully back into the fold. Obama managed the Copenhagen Accord – voluntary and hence not needing Senate ratification. Biden rejoined the Paris Agreement. Both presided (with Trump) over the greatest expansion of US oil and gas production, with the US becoming the world's largest oil producer. They were the great fossil-fuel presidents.

With Trump's re-election, the China problem became even bigger. The US has not only withdrawn again from the Paris Agreement but has doubled down on its hostility to global carbon agreements and the COP process, especially now shale oil and in particular shale gas have given it a huge competitive advantage in energy. China, ever playing the geopolitical game, has moved into the vacuum, claiming it now is the global climate change leader, cornering the market in critical minerals, whilst at the same time expanding its dominant fleet of coal power stations and holding its rank as the world's greatest carbon polluter, now by some clear margin, and with over 50 per cent of the world's coal burn.[7]

The other roll of the dice at Kyoto was to place the EU at the centre of the COP game. The EU had many political reasons for 'leading' on climate change, as well as a very fortuitous position on its emissions. EU member states (especially Germany) had seen the green political movement emerge, so that, from 1998, the Green Party would either be part of the government coalition or its fortunes and its pivotal voters would determine who won the elections. The Greens were overwhelmingly anti-nuclear, and the Red–Green coalition in Germany pushed through the new 'nuclear consensus' between government and the utilities which started the phase-out of nuclear power – ironically to the considerable benefit of coal. Add to the German placating of the Greens the EU's desire to reconnect with the young (a great political concern amongst federalists) and the stage was set for the EU and the Commission to take on the climate change mantle.[8]

The added attraction to Germany and the EU more generally was the belief that the future was indeed green. With the launching of the *Energiewende* in Germany in 2010,[9] the aim was no less than an industrial renaissance, with renewable energy companies growing quickly to dominate global markets. That this fantasy would collapse in the face of Chinese competition, and that the market created in Germany for Chinese solar companies, in particular, helped bring this about, was still to come. At the time, it made the Germans and the EU fully pro-Kyoto and pro-climate targets for developed countries. Germany was to be the great clean-energy superpower of the future, with German industry in the vanguard.

What made such targets all the more appealing is that it appeared that they would be easy to achieve. Why? As the Berlin Wall fell in 1989, the base year of the carbon targets of 1990 coincided with the collapse of the rust-bucket industries in East Germany and amongst the Eastern European countries that were expected to join the EU.

It was too good to be true, and too good an opportunity to be missed out on. This was the great attraction of Kyoto. The problem was that the US was out, China was in the developing countries category, and in due course both Canada and Japan would drop out.[10] This meant that Kyoto looked like being a Europe-only protocol. Indeed, it would not have even got off the ground had the Europeans not persuaded Russia to join so that the 55 per cent minimum threshold could be met.[11] Russia was the ultimate rust-bucket case in the base year of 1990, and, better still, the EU had something Russia wanted in return – the support for its membership of the World Trade Organization.

The EU proved up to the task of meeting the initial targets and set them into the catchy slogan of '20-20-20': a 20 per cent reduction target by 2020, a 20 per cent renewables target and 20 per cent for energy efficiency. Better still, the EU was on a seriously negative path on the industrial front and gradually closing down much of its energy-intensive industries, switching to imports. Its carbon production went down, but its carbon consumption went up, thereby, at a global level, negating some of its impacts on global emissions and the ppm. Nowhere was this more apparent than in the UK and, surprise, surprise, under the Kyoto and subsequent Paris targets, the UK became the poster child of carbon production territorial emissions reductions.

The path was now clear for the Kyoto Protocol coming into force. The US was out, China was not seriously in, and the targets measured carbon production not carbon consumption. Not much has changed since.

The Holy Grail of a Legally Binding Treaty

The UN always envisaged that it would go beyond the voluntary nature of the targets under Kyoto and move to legally binding targets and a global treaty. In this, it greatly exceeded the UN's more general remit. For all it becoming the focus of global government, as many progressives proposed, the idea that the UN could legally impose its framework on the nations of the world, or at least beyond the small and powerless, was at best a joke and at worst a very dangerous game. The UN has no troops, it has no military power, and the international courts work only as long as the major powers allow them to do so. Indeed, they have probably exceeded what is and will be tolerated. Placing the Prime Minister of Israel and the President of Russia under arrest warrants is not credible. Can you imagine the world's powers standing by if Putin is arrested and locked up whilst being tried in The Hague? The ex-President of Serbia perhaps, but in the case of the Israeli Prime Minister, the US is likely to resist, and in the case of Putin, the Russians and the Chinese are just two of the possible objectors. The most that can be achieved is to make their international travel options a bit limited.

When it comes to climate change, over-reach for the UN is harder to resist and some countries seriously urge it to do just this, not least the UK. For those for whom the targets are easy, why not use the UN to bring others forcefully into the fold? That the others include both Russia and the US seems to pass the UN by, and further that the US pays the largest share of the UN budget is an accident waiting to happen.[12]

Notwithstanding this obvious roadblock, the UN pressed ahead with its aim to attain a legally binding treaty, notably at the Durban COP in 2012.[13] It failed there, but undaunted, the UN pushed ahead for a legally binding deal at Paris. All it achieved was a legally binging agreement to come up with further targets later on at subsequent COPs, but not actually enforceable targets. Even compliance with this modest requirement has been patchy and probably will remain so.

The euphoria that the Paris Agreement[14] generated is remarkable, and that this excitement remains in the face of mounting evidence of failure is all the more remarkable. The Paris Agreement was set in the context within which the agreed commitments were not expected to add up to meeting the 2 °C target, as they had never been in previous or subsequent COPs. With no coherent plan to meet 2 °C, the delegates agreed that there should be a new target of limiting warming to 1.5 °C. Despite this being even more implausible, this became the target to which all the 'Paris-compatible' plans for banks, other financial institutions and companies were set.

These overarching temperature targets could only be assessed *ex post*, since they are averages, and hence the fiction of the world being on target could be maintained for several years after they had in fact been breached. In the case of 1.5 °C, this was breached within a decade of the Paris Agreement being signed, but probably won't be formally admitted for years to come.

As to the holy grail of a legally binding agreement, the climate community hangs on to the consolation that the parties to the agreement were committed to a 'legal' requirement to offer subsequent further NDCs. How exactly this commitment is to be enforced remains a mystery.

None of this prevented the Paris COP being the high point and claimed as a great achievement by world leaders and the climate community more widely. This was the moment when the cacophony of boasts about saving the world would peak.[15]

In reality, it was better regarded retrospectively as the moment when the COPs' route floundered. The writing was very publicly on the wall for the 2 °C target, if the happy delegates had troubled to look.

There was to be one more 'great leap forward'. The Glasgow COP in 2021 was the last time the major leaders turned up,[16] and it was the moment for Johnson to trumpet to the world the UK's carbon emissions cuts and its world leadership on climate change. Never mind that he saw fit to fly back immediately it concluded just to have a dinner with his chums amongst the journalists at the Garrick Club in London. This was the Johnson who claimed that there was no need to change our lifestyles, let alone reduce flying and other consumption-based lifestyles.[17] Climate change and ever-greater GDP and associated ever-greater consumption were part of the 'cakeism' for which he proudly claimed authorship. Nowhere was this more apparent than when it came to climate change: fewer emissions, greater consumption, and no individual sacrifices.

Sadly, Johnson never took the trouble to analyse why the UK emissions had fallen so much. If he had, he would have noticed not only the exit of energy-intensive industries, but also the failure of new energy-intensive investment in the UK. If he had looked at the carbon consumption data, he would have realised that the UK's service-based economy rested upon the import of carbon-intensive goods (and even services) from elsewhere. He would have seen that some of China's emissions were caused in the UK. After he was forced out of office, the petrochemical plant at Grangemouth and several other refineries, and Port Talbot and Scunthorpe steelworks would be dramatically scaled back, and the car industry would fall back to an output not seen since the late 1940s. What was left of the fertiliser industry would be gone, joining the exit from aluminium, and glass and fibreglass. These headline casualties were joined by smaller businesses, including pubs and shops. He might even have noticed that the UK was en route to the highest industrial electricity prices in the developed world.

Losing the Battle

The Paris and Glasgow COPs were succeeded by a series of meetings which, at best, trod water. Instead of a ramping-up of efforts and giving an even greater role to the UN, what happened was a clutching at straws in the form of side agreements. These were 'coalitions of the willing' on things like methane and coal, mostly missing the main polluters in action.

The problems confronting the COP process were all the more apparent as subsequent meetings were held in countries with other priorities. The meetings at Sharm El Sheikh in Egypt and then Baku in Azerbaijan reflected the continuing role of the over 80 per cent of fossil fuels and the interests of developing countries. Azerbaijan was never interested in getting out of oil, and Egypt had new and crucial gas fields to exploit. Brazil has lots of oil resources and, as noted, aims to be the fourth-largest producer in the world. More generally, the developing countries coalesced around the understandable claims made by India: you developed with fossil fuels, but you want us not to. Very well, pay us not to do so, as compensation for forgoing this opportunity.

In the meantime, the shift towards the emissions projections for key developing countries highlighted the difficulties ahead. India emerged with the world's largest population, and with the ambition to imitate the Chinese economic miracle. The basis of its industrialisation is coal, as China's had been and continues to be. Although India pledged to get to net zero sometime after 2060 and probably 2070, and although India has great solar potential, its coal is abundant and very cheap.

The future emissions, the future destruction of the ecosystems and the capacity for sequestration lie not with the UK or the EU – or even the US – but with countries like India, China, Indonesia, Brazil and Nigeria. The Middle East and Sub-Saharan Africa, plus Latin America and Southeast Asia, are where the future of the climate will be decided. None of these countries prioritises climate change in the way the UK and EU member states have. They have many other challenges and these are almost all more immediate. India's GDP growth rate points to doubling the size of its economy within a decade, as does Indonesia's. This extra economic activity is not going to be met with solar and wind alone, let alone meeting their energy demand now. India already produces 1 billion tonnes of coal and plans to take its coal production up to 1.13 billion tonnes by 2029–30.[18] Indonesia plans to carry on with its great coal expansion, not least to power its refining of nickel, ironically to provide one of the critical mineral inputs to the batteries for EVs. It also plans to ramp up the clearing of its rainforests for agriculture, including for producing biofuels.[19]

China

Never mind, say some in the climate community. The great hope is China, which they expect to take climate leadership, especially in the context of Trump's retreat from the US's multiple global roles. China will continue to dominate solar panel and wind turbine manufacture; it will dominate the world's EV and battery markets and it claims its emissions will peak this decade. It will, it is claimed, step up to the plate, as the US steps down.

As the world's great polluter of the atmosphere, as the burner of more than half the world's coal, rapidly expanding aviation and petrochemicals, and as the country leading on ecosystem destruction at home, and increasingly abroad too, with the extraction of minerals and the imports of intensive agricultural production, and with its Belt and Road[20] approach to critical minerals, such a transformation is both necessary and would be welcome.

For China, an energy mix of coal, nuclear and renewables makes a lot of sense, and it can claim credit for the renewables bit, pointing, as with India, to the increased renewables capacity. This rosy picture belies the fact that the energy generated is much less, because of the intermittency. Having similar capacity does not mean having half the total energy. The system remains grounded on coal, with nuclear now being added at scale.

China has other happy stories to tell. Having largely completed its great construction- and infrastructure-led economic expansion, building is falling back, and *pari passu* so are the emissions in these areas. It is less the switch in energy and more the change in the composition of the economy that is making its impact on emissions felt. Add a declining and ageing population and a slowing growth rate, and the prospect of China's emissions peaking might finally be coming into sight, if they have not already done so.

This creates room for China to push for climate leadership, saying it is no longer increasing emissions. But with China at over 30 per cent of the world's emissions, the climate community should pause to reflect on what a disaster just plateauing emissions would still be. No doubt there will be lots of great speeches and celebrations as and when this happens, but it should be more a wake than a party. China's proposed NDC at the Brazil COP points to a very long tail of carbon emissions, one incompatible with halting the rise in the concentration of carbon in the atmosphere.

The US Withdraws Again

For many in the climate community and especially for activists, it is easy to claim that China is the good guy, compared with the evil Satan of the US. The pro-China camp now includes not just the usual suspects but also serious climate scientists and economists. Trump adds another dollop of spice to the anti-US story. Trump is one of the few world leaders to call climate change a hoax. This appeals to his voter base and allows him to promote 'Drill Baby Drill' for oil and gas, and to turn a blind eye to the tech giants now considering coal and gas as part of the route to meeting their growing electricity demand for data centres and AI. Dismantling the (very limited) Biden and Obama climate change measures is all part of the political sport. Trump has been gutting Biden's Inflation Reduction Act 2022 and has again withdrawn from the COP processes and attacked the grounds for the Environment Protection Agency to regulate climate pollution.[21]

None of this is good news from a climate perspective, but it does need to be put into context. As noted, it was Obama and then Biden who presided over the greatest expansion of fossil-fuel production in US history. These are the 'Drill Baby Drill' US presidents when it comes to results. The Inflation Reduction Act was not entirely or even mostly focused on 'clean' energy, and Biden retained most of the tariffs from Trump's first presidency. What Trump cannot be accused of when it comes to climate change is hypocrisy; Obama and Biden can. Judged by results, Obama and Biden have as much carbon on their hands as Trump has, if not more.

Perhaps this is a little unfair to both Obama and Biden. Both moved on regulation of carbon emissions, and both tried to address coal – though both ran into Democrats like Joe Machin from coal constituencies.[22] But even here it is gas that did for coal, just as gas was doing for coal in the UK. The US developed abundant and very cheap shale gas which left coal with little chance of competing. This was the main reason for emissions reductions in the US (as it was in the UK). The switch from coal to gas for electricity generation rested largely on the gradual closure of existing old coal power stations.

There is a sense in which US climate policy shows a remarkable consistency back to Clinton and his inability to get Kyoto through Congress. Across the political aisle in the US Congress and Senate is a deepening suspicion and even hostility to China, and for understandable reasons. US politicians widely see China as the great threat to the US, and the control of critical minerals and their refinement adds to the deep resentment of the theft of intellectual property (IP) and the deliberate use of large subsidies which undermine US industry.

As Clinton realised, there is little immediate sense in the US reducing its emissions if China does not do so as well.

It takes two to tango, and now the US sees China as flexing its critical minerals muscle against the US. Why would the US increase its exposure to China by going hard down the renewables and EV route before it has the mineral capability to avoid the stranglehold that China has already developed and has used in its tariff disputes with the US, and threatens to tighten? With a Taiwan invasion looming, from a US perspective it does not look sensible for American politicians to play even further into China's hands.

Remember the free-rider problem. It has multiple dimensions beyond just climate change, and it is not necessary to go with Trump to see that the US can reasonably claim that China has been more widely free riding on the US and wants to do some more. The Europeans admit they have been free riding within the North Atlantic Treaty Organization (NATO) on the US, and now the Europeans want the US to jump back into the COP process. Why would it? And further, the US can argue that, as paymaster for the UN (and the International Monetary Fund and the World Bank), why should it underwrite further expansion of the scope and budget of the COP secretariats?

COP30 in Brazil

If the contradictions at the heart of the COP process were revealed in Egypt and Azerbaijan, the Brazil COP sets these out in the full glare for the climate activists and the climate community to see. Tens of thousands fly to Brazil. They get to the COP via the new road cleared through the Amazon rainforest. They may even stay on the two cruise ships moved nearby.

The Brazilian government places itself in the top ten world oil producers, with the aspiration to be the fourth-largest oil producer in the world.[23] It has granted licences for oil drilling at the mouth of the Amazon, and it plans many more.[24] Brazil has relaxed the restrictions on development of the Amazon and presides over the continued clearing and burning of the great carbon sink of the Amazon, some of which is now a net emitter of carbon.

It is hard to make this up. The great schism between the US and China is on display, as very gingerly China steps up to a possible 'leadership' role, and further deepens its trade relations with Brazil, buying yet more intensively grown soy beans from cleared lands, and as it engages with Brazil and especially the lithium triangle of Argentina, Bolivia and Chile for raw critical minerals, preferably to be refined back in China.

After COP30, the future of the COP process to gain a legally binding global top-down agreement based upon enforceable NDCs may well be slowly buried. No doubt it will live on as a technical exercise, and a reduced-form (because of a reduced budget) IPCC will continue to function in the background. World leaders have other things on their minds. As the tensions remain between Russia (and Ukraine) and China (and Taiwan and the South China Sea Islands), with the emergence of India as the leading developing country gradually overtaking China, and as China's economic growth might decline in a sea of debt, reduced population and the sorts of difficulties that Japan experienced from the late 1980s until now, the COPs may slip further into the background – just one part of the bigger geopolitical game.

Why COPs Will Never Solve the Problem

Few can carry on with the illusion that the COPs are the route to solving climate change. There is not going to be a legally binding enforceable global treaty, and the COPs in any event cover only half of the problem. They largely leave out the natural environment and sequestration. In hindsight (and actually pretty obviously at the time, despite the blindness of the climate change community and especially the activists), they were never going to be much more than a convenient and at times useful forum for global engagement amongst political leaders. At times, they have been worse, providing the illusion of progress and the forum to claim leadership when nothing could be further from the truth of what has in fact been going on. Make a speech at the COP, claim to be saving the world and then go home and concentrate on other more important things is not an entirely unfair critique of what has too often been going on.

The fundamental point is that the world is never going to see a global governance regime, full stop, and certainly not for climate change. The world of nations and superpowers is back, even if the end-of-history brigade thought that the fall of the Berlin Wall and the gradual opening of China post-Mao was going to lead us into a new liberal global order, and that free trade was going to usher in stability and peace, in the old Cobdenite story of trade making wars too expensive to contemplate. Russia was never going to join the EU or even NATO, and China's economic growth was never going to translate into a liberal democracy. It is now hard to remember that when the UNFCCC and Kyoto were being developed, serious people at the time actually thought all this was going to happen.

Rather than the COPs doing away with free riding, they never have and never will. Which brings us back full circle to the underlying difficulty. The real foundation of the COPs is Brundtland, which is quite right to make the demand that the developed countries should pay the developing countries not to develop via coal and the other fossil fuels. Heaps of ultra-cheap coal to be shovelled up is a temptation not to be lightly cast aside, and practically impossible for developed countries to compensate the developing countries for.

In addition to the recognition that renewables need subsidies, as highlighted in Chapter 6, the genie is let out of the bottle by the demand for big wealth transfers from north to south – the old Brundtland demand. This is at the heart of what the UN is all about, and it is very unlikely ever to happen at scale.

Transfers from north to south are more likely to come via the exploitation of raw materials in the south to promote economic growth in the north. Money flows for cobalt in the DRC, for lithium in Argentina, Bolivia and Chile, and for copper in Tanzania and Mongolia, just as it once flowed for sugar cane in the Caribbean.

Brazil now wants money from oil and land for greater agricultural surpluses as the rainforest retreats, and Sub-Saharan Africa is seeing agriculture intensification for overseas markets like China, and the large-scale release of carbon from its soils that this is causing.

As for the US and the Europeans, foreign aid is being reduced not increased. The aim of 1 per cent GDP going as aid, promoted by Brundtland, is not getting delivered. Indeed, much of the remaining aid is being used for the benefit of the donor countries. To pay India not to develop through fossil fuels will cost much more than this. Paying developing countries not to go down the fossil-fuel route is not going to work. Transfers in the name of climate change amount to less than the annual dividend of Saudi Aramco.[25]

In the background there is also the problem of the great oil and gas producers and their economic interests. Russia is never going to be serious about getting out of oil. No activist group bothers to demonstrate in Russia and demand that Russia 'just stops oil'. It won't work in the US, now that, with production at over 13 million barrels a day,[26] the US is the world's largest oil producer, and for all the talk of 'transformation' and Vision 30 in Saudi Arabia, it (and also Iran, the United Arab Emirates and Iraq) is not going down this route either. Brazil is now firmly in on the oil act, as are several other Amazon countries.

It is not hard to conclude not only that the COPs won't work, but that nothing much will at the global level. That may well be correct, but it is not a reason to give up. It is better to think through the alternative – bottom-up – options for addressing climate change. Fortunately, there are good things that can be done here. The irony is that by concentrating all the efforts on the top-down UN approaches, these alternatives may not get the attention and traction they deserve.

In any event, it is hard to see the COPs carrying on as the great spectacles that Paris and Glasgow provided. The great days of the COPs are over, even if the process limps on. COP30 in Brazil served to demonstrate this climate realism.

10 UNILATERALISM, BOTTOM-UP AND NO REGRETS

All climate change policies are ultimately national, and in practice most are unilateral. Even the EU policies are only what can be agreed by its nation state members. Chinese and US climate policies from time to time pay some lip service to the COP agreements, but since they are unenforceable, they are also best seen as national too. Russia and India have always taken a national approach.

Does this matter? Must the climate policies be global to get around the free-rider problem? Perhaps surprisingly, the answer is no. A host of unilateral policies is available that make national sense and which can form parts of possible coalitions of the willing. Many are no-regrets.

Pure Altruism and Unilateralism

Suppose a country decides it no longer wishes to be responsible for causing climate change, regardless of what others do. Suppose it does so in the full knowledge that its actions might make little difference, that it will face the costs of its unilateralism but still also face the costs of climate change.

This is unilateralism in the name of pure global interests. It is in the interests of everyone else that a country takes this path, and especially if they themselves don't. Pure unilateralism in effect treats all citizens of the world as its concern and wants to do no harm to them, whatever their nationality, and whether or not they reciprocate. It is a universalism of concern, with no preference for the interests of those in its own nation state. Many progressives think like this, as do many in the climate community. The altruistic country may hope that its actions encourage others to follow its moral example, but its path does not depend upon their reciprocity.[1]

It is important to recognise at the outset what it would take to unilaterally no longer cause climate change. When, for example, the UK Climate Change Committee (CCC) said that if the government adopted a 100 per cent net zero territorial carbon production target for 2050, it would indeed mean its own citizens were no longer causing climate change, as part of its advice (better described as advocacy) for this amendment to the Climate Change Act in 2019, this is what it meant.[2]

Scratch beneath this advocacy, the only way that a net zero carbon production target could mean what the CCC claimed it did would be if everyone else – or at least every country that exported to the UK – also not only adopted this target but met it too. That is a forlorn hope and very unlikely to happen. Thus, we are left with the harder reality: unilaterally being sure of no longer causing climate change requires that the target is for net zero carbon *consumption*. This would be the right target.

Carbon consumption means exactly what it says on the tin. All our consumption must be net zero, wherever the goods and services are produced. For a country like the UK, this would be very painful. The gap between carbon production and carbon consumption is a very big one. It brings into play all the imported carbon in consumption goods.

We could make the target even tougher and include the carbon embedded in what we export, in circumstances where we are unsure about whether the importers of our exports will also take this carbon into account in the pursuit of their own net zero carbon consumption target. In practice, they rarely will, and hence the carbon embedded in our exports is going to cause further climate change. It would be a huge challenge for oil and gas exporters.

You can see where all this is leading. A unilateral carbon consumption net zero target is going to make a significant dent in our consumption. The difference between the current consumption and the net zero carbon consumption reflects the extent to which we are living beyond our environmental means – or at least just the climate change bit. We are doing other non-climate environmental damage too. The fully sustainable economy, described in *Legacy*, on a unilateral basis, will be a significantly lower-consumption economy.

This has not dawned on many of the climate community and almost all the climate activists, or, if it has, they are generally keen not to advertise it. If, for example, we just stop oil and extend this to just stop carbon, the target is much of the public's current consumption. Demonstrating in favour of cutting living standards is going to be altogether tougher than throwing paint at classic works of art, and it would have painful implications for their own personal consumption.

It is a problem that is not unique to climate change. Religious believers are challenged by the tenets of their beliefs. Christians can try to follow the dictates of the Ten Commandments, and they can give away their worldly goods to the poor, thereby dramatically reducing their own consumption. Ideologies set out moulds of perfect societies, such as that depicted by Marx and Engels in their *Communist Manifesto*,[3] but as with many attempts at founding radically new societies and new ways of living, the going is often very tough. The disciples preach on how we should behave, but like those flying to COPs, find it hard to practise it themselves.

Pure altruistic unilateralism on climate change, whilst it has an austere ethical grounding, is not going to work, unless that decarbonisation is going to deliver cheaper electricity and hence lead to an energy cost-competitive advantage. To work in practice, it must be all altruistic glow, but with little pain. This is unlikely to be the case, except in very special circumstances, notably in parts of the world with abundant solar resources. Even here, many carbon-intensive goods will be imported and tourism is pretty ubiquitous.

Assuming that renewables are going to be more expensive, there are fortunately ways around this, without abandoning unilateralism. These are carbon taxation and carbon border adjustments to make people pay for the pollution they cause. Together, these point towards a wider coalition of the unilateral willing, perhaps the only way of getting beyond the single nation state to bringing many into play and hence starting to encroach on the global dimensions of climate change, and all without needing to bring the UN into the picture.

Carbon Taxation, Tariffs and Trade

Efficient markets are ones that internalise all the costs. This means that the costs of pollution should be part of the price of energy. Put the other way around, not to price pollution will be inefficient, even if it has the free-rider advantage.

A uniform carbon tax reflects the fact that carbon is just carbon: it does not matter what the process that produces it is, and location does not matter. If the polluter-pays principle is to be applied,[4] such that all the carbon consumed is captured, then a uniform carbon tax is the way to go. Whether the steel is made in China or made in Port Talbot, the carbon content attracts the tax. Made in China includes the coal content of the processes that produce Chinese steel, and the costs to transport that steel halfway across the world. Ditto solar panels, wind turbines and masts and all the critical minerals for batteries and EVs.

In addition to internalising the carbon emitted to make the stuff we consume, there are two other consequences of unilaterally going for a carbon tax. It does not distort trade, and it raises money. If not internalising pollution costs distorts markets, then adding these costs back in removes this distortion. Carbon taxation, and pollution charges generally, improve the economic efficiency of markets.

It is remarkable that in all the controversy over Trump's tariffs, there is little discussion of their environmental dimensions. On the one side are the free traders, as if markets without tariffs are efficient, on the other are the tariff advocates, who favour home production over imports and a balancing of the current account of their balance of payments.

Take the biggest element of the Trump tariffs: the Chinese dimension. China has used export trade as the main early motor for its great GDP growth. Chinese exports have embedded a lot of carbon. It has engaged in subsidising exporters, protectionism of its home markets and IP theft. These are all distortions to trade. In this, it is not alone. This is how Japan's economic miracle worked too, before it collapsed in 1989.

Trump's argument is that this is not a level playing field and he is right. The obvious first-best solution would be for China to remove its subsidies, open its home markets and honour IP rights. This is never going to happen. Export subsidies are part of China's industrial policy, and it has successfully used this policy to build up great solar companies and a host of other industries behind its subsidy walls, and then through aggressive global pricing has wiped out the targeted industries in the US and the EU.[5]

The next Chinese targets are batteries and EVs, having cornered markets in critical minerals and their refining. It is, and probably will continue to be, an incredibly successful way to grow China's economy. The Belt and Road subsidies have extended the benefits to China of this interventionist policy to gain greater global power too, as well as to ensure its supply chains for food and minerals. It is ironic that Trump's critics fail to recognise that his tariffs have much in common with what China has been doing for the last three decades.

Whether Trump's tariffs, whatever they turn out to be in practice, are the appropriate response to the challenge it sees China presenting it with is open to debate. There are arguments for and against Trump's tariffs. But the one illegitimate attack on Trump's approach is to claim in simplistic terms that economic theory favours free trade, where free trade means no tariffs. Simply quoting Adam Smith, as his critics do, is to use arguments from a long-past world in which there was no significant government spending. The nineteenth-century British corn laws case was indeed simple. The British state did not subsidise agriculture, so tariffs were the prime protectionist instrument. In the modern world, the state is *the* main economic player, a reality typically ignored by free traders, and the role of the state in the economy affects prices and competitiveness.

The ways in which the distortions to trade in China affect the global economy can be seen in the pre-Trump world. As noted, China's great economic rise is probably also the greatest environmental disaster in human history. It turned China from a country with a negligible carbon footprint into the world's greatest carbon polluter. It wreaked serious damage on its ecosystems, including the great rivers and the South China Sea. It is about to do yet more damage with its dams in Tibet. This is the price to the global environment, as well as to the ecosystems within China, of the great economic growth of China. China did not pay for the massive pollution it was causing to its own population, to the South China Sea and to the world's atmosphere. This may well be about to be repeated by India, Indonesia and other developing economies.

In all three cases, their trade strategy has significant mercantile dimensions. Indeed, they have the best of both worlds: they can be mercantilist, while exploiting free trade with the US and the EU. They have big markets to go after, whilst protecting their home industries. In the case of China and Indonesia, home-grown production is linked to the idea of self-sufficiency. For Indonesia, it wants to capture more of the supply chains and hence insists that its nickel is refined in Indonesia. In China's case, its self-sufficiency ambitions extend not just to energy and minerals, but to food production and supply chains, chips manufacture and much more.

The mercantile approach is the stuff of trying to gain geopolitical and military dominance. China has followed this very closely. Its energy policies are designed to overcome its own weakness – it has little of its own oil and gas. Hence it promotes coal, nuclear and renewables as a self-sufficiency strategy.[6] This energy will be there if it faces a blockade of fuel supplies after an invasion of Taiwan. By contrast, a free-trade US is extraordinarily vulnerable to interference in the supplies of critical minerals and, increasingly, high tech, not least if the supply chains from mainland China for the minerals and Taiwan for chips are cut off.

Europe has witnessed this too, with the dependency Russia has been able to impose through its gas exports. Although US shale gas has come to the rescue, and remarkably more quickly and in greater volumes than was anticipated, the implications for trade are apparent. That is why the EU aspires to cut all supplies of gas from Russia by 2027.[7] The irony here is that if the climate community had had its way, shale gas would be banned not only in Europe, but also in the US. It is shale gas that helped to save the EU and thereby help to hold the line in Ukraine. The lessons will not have been missed by the Chinese. China does not have much shale gas or oil. If it did, it would almost certainly have developed this industry. The energy superpower is the US, not China.

A carbon tax redresses one dimension of carbon damage. It is a good thing to do in the context of efficient markets. It does not violate the World Trade Organization rules, which are designed to promote free trade. Many countries have been gradually introducing carbon taxes, howbeit always in a partial way, and often replicating some of the worst features of partial tariffs. Typically, countries exclude agriculture from carbon taxation, and indeed many subsidise fossil-fuel inputs to agriculture. An example is the exclusion from diesel taxation for farmers. Renewables are excluded as if there is no carbon emitted, ignoring their far from green supply chains. EV batteries and all the minerals and their refining that go into the renewables are typically excluded.

Even within the fossil fuels there are distortions. Coal tends to get more favourable general energy taxation and only hit with carbon taxation when burnt in electricity power stations and energy-intensive industrial plants in the EU. Gas gets taxed more lightly than oil, and so on. One distortion is layered on another.

The EU ETS is a fixing of quantities to produce a price for required carbon emissions permits, and, as such, it is a quasi-carbon tax. Over time, its scope has been widened, but still a great deal is left out of its grasp.

Pick-and-mix carbon taxes and ETS schemes have a further big distortion. They tend to be tailor-made for lobbying and capturing by vested interests. Farmers excel at this, but every politically sensitive sector pleads its political importance, and especially where voting is on a geographical constituency basis.

The gap between what an efficient carbon tax would look like to assist in the unilateral pursuit of net zero carbon consumption and what we have is huge. Hence the opportunity: the scope for improvement is correspondingly large, in both improving the functions of markets and finding the cheapest ways to decarbonise.

The Money

Further encouragement to take up this opportunity comes from the money. After the great financial liberalisations from the 1980s onwards, and the associated financial engineering, many governments are now struggling to balance their internal budgets. This is in a context in which taxation is already high, partly as a result of the global financial crash back in 2007/08 and then the Covid pandemic expenditures. Put simply, governments are running out of things to tax, and electorates are proving reluctant to endorse conventional tax-raising governments. The easy route of borrowing instead is no longer an option. In most countries, government debt is roughly twice what it was before the 2007/08 financial crash.

Carbon taxes are what might be called virtue taxes. Instead of distorting labour and capital markets, they correct the externality, making markets more efficient.[8] Carbon taxes may be one of the last refuges of tax-raising governments.

Energy has been something to tax for a long time, and oil in particular. There are lots and lots of energy taxes, from taxing oil and gas licences, to taxing the refined products. If there is a switch in transport from oil to electricity, and a switch from oil (and eventually coal) as a fuel for electricity generation to gas, taxation of oil will fall, and governments will need a replacement.[9]

The money raised (and, conversely, the money lost) creates an income effect from the tax. What the net effect of the tax is depends upon what the revenue is spent on. One option is to just give it back again as a general benefit or as a reduction in other distorting taxes. This results in a change in the relative prices of goods and services, neutralising the income effect. Instead of distorting labour markets by taxing labour, carbon could provide the revenue instead. Another benefit flows to the competitiveness of the economy.

Eventually, were there to be a comprehensive move from high- to low-carbon energy, the tax would start to lose its grip. Complete net zero carbon consumption globally would lead to zero carbon tax revenue globally. For the many reasons set out in this book, this is not going to happen for many decades, if ever. Carbon taxes could raise lots of money for many years to come.

Tax revenue from tariffs was once the prime source of money to governments. Trump sees it as being large enough to reduce labour taxes. It is not impossible to consider directed tariffs on things like steel and cars as proxies for carbon taxes, and in particular taxes on coal-intensive production. Even general tariffs against China, India and Russia could have a big implicit carbon impact.

The money leads to a conclusion: even if politicians like Trump are not at all attracted to the idea of carbon taxes, the impact of their policies might have some carbon effects.

Carbon Border Adjustments

The unilateralist in search of no longer causing climate change needs to make sure their carbon imports are covered. Carbon imports need to be treated in the same way as home territorial carbon production, and not as a get-out-of-jail card for deindustrialising countries like the UK. If the chosen instrument is a carbon tax, then it follows that it should be applied at the border. There would be a carbon border tax to complement a domestic carbon tax.[10]

This gives the virtuous unilateralist altruist the net zero carbon consumption result. The outcry from those exporting to, say, the UK under such a regime is that this is just protectionism dressed up as environmentally good. They will – and do – scream loudly. Many did at COP30 in Brazil against the EU's carbon border adjustment mechanism (CBAM).[11]

But here the magic happens: the carbon border tax is an incentive for other countries to join the unilaterally willing. Why? Because the carbon border tax can be avoided if a carbon tax has already been paid back home in the exporting country. If, say, China levies a carbon tax on its steel production that is equivalent to the carbon tax in, say, the UK, then at the border the carbon has already been internalised in the price of the exported steel via the Chinese carbon tax. There is no case for double taxation.

This only works if, in this example, China does in fact have an equivalent tax, and one that is transparent and verifiable and not offset by other often less visible subsidies. Provided that both sides play by the rules of a level playing field, there is a massive incentive for China to impose an equivalent carbon tax. Why? Because the money from the tax goes to the Chinese government and not the UK government. Why pay a tariff to a foreign government when you can keep the money yourself?

This issue is reflected in the way the Trump tariffs work. The tariff is levied on the importer, not the exporter. The result is that the price goes up in the US, and US citizens end up paying the tariff (the tax) to the US government. The importer loses out because it loses market share as its products are now more highly priced. But the exporter – for example, the Chinese government – does not get the money. In the carbon border tax case above, China does get the money if it imposes the equivalent tax.

This is a very powerful incentive effect from the carbon border tax. Suppose you are a Kenyan rose or bean grower, flying your products into the UK and other EU markets. Suddenly the relative prices have changed and you are charged a border tax at the destination airport. The incentive is to immediately tax the carbon emitted in Kenya in growing the roses and the beans and pay it to the Kenyan government. This means that the Kenyans are not out of pocket, other than as a result of a contraction of these industries if the carbon tax is high enough to reduce purchases in the importing country. In fact, in this example, it may not turn out this way. Why? Because the costs of production in Kenya may still be lower than the addition of the carbon price would make them. Heat and growing seasons and land may still leave Kenya with a comparative or even absolute advantage once all the costs including the carbon tax have been taken into account. The ultimate impact depends upon the substitution effect from higher prices.

Crucially, Kenya gets the money from the carbon tax and has the political lever from its electorate to impose the domestic carbon tax because otherwise it would simply be lost revenue.

The Political Economy of Carbon Border Adjustments

The carbon border tax encourages the exporters to impose a carbon tax. This is the route to an expanding circle of countries included within the coalition of the willing. It is a bottom-up route to tackling the global dimensions of climate change and it does it by raising lots of money for the participating countries.

Those that rule out other taxation options may choose carbon taxes anyway. In doing so, they have an incentive to align their taxes with those of the coalition of the willing members to escape the border adjustment.

Those with energy taxes that are rough proxies for carbon – notably energy taxes that fall on the fossil fuels – have an incentive to fully convert these to carbon taxes and then align with the coalition of the willing.

Gradually more and more countries join to maintain market access. What matters is how big the market is of those in the coalition of the willing. The EU is big – still over 15 per cent of world trade – and especially important in services (which by the way emit lots of carbon in their supply chains).

What would transform the bottom-up coalition of the willing is if the US were to join too. Then around 30–40 per cent of world trade would be captured, at which point the incentive mechanism creates a snowball of countries wishing to join too.

It is a big *if*, but not completely absurd. One reason is that its access to carbon border adjustment countries' markets is affected. Were China and the Far Eastern countries to join, then US corporations might lobby hard for the US to join, resulting in an approximation of the current tariffs to what a carbon border adjustment would look like. To the extent that Trump has concentrated on energy-intensive goods and services, and wants some of these re-shored, the gap may not be enormous, and there is nothing to stop tariffs being added on top of a carbon border tax. It is a route too for a future Democratic government in the US that finds it hard politically to undo Trump's tariffs and do without the revenues and wants to get back on board the politics of climate change. Converting Trump's tariffs into a carbon border adjustment might appeal to a future US government, especially if the revenue effects are not very different. Continuing Trump's strategy would increasingly stress home production over imports, and that reduces carbon-intensive imports further.

The Hard Sell on Climate Change

Will the unilateralist approach work? Won't the free-rider incentive dominate? The most ardent members of the climate community have begun to understand that their head-on strategies are not convincing the voters. The political backlash against net zero has been accelerating. Whilst voters are happy to support climate change policies when they believe the stories about there being no cost to them personally, that net zero carbon production targets are win–win, they are less convinced when the costs land on their bills, and domestic industries close down.

Telling optimistic stories about win–win is a very dangerous game. It is avoiding the fundamental reality: if the pollution is not being paid for, and if it has to be paid for to correct for the pollution, then it has an inevitable cost of climate policies implication. Telling the public the truth – that it will be expensive to achieve net zero and that the free-rider incentive remains powerful to all – risks the reaction that since it isn't going to work, climate realism points to focusing on adaptation to a much warmer world.

Which brings us back to ethics and the bottom-up unilateralist approach. For unilateralism to gain a grip, it has to work, in the sense that it has to be true that, as a result, people will no longer be causing climate change. They have to believe that their actions are having positive consequences on what is a global problem. They have to believe, too, that in due course technology will help out.

There are examples of when the electorates have chosen to sacrifice their standards of living for a greater cause. War is the obvious example. The two great world wars of the twentieth century entailed very sharp reductions in living standards, with punitive tax rates, asset confiscation and even rationing. The greater cause was national survival, as it is now in Ukraine. Climate change is even more challenging, because the national benefit comes only if others follow suit and it is largely in the future. That probably means that the sacrifice has to be limited. Not too much, not for too long and with a fair technology wind. Having a greater coalition of the willing helps. Having others making sacrifices too adds to the sense of solidarity.

The other side of the pressure to join a coalition of the willing is the consequence of not acting, of being clear how it will otherwise end. To that grim possibility we now turn.

11 WHAT HAPPENS IF WE DON'T ACT?

Business-as-usual is easy to work out when it comes to climate change: just add 2 ppm every year into the future. This takes us from around 425 ppm in 2025 to 475 ppm in 2050. Accelerate to 3 ppm every year, and that takes us to 500 ppm. That is within spitting distance of a doubling of the concentration of carbon in the atmosphere since the Industrial Revolution got going, which would be 550 ppm.

Given the likely increases in the demand for energy from AI, data centres, air conditioning and desalination, and the increase in population of, say, another 1 billion, add economic growth in India and Indonesia of, say, 6–8 per cent per annum, and low-carbon electricity will struggle to cope with all the extra demand, but not make much or even any inroads into existing demand for oil, gas and coal. Within the fossil fuels, oil demand will probably go up, driven by plastics and petrochemicals, even if it loses out in transport; coal may well peak, but hold its own, and gas demand is likely to increase significantly, not least to generate electricity. This is a realistic picture of our energy future, one where there are lots more renewables and even nuclear, but no transition from fossil fuels. It is not optimistic or pessimistic: it is climate realism.

Whilst this is very bad news on the emissions front, it could be even worse for sequestration. Project forward to 2050 the sheer scale of destruction of the great rainforests. Picture the Amazon being cleared and burnt at the current rates. By 2050 another 60 million hectares may be gone.[1] A similar story can be told for the Mekong, with much already gone, for the Congo, for Indonesia, and for smaller rainforests, such as

Queensland, Australia. The damming of the great rivers on the Tibetan plain by China imperils the crucial water supplies of Bangladesh and India and can only cause more ecosystem damage. Meanwhile, the temperate rainforests plus the great forests of Siberia continue to be depleted. Fires, in part the result of climate change, make matters worse.

Climate change acidifies the oceans, reducing their ability to absorb carbon. These great carbon sinks may not be able to cope with much more carbon. Add all this together and it is more emissions plus less sequestration that pushes the stock of carbon in the atmosphere ever higher. None of this can be dismissed as alarmism. It is just a realistic take on the path we are on and have been on since 1990.

What will this mean for global temperatures, for regional temperatures and for sea levels? There are lots of scenarios, with, for all its shortcomings, the IPCC leading the way.[2] What these tell us is that there is a great deal of uncertainty. It could be just over 2 °C global warming, or it could be as much as 4 °C. You can scare yourself at the bottom end and terrify yourself at the upper end. If energy demand doubles by, say, 2050 and fossil fuels hang on to even, say, 60 per cent market share (down from over 80 per cent now) of much bigger economies, that is a considerable absolute increase in the fossil-fuel burn. Peaking out on coal, gas and oil at the current levels is what delivers at least 2 ppm per annum. To hold the line at current temperatures, we have to run uphill very hard – not just replace existing fossil fuels, but also compensate for the much higher aggregate demand for energy. It would almost certainly require very large-scale emissions reductions, very large-scale sequestration increases and massive deployment of CCS.

A Warmer World up to 2 °C

Even sticking to what we can be sure of, we know that the global temperatures are going to rise, and for some time to come. The overall stock of carbon in the atmosphere lasts for a long time, even if some gases, like methane, fall out quite quickly. That stock is no longer being sequestrated at the past rates, adding to the numbers.

What will this world be like? The climate community has put a lot of effort into telling scary stories about a hotter world – of heatwaves, droughts, floods, plagues and famines. Every extreme weather event (and many non-extreme ones) is treated as an illustration of what is to come, giving rise to extreme reporting.[3]

It is hard to sift through this cacophony of shrieks and alarms. Never mentioned are the benefits from climate change. Warmer winters in northern regions mean fewer deaths from the cold, longer growing seasons and greater access as ice retreats. Heating costs fall.

The opening up of the Northeast Passage in the Arctic is a great boon to Russia and to shipping, cutting off significant time and distance on trade routes from the Pacific to the Atlantic. Less ice also means more access to the mineral resources of the Arctic, and to its fish stocks. To even mention such benefits is a heresy to the climate community, and the activists may even try to cancel those who dare to do so.

The more complex weighing of costs and benefits points to a much more complex and inconvenient conclusion, which may make it even harder to get action on climate mitigation. Up to 2 °C warming might, on balance, turn out to be not that bad and even for some economically positive.[4] This calculation takes account of the fact that most of the world's wealth is in the Northern Hemisphere, and notably in North America, Europe, Russia and China. All of these will have some benefits from a slightly warmer climate, notwithstanding the heatwaves.

For the rest of the world, and especially the tropics, the story is not likely to be so positive. These poorer regions of the world will face temperatures that can be made bearable only with air conditioning and they will need lots of desalination. Without the infrastructures to cope with these emerging challenges, and lacking the wealth to pay for the necessary investment, it is understandable that, since these countries are not the primary cause of the rising temperatures, they demand loss and damage compensation from the Global North. This they are not likely to get. The results for them are skewed to the negative, and in some cases sharply so. But for most, having already experienced 1.5 °C warming, it has not yet been catastrophic.

A Hotter World: Above 2°C

It is above 2 °C that things are likely to get tough and nasty for almost everyone. Parts of the tropics might become uninhabitable and then there are only two options: move or die. This is when large-scale migration gets going, and possibly more starvation, as subsistence agriculture wilts away under the heat.

For people in the tropics, it could be really bad. There is no other way of putting it. But is it also really bad for the northern developed regions of the world? It is not so obvious. Wealthy societies could begin to literally live indoors. Many already do, moving from centrally heated and air-conditioned houses to heated and air-conditioned offices, using air-conditioned transport to get between them. With enough technology and wealth, it is possible to live in climate capsules. It is also possible to have plentiful water with desalination, and crops and livestock can move indoors. Indeed, indoor farming is already replacing the precarious exposure to the outdoors.

Such adaptation is possible in even hotter areas. A glance at the United Arab Emirates including Dubai, in particular, shows what is possible already in places where temperatures can exceed 40 °C. Recall the new Neom city being built in Saudi Arabia. Its grandiose ambition reflects Crown Prince Mohammed bin Salman's utopian 'Saudi Vision 2030'.[5] It stretches out what is technically possible with wealth that is practically limitless. Though it is a failing vanity project dreamt up by consultants, it does illustrate a futuristic 'vision' for the very rich, and for very rich countries. Much of Saudi Arabia already copes with what elsewhere would be regarded as extreme heat.

For the global elite, it may indeed be possible to survive and prosper in a much hotter world beyond 2 °C. This is the rationale behind Bill Gates' recent statement that we can live with climate change.[6] But mostly for the global elite. It takes the gated capsule communities they have already been building to provide a cocoon for them and their dependants. There is a whole cult of this sort of thing already in swing. It is what lies behind Musk's idea of a community living on Mars, having trashed this planet first.

The elite's problem is whether they can keep the masses at bay. That looks unlikely, and climate change much beyond 2 °C will turn out to be a strong challenge to those on the left of politics, and indeed to democracy itself.

Tipping Points

Before considering the politics, there is one further twist. Things could turn out much worse (or indeed much more benign) than the current models suggest. Why? Because the trend in temperatures and in the concentration of carbon in the atmosphere could be non-linear. There could be inflection points, tipping from one climate to another.

To see how this might happen, let's start with the carbon concentration. The pathway has been around 2 ppm on a pretty linear trendline since 1990. What if it turned sharply up to over 3 ppm? If the causation runs from ppm to temperatures, then the projected 2–3 °C warming, bad though it might be, could increase to something much worse.

How might this happen? It requires a sharp increase in emissions and a sharp reduction in sequestration. All sorts of scary scenarios have been suggested. Emissions might spike sharply upwards from the melting of the tundra, and a corresponding release of the methane contained with it. Methane has a short life in the atmosphere, but with a much greater forcing effect. The causal chain goes from fast methane release to sharp temperature rises, to more carbon and methane releases as more tundra melts.

The Arctic offers a further possible tipping point. The melting ice and snow reduces the whiteness of the Arctic, which in turn reduces the bounce-back of solar radiation. The albedo effect diminishes, and temperatures rise, melting more ice and snow.

These are all possible emissions tipping points. On the sequestration side, the worry is that higher temperatures trigger ecosystem collapses. A warmer climate might dry out the Amazon, whilst more ppm might further acidify the oceans. These changes hit the sequestration hard, and ecosystems once in decline may go one way. Couple this with the great extinction event we are already causing, linked to but separate from climate change, and a world of gradual warming translates itself into something much worse.

What about more benign tipping points? The natural way of causing rapid climate cooling has been volcanic activity. Great eruptions spew out ash and gases high into the atmosphere, and these act as a reverse greenhouse effect, causing global cooling. They have in the past caused upheaval, crop failures and famines, and associated wars and conflicts. They might even have caused the Black Death in the mid-fourteenth century.[7]

On a longer-term perspective, it is the changes to the Earth's rotation and changes to solar activity that have caused cooling (and warming). Ice ages are the consequence, and the 'snowball Earths' come from the increase in the albedo effect; these are longer term. We may be between cold periods within a cycle of ice ages, but this is unlikely to come to the rescue soon enough. In the 1970s a genuine fear was of a new ice age. The main concerns were the role of aerosols, reflecting back solar radiation and the long-term

Milankovitch cycles. *Time Magazine* ran a front cover in 1974 on 'Another Ice Age?' It may have been well founded but not in time to halt the global warming we are causing.

That only leaves two possible benign tipping points: geoengineering, which may be resorted to if, as and when the temperature increase accelerates and the ppm keep going up, and a dramatic and rapid technological breakthrough on the energy front.

Geoengineering of the atmosphere is theoretically possible, and as we saw in Chapter 8, it is practical on a very small scale. The composition of the atmosphere can be manipulated, but as yet the costs and political risks are huge. It is unlikely to deliver, if at all, until at best late in this century, and would require a great concentration of resources to do so.

A technology breakthrough is repeatedly promised in energy, and most claims are associated with nuclear. Once it was going to be too cheap to measure, and now we are told that nuclear fusion is going to deliver unlimited energy. Again, theoretically this is a possibility, but this promise has always been about 30 years in the future. To impact on climate change, fusion has to be deployed at scale around the world and especially in developing countries to offset the rising emissions from their economic growth and development. It also has to be controlled.

From Science and Modelling to Politics

If you are a betting person, the overwhelming odds are on climate change continuing on past 2 °C warming. After that, any bets are really speculative gambles, not amenable to the assignment of meaningful probabilities. The science gets us so far, but further out so much is on our hands that it is the politics that takes over.

The great UN COP conferences and the UNFCCC aim at building a cross-country consensus, bringing left and right together and democrats and dictators to the table. The IPCC was set up as an attempt to create a foundation of facts and hypotheses and models and scenarios around which all could coalesce.

It has been a great ambitious project, and it has had some limited success. Very few dispute the fundamental science of global warming. True, Trump does not agree, and Putin is not on the same page either. Some still say it is a hoax. But even these few are surrounded by people who largely think otherwise. It is reasonable to conclude that the scientific argument on the theory of the greenhouse effect has been won.

What has not been won is the debate about how much is caused by humans, and by which humans, and how tight the causation is from ppm to predictions of temperature increases. This is a political and media minefield of competing claims, with some concerned scientists going much further than the science and the evidence dictates to campaign for actions and policies.

Climate change is one of the great political games of our time. This game has been played out between the left and the right in democracies and between different geopolitical strategists in countries such as China and India. It is a game about popularity and votes, and, not surprisingly, it plays into the resurgence of the popularist right.

In some countries there never has been a political consensus about the broad framework of climate policies; in others, where consensus was carefully and painstakingly constructed, it has broken down. The US is in the former category; the UK in the latter.

The reason the political divides have opened up is partly the consequence of the tactics and policies of the progressive political left, and partly from a deep division about the role of the state and the arguments around socialism. Some on the left see climate change as caused by evil capitalist companies and argue that the state should step in to regulate and nationalise them, and then direct them on the correct pathway. The radical left goes further and demands direct action against the oil companies (usually the Western oil companies). Those on the right see climate change policies as back-door socialism, with all that entails. They see it as part and parcel of state control and link it (as do the progressives on the left) with other causes, like DE&I, Black Lives Matter and transgender rights – even rights for rivers and trees.[8]

I exaggerate to make my point; there is much more to this than whether people are pro- or anti-climate change policies. What is really at stake is the kind of political, economic and social organisation of society.

The left knows that, despite their appeals to 'tax the rich', there is now little political mileage behind genuine socialism and the levelling-down that people fear it might bring. They dress up climate change as an economic opportunity, a way to boost economic growth through state actions, and therefore a route to cheap energy. For this, they need a narrative not just about the evil of fossil fuels, but that relying on fossil fuels for over 80 per cent of our energy exposes us to what they predict to be inevitable high and volatile oil and gas prices (they rarely claim that coal prices are inevitably going to be high and volatile). Peak oil added more spice to this story.

The left can therefore justify their interventionist policies by claiming that net zero policies are win–win: clean energy that is also cheap. They then throw in the claim that it is also home-grown, failing lamentably to tell supporters about the global supply chains, and all the pollution embedded in them.

It helps the left to claim that China is leading the way. The appeal today of China amongst the left follows a pattern similar to the enthusiasm of the left for Soviet Russia in the 1920s and 1930s,[9] and Trump's arrival allows them to see the US as the great capitalist Satan, whilst staying silent on China's overall environmental record and wider concerns about Tibet, the Uighurs, and actions in the South China Sea.

All of this makes it much harder for the left to face up to the challenges of climate change. But it has not been without its political successes. The left convinced many in the centre and centre right that their narrative was correct. As a result, centre-right governments in Germany (Angela Merkel) and the UK (David Cameron, Theresa May, Boris Johnson and Rishi Sunak) pursued very similar policies to those advocated by the left. But neither side got effective action and instead they all got more warming. Together they created a very sharp political dividing line, which can be exploited by the far right, which is anti-net zero and anti-climate policies throughout Europe. Trump takes a similar line in the US. The mainstream political right is now being pulled away too.

In simple terms, the voters in the democracies have found out that the claim that renewables are much cheaper and that energy prices are going to go down for households and businesses as a result of fast-track net zero policies is not correct. It is true that Putin's actions in Ukraine led to a further tightening of a price spike in gas that was already under way,[10] but it is not true that the US with its greater reliance on fossil fuels suffered as a consequence. Ditto for Iran.

It is Europe that lacks international competitiveness, and that has the highest industrial and domestic electricity prices, not the US. Trump's emphasis on fossil fuels, his 'Drill, Baby, Drill' mantra, offers the US the great geopolitical advantage: cheap abundant oil and gas and energy self-sufficiency, and indeed the opportunities for large-scale energy exports. It is the US that has cheap energy that is home-grown and secure. Little of this is on offer in Europe.[11]

The EU and the UK have in fact doubled down on their climate policies. Net zero electricity has been pushed hard, oil and gas exploration in the North Sea by companies in UK waters squashed with windfall taxes and prohibitions on new oil and gas licences, and the EU ETS tightened. Deindustrialisation continues, and few energy-intensive industries are choosing the EU (and especially the UK) as places to invest. The UK gas gets imported from Norway by pipelines, and from the US and Qatar via LNG. In Eastern

Europe, cheap Russian gas remains an enticement, and some have never stopped using it.

After two decades of the consequences of the financial crisis and then Covid, these particularly self-inflicted energy costs have spawned a cost-of-living crisis. Energy costs pervade everything. Energy is more important even than labour costs. Flatlining living standards with low productivity and low economic growth mean that the costs of net zero policies bite hard, and the fallacy of focusing on the marginal costs of wind and solar, and not the system costs of these intermittent technologies, does not convince voters. They are not fools, and they live the impact of the costs of these policies in their household energy bills and in making their jobs more precarious. It is therefore no surprise that they increasingly support political parties that either oppose outright net zero policies or at least wish to slow them down.

In doing so, voters in Europe and in the US see climate change policies in the broader focus of the progressive left agenda. They see immigration on the same page, not a separate political chapter, not least because the same people who want to go fast on climate change also often favour open immigration. They see DE&I policies, Black Lives Matter and climate change as part of a programme of a left agenda. The UK Green Party expounds wealth taxes, open immigration, widespread state controls and nationalisation. It is therefore an easy step for the right to headline both anti-net zero and anti-immigration on their billboards. The scope for consensus and cooperation has been blown apart, as the central ground of politics fades.

The UN, the Progressive Left and Utilitarianism

The progressive left adds to the dividing of being pro-net zero and pro-immigration, with being pro- the internationalism of the UN. It does not help to create a broader political consensus on climate change where the UN does not see itself as a federation of nations, but rather as a supra-national body, going beyond the nation state. Nowhere is this clearer than when it comes to the COPs. Most of the tens of thousands who turn up to these events are of the left, and most are internationalist.

There are indeed good philosophical reasons for grounding an ethics and a politics on internationalism, and regarding all humans wherever and whenever they live as being fundamentally equal, with equal rights and equal responsibilities. This is at the heart of liberalism – each individual matters equally. It is what lies behind, for example, the analysis in Stern's famous *Economics of Climate Change*.[12] If when you live and where you live is not relevant, then future people, however far into the future, matter as much as we do now, and those in Gaza and Somalia matter as much as those in London and indeed those in your own family. Utility is what progressive liberals on the left want to maximise, not the specific rights and responsibilities of people with homes, families and countries as their primary focus.

Utilitarianism and progressive left politics do not sit comfortably with the nation state. Nation states point towards bottom-up approaches not top-down ones. Interestingly, it is here that those on the progressive left depart from those on the far left, mirroring what is happening on the right. The far left is very nationalistic. The dominance of the state as the director of the economy and society and forced equality and social surveillance and conformity, and the suppression of the law to the interests of the state that can be found in Russia and China are a million miles from the ideals of utilitarians on the progressive left. Yet they tend to favour China as they once did Russia, and it is notable that some in the climate change community want to 'go beyond' democracy because it is not giving them the results that they would want to impose. Ironically, the US, China and Russia have all developed an elite class with fabulous personal wealth. The difference is that those elites in Russia and China are wealthy because the state allows them to be, in exchange for unswerving loyalty to the great leaders. In the US, the tech billionaires have an element of legal protection and don't end up in jail or dead if they challenge their leader. It helps that they are the founders of great businesses too.

Life Goes On, But Not As We Know It

The outlook on climate change is bleak. This is not pessimism. It is realism. The politics is running away from the progressive left as the promises of the COPs and the transitions and the claims about 'cheap' renewables get swamped by the evidence. There will be more wind and especially solar. The wall of increasing energy demand will require these, and also more nuclear and more fossil fuels to power the world economy. It will require more and more and more.[13]

Climate change is not our only or indeed even a separable problem. Biodiversity is taking a hit too. Ecosystems are being destroyed in the name of economic progress and as a result of population growth, even as the latter slows down. Add the loss of biodiversity and the destruction of the core ecosystems of the Earth, and the fabulously wonderful abundance and hospitable climate that we enjoy will deteriorate. It is and will go on doing so for the foreseeable future. Again, this is realism, not pessimism.

This is not, however, the end of life on Earth, just a lot less biodiversity on Earth and a less good climate for us humans. In geological time, we are just a blip and have not yet been around for the usual life of a species – around 1–10 million years.[14] We have eliminated all the other humans in the *Homo* category. They are all gone, helped to extinction by us. We are helping a lot of other species go extinct too.

In the very long run, climate change is the motor for increasing biodiversity. Climate change cleans out many specialists adapted to their current climate. It creates new ecological niches and it increases competition through natural selection, the engine of evolution. Life on Earth will go through many episodes before our sun dies and, with it, life on Earth – in around 4 billion years' time.

Climate change is not inevitable: climate change does not have to go on at its current breakneck speed. Extinction and the destruction of ecosystems do not need to be the way our planet goes except in the extremely long term. Both are solvable problems. But they are not solvable if we humans are driven by that desire for more and more and more, and the GDP growth that reflects it. The sustainable economy, which I describe in *Legacy*, is eminently possible, but it would require a very different politics from that advanced by the far left, the progressive left, the centre right and the far right, and a much more honest debate and discussion about the models, the predictions and the claims about costs. Propaganda, lobbying, the pursuit of vested interests and ideology are not our friends in addressing these problems.

12 HOW NOT TO WASTE ANOTHER 25 YEARS

We probably will waste another 25 years, but here is how we could avoid doing so.

Stopping climate change and biodiversity loss is a huge undertaking and especially so since it has to be achieved in a matter of a few decades. Despite the political rhetoric and the claims of many in the climate community, nothing much has been achieved since 1990. The 30 COPs on climate change have not made much difference, and the 16 COPs on biodiversity have had a similar negligible impact.

It is not for lack of goodwill, but rather costs that have stood in the way. Progress is going to cost a lot. It is impossible to know how much, but it will test the willingness of people to pay, and test politicians to persuade us to do so. So far, there has been a 'happy clappy' approach – tell people it is all going to be win–win; the problems get solved and the prices go down. They haven't and they don't.

It is imperative that the least-cost pathways are found, about which we need to be brutally honest. There is very little money to waste, yet we are wasting much of the resources being deployed so far, and with little net gain. To have any chance of getting on the sustainable consumption path, it will need to be extremely efficient. 'Stop the waste' is a good slogan to start with.

This is doubly important given the scale of the challenge. Going from over 80 per cent reliance on fossil fuels to a small residual, dealt with by CCS or other sequestration, is a huge ask, and especially since there will most likely be considerable growth in electricity and energy demand as the world digitalises and adds data centres and AI and eventually quantum computing. It's a massive undertaking, probably beyond anything humans have ever taken on, and the resources available to tackle climate change are small in comparison. Switching from a peacetime to a wartime economy with the great mobilisation of resources in the First and Second World Wars are possible comparators, but neither involved a switch in the entire energy system. Net zero in 25 years is on this sort of scale. Protecting nature may be even bigger, given how much land use would have to change to one that protected ecosystems and halted the scale of the destruction.

So far, a remarkable amount of money has been spent with little or no impact, and some spending has been perverse. Part of this is because the spending is typically trying to address multiple objectives at the same time. It is not just net zero, politicians proclaim, but *also* 'economic growth' *and* increasing consumption *and* achieving geopolitical ambitions. We need to concentrate ruthlessly on the tasks in hand. Every item of spending has to answer the questions: How does this reduce global warming? How does this reduce global biodiversity loss? Diluting the objectives dilutes the progress.

'Do everything' strategies appeal to politicians, for they have the convenient effect of giving out prizes to all the technologies and lobby groups. Backing wind *and* solar *and* nuclear *and* CCS *and* hydrogen, as well as energy efficiency *and* EV production *and* heat pumps *and* anything else that can muster up a lobby group keeps the maximum of interests on board, but it inevitably spreads the jam very thinly.

Focus on the Global Impacts, Not Territorial Emissions

Take the UK. Solar is never going to make much difference compared with sunnier countries like Spain. The UK is never going to build a significant solar panel industry. But the

UK's offshore wind industry has one of the best locations in the world to develop the technology, and the build-out has gained many insights into how to run a logistics support system. The North Sea is shallow, well studied and the wind flows are good. It also has lots of depleted oil and gas wells, lots of pipelines and a supporting oil and gas infrastructure onshore. It is a great place to try out CCS – if it doesn't work in the North Sea, it is probably not going to work globally, except in very specialist circumstances.

The UK has world-leading research capability. It still has world-class universities. New technologies are going to be needed and the UK has the potential to contribute greatly on the science.

If the question is how to contribute to tackling climate change, the UK should probably focus on R&D and CCS, given we already have more than enough wind. Money should be spent on these instead of on yet more offshore wind and onshore solar and it should avoid biomass. This focus has got nothing much to do with minimising UK territorial emissions; it has to do with helping to mitigate *global* warming.

R&D and CCS should not be pursued primarily for competitive advantage. They are not primarily 'growth' stories, though a growth case can be made for some of the R&D. On the contrary, they should be designed to create global public goods, making the research and the technological advances freely available to any country that wants to use them to further its decarbonisation. This is where a central mistake gets made: if you believe that the renewables will be cheaper than fossil fuels, then pursuing a unilateral policy is justified in terms of competitive advantage, and hence the benefits to global warming are additional and indeed incidental. It is possibly true for China and its solar panel manufacture, batteries and EVs. Sadly, it is not true for the UK, and resources are not infinite. Hence the need to focus. A lot of solar, batteries and EVs will happen anyway, but these need to be put in context. Solar and

EVs will contribute, but they won't crack climate change except at the margin. Recall how great the energy demand growth is likely to be, and set solar and EVs in this context. Important, yes; game-changing, probably not.

Other countries have comparative advantages and expertise to bring to the global climate change problem. They should each concentrate on what they can do best to tackle global warming, contributing to the global public goods.

Avoid Costly Mistakes and Stop Digging Holes: Learning from the German and UK Mistakes

This is no time to waste money. Yet that is what has been happening, sometimes on a grand scale. Recall the discussion in Chapter 9 of the most egregious waste in Germany. Germany swallowed the whole renewables story. It has been a lobbyists' dream. Born of the green movement and especially the Green Party, the original rationale for the *Energiewende* was that it would be a brilliant industrial strategy, and Germany would not only move towards cheap renewable energy, but also create new global businesses, renewables equivalents of the Apples and Amazons and Googles and Microsofts of the US-dominated tech world.

If only, but it was not to be. As soon as the details were filled in, the *Energiewende* sowed the seeds of Germany's energy disasters: more coal, greater reliance on Russian gas, premature closure of nuclear and high prices, without any significant German companies emerging.

How could this have happened? The German population were sold a story which just happened to fit the electoral arithmetic. The Green Party emerged as a coalition partner contender, and it had its price: closing the nuclear industry and building lots and lots of renewables.

The Greens got what they asked for. Premature closure of the German nuclear power stations must rank as one of the worst single energy policy decisions made within the EU, perhaps even globally. Whereas it is understandable that Japan closed its nuclear power stations after Fukushima (though even this may be in hindsight viewed as a serious mistake and already by 2025 ten reactors have been reopened), in Germany it was pure politics, born out of the anti-nuclear movement against nuclear weapons, and reflecting the front line that West Germany faced against a possible nuclear war between Russia and the US.

Pacifism has a deep ethical foundation, and pacifists who oppose military nuclear weapons typically will oppose civil nuclear power. But in Germany the policy was closing *existing* very well-regulated nuclear power stations in its industrial south, without removing the 'threat' of nuclear accidents, given its close proximity to nuclear power stations in France, and ironically its reliance on exports of French nuclear electricity to keep its lights on after its own nuclear power station closures, as the intermittent renewables were added to its electricity networks.[1]

The impacts of withdrawing reliable baseload were not thought through. Without nuclear, German industry was very exposed to intermittency and indeed just having enough electricity generation. The result was that Germany switched from nuclear to coal. It is hard to make this up. 13 GW of new coal was added to its electricity system from 2000. Even this was not enough and the German industrial dependency on gas grew too. Just stand back and take this in: the *Energiewende* exit from nuclear led to a switch to fossil fuels. This *increases* global warming.

To this mistake was added a second greatly misconceived policy: the *Energiewende* embarked on a huge expansion of solar. This is Germany we are discussing, not exactly renowned for its sunshine in the cloudy and dark Germany. This is not Spain or North Africa. Germany spent a considerable share of its €200 billion of a carbon transition budget on solar. Not only was this very expensive, but it diverted monies that could have been better spent actually reducing global warming. The idea was that this would kick-start the German solar industry, which would then take on the world. What it actually did was kick-start the Chinese solar industry, which then wiped out European (and indeed US) solar companies.

All this is indeed very hard to make up. It has ended in tears: the broad consensus around the *Energiewende* in Germany, reflected in Merkel's sudden reversal of her position on keeping existing nuclear power stations open, has now cracked open, as it has across Europe.[2] The rise of the German right (both the mainstream right and the far right, Alternative für Deutschland, AfD) has been associated with two main policies: anti-immigration and anti-net zero. For the mainstream German Conservatives, energy prices are a big priority.

Worse for Germany, the reliance on Russian gas without nuclear led to an energy debacle, as both Nord Stream gas pipelines were blown up and Germany's long-term reliance on oil and then gas from Russia turned out to be a big mistake (though it could repeat it). Solar panels and now EVs from China, and gas from Russia, plus keeping the old coal power stations going, provides a sad example of how misconceived the *Energiewende* was and still is. Think how much could have been achieved on the climate front if Germany had pursued the opposite of the *Energiewende*, especially in R&D and on the nuclear front.

In the UK, with its own '*Energiewende*', the target was closure of coal, not nuclear. So far, so much better. But the UK did not exit reliance on coal: on the contrary, its high industrial energy prices pushed out its remaining energy-intensive businesses, so that it relied more on Chinese coal to produce the stuff that is now imported. The UK claims to have exited coal. It hasn't. But it has had to live with the impacts of closing coal power stations, as Germany has had to do with its closure of nuclear. The result in both cases: greater reliance on gas. In increasing its reliance on gas, the UK has nevertheless also chosen to 'virtue-signal' by stopping future oil and gas licences in the North Sea, to be replaced by US and Middle Eastern LNG and ever-greater reliance on pipeline gas from Norway. Obviously, LNG is environmentally much worse than pipeline gas.[3]

The reliance on gas in the UK is understated but very real. The policy of building 50 GW of offshore wind by 2030 means that the gas power stations are all going to be extremely intermittent too. When the wind blows, the price will collapse and the gas stations will be rationed off the system. But they will become more important as they are used less. As noted in Chapter 6, NESO has estimated that a full 35 GW of gas will be needed by 2030, but that it will only run about 5 per cent of the time. The implication is clear: there is little incentive to keep a gas power station going and none to build new ones. There will have to be a subsidy to keep them on standby.

This has one further damaging consequence. Drax, one of the biggest polluters in Europe, is needed not just because of the accounting trick we met earlier that it is not counted in the UK's territorial carbon emissions numbers, but also because it is a large flexible power station that can behave like a coal station in maintaining security of supply. Indeed, the similarity to a coal power station is considerable: it is an old coal power station, it is burning wood like coal, and it is very polluting, including not just carbon but also PM2.5. Having got the UK energy system into a position of increasing intermittency, the irony is that Drax keeps on polluting because it keeps the lights on, and it has to continue to be heavily subsidised to do so.

Perhaps the biggest mistake is to set almost impossible short-term net zero targets. The UK excels in this. It has been targeting a net zero electricity system by 2030 as another example of how it is 'world-leading' on climate change. Put aside the impacts of this for security of supply, and think of the practicalities. This is a 'whatever it costs' policy, in a matter of 65 months from the general election in 2024. The 50 GW offshore wind required by 2030 renders the whole system driven by intermittent generation, well before any solution has been dreamt up for the low-wind/no-wind situations.

The impacts are multiple. High costs are baked in through to the 2040s at least, the economy will be distorted by the diversion of labour and capital to this grand project (as war expenditure does at times of conflicts), and the lights may even flicker. In consequence, it has already shattered any remaining political consensus on net zero, with the Conservatives and Reform parties now explicitly both against this specific target. This in turn raises the cost of capital, as policy uncertainty goes up.

These examples illustrate a much broader point: one of the reasons so little has been achieved so far is that the politics has driven towards high costs and impossible targets, and prejudices for and against specific technologies have exacerbated the costs. The good news is that it is hard to think how it could have been worse, and that points to the enormous scope for improvement. Just stop digging an ever-deeper hole should be a climate change policy priority.

Take the System Approach

These mistakes cannot continue if our great environmental problems are to be addressed. So how to do it, apart from the obvious focusing on the global problem at hand, specialising in comparative advantages, and 'just stop digging'?

Take the system approach to these system problems which need system solutions. A wind farm here and a solar farm there are not going to solve climate change, nor is a clump of trees as a carbon offset going to fix biodiversity or climate change. Individual small-scale projects can be helpful, but largely as part of a system approach, not as discrete and isolated interventions.

These system approaches need to have the system objectives in mind. It cannot be repeated too often that climate change is global and hence it is the reduction of carbon consumption not carbon production that is the key objective. Natural sequestration and biodiversity are all about ecosystems, and some ecosystems are more important than others.

Setting the wrong objectives will lead to both higher costs and lower improvements. Let's say that the system objectives are derived from the overarching requirement to leave the next generation with a set of environmental assets at least as good as those the current generation inherited, as set out in my *Legacy* book. This is, in one sense, easy for government and citizens to sign up to, in the hope that, given it is a long way into the future, it does not necessarily require immediate action – and costs – now. That will not do, however, because it takes a generation to significantly change the atmosphere and the ecosystems, and hence it requires continued action and costs now.

In order to define a least-cost pathway to achieve these broad requirements, there needs to be a clear definition of what that end point will be in terms of ppm of carbon in the atmosphere and how much biodiversity there will be. We will also need a baseline for the starting point and a minimum threshold at the end point.

Let's make it even more practical: let's say that the baseline is where we are now, given that it would be a huge achievement relative to the trends identified in earlier chapters to even hold the line. Let's say that a generation is 25 years, and make the target date for the atmosphere and the natural ecosystems to stabilise back to the current levels by 2050. It would not, of course, be 'optimal' to cement in around 425 ppm carbon in the atmosphere, and there are good arguments for going lower and some would say faster too. Yet there is very little hope that we will in fact do better, and the current trends mean we will be doing considerably worse by 2050.

Just to be crystal clear about what can and cannot be achieved, recall that if the world's economies continue growing at, say, 3 per cent per annum, the total world economy will in 2050 be *twice* the current size. So, in 25 years, it is to be assumed on this trajectory of economic growth that we will be dealing with an economy the current size *and* another one the same size too. That is an enormous aggregate amount of extra consumption and, with it, a major increase in the demand for energy. Even if the share of fossil fuels in global energy demand were to halve in 25 years, the total emissions from fossil fuels in the absence of enhanced sequestration would be roughly the same. It might be a bit better: a switch towards gas from coal and oil might reduce overall emissions a bit, provided the methane from the gas is captured.

What all this means is that to achieve the intergenerational requirement by 2050 will require a much faster exit from fossil fuels, probably reducing the share to around 20 per cent or less. This means that renewables plus nuclear plus hydro will have to go from less than 20 per cent to 80 per cent in 25 years. Much of the supply chain systems for renewables would need to be cleaned up, and especially mining and refining critical minerals. You can see why trying to get below the current baseline is a pipedream. The real challenge is to even begin to cut into the IEA's business-as-usual projection and Exxon's forecast of the oil demand holding at 100 mbd in 2050.[4] On current trajectories, oil demand may be even higher in 2050 than now (over 100 mbd), gas may have gone up a lot, and coal may even be roughly holding its own. Recall, as with other 'transitions', the coming of a new energy source has historically been accompanied by an associated *increase* in the demand for the existing ones – wood, coal and oil have all increased demand as each new fuel comes along. Gas may cut into oil's share of energy demand, but the overall demand for oil may nevertheless hold its own or increase. The low-carbon technologies will do extremely well to power the extra demand, but to stabilise the climate, they need to cut deeply into the existing demand for fossil fuels as well.

Ecosystems protection is similarly on a sliding pathway. Holding the line at 2025 levels might be helped by some new tree planting and some broader carbon credits, but even if these really offset carbon loss (which most don't, for the reasons we have explored in earlier chapters), the current policy developments are all about trying to stop the rot going forward, and not offering any serious prospect of reversing it. As with the climate, holding the line at today's depleted baselines for ecosystems would be a huge achievement. As yet, 30 per cent generally and credibly protected land by 2030, the objective to come out of the COP15 on biodiversity, is a pipedream.[5]

Think of what it would take for the Amazon in 2050 to have the same extent and quality of rainforests as it has today. This is not about slowing down the burning; it is about stopping it now. Given that rainforests and most ecosystems take many decades to even centuries to form and establish their complex biodiversity, the destruction has to stop immediately, because there is not much prospect of reversing subsequent destruction this century, if ever. Yet the ecosystems face the same relentless consequences as the climate from economic growth. If consumption is twice its current level in 2050, then it is inevitable that the pressures on ecosystems for development and resources will increase, *pari passu*. Worse, the efforts to slow climate change will require large-scale mining and water resources, before the growth of air travel and global tourism adds to the pressures. As with the 425 ppm, halting the destruction of ecosystems is a huge ambition, and yet it is a necessary one if the next generation is to get as good a biodiversity as we have now. As with geoengineering, the Noah's Ark strategies will not crack this problem by 2050, and offsetting would do well to avoid causing even more damage rather than reverse it.

We have to accept the existing baselines for now for all practical purposes. This gives us the endpoints for 2050. The tasks are how to hold the line at 425 ppm and at the current rainforest and other ecosystem extents. It means a very sharp reduction in fossil fuels and it means an immediate halt to ecosystem destruction. Both are incredibly urgent.

The achievement of such targets is outside previous experience in human history. A transformation of energy systems on this scale has never been achieved in such a short time, and never has the protection of a national park here and there added up to an overall aggregate protection of biodiversity. It must follow that the undertaking is hugely costly, and one that will require massive efforts made by nations and regions, some of which are in imminent danger of war.

The only alternative is geoengineering at massive scale and quickly. That means CCS for most emissions, with added DACS. Both technically work, but good luck assuming they will be rolled out at scale by 2050 or later.

As explained in *Legacy*, what has to give in these circumstances is consumption. Resources have to be directed to the immediate tasks in hand. This is where it is dishonest to trot out the political win–win arguments, that it can all be done, done very quickly, and with lower costs – faster and faster decarbonisation and lower and lower bills. Not only do politicians trot out this rubbish, but extraordinarily many people believe it, excited by the spin and lobbying supported by the media. It is not only not true; it is positively dangerous.

To get from here to 2050 will require the sort of planning that goes with wars. This is a whole-system change, not piecemeal replacements of assets. The amount of capital required is on a scale not yet witnessed even in the global financial engineering of the last three decades. Savings will have to be carved out of what would have been consumption, because savings have to equal investment. No ingenious bit of 'green finance' can escape this reality.

Designing the Systems

If the Rubicon is crossed and the path to the 2050 ambitions is set, the next step is to design the systems changes that would be needed if we are serious about achieving them. The energy bit is conceptually remarkably simple: the complete global energy system has to switch from over 80 per cent fossil fuels to, say, 20 per cent in 25 years. This means that the system has to be overwhelmingly based upon electricity, and there has to be an enormous increase in the amount of electricity generation – both to replace the oil, gas and coal and to take up the prospective doubling of demand if the world economy is to double in size by 2050, and AI, data centres and cyber technologies are to move to the central place in this future economy.

If you are still on this line of argument, the next step is to realise that all of this could not be achieved with solar panels and wind farms – some, yes, and probably more solar than wind. In order to replace the energy needed for heating, transport, steel, petrochemicals, fertilisers and aluminium, and to power the huge expansion of mining for batteries and generating equipment, there is no escape from the need for very large-scale, high-density firm electricity generation. As yet, there are possibly only two technologies that could do this: very large-scale hydroelectric and a massive expansion of nuclear.

You can see the problem immediately with the hydro. Most of the world's largest rivers would have to be dammed, and the consequences for ecosystems would be dire. The example of the Mekong is already one that starkly reveals the scale of destruction that large-scale dam building can cause. The Congo and the Amazon are already under pressure from large dams too. It is not hard to imagine a very large hydro-damming programme over the next 25 years being one of the greatest causes of rainforest and ecosystem destruction (and destruction in temperate areas too).

That leaves nuclear. Theoretically, it could do the job, and indeed surpass the task in hand. France and Japan have already shown how much can be done. Now China is leading on nuclear, with others following. Yet it is obviously not a simple silver bullet. Massive and rapid nuclear expansion may be possible, but the timescales are very challenging and the waste has to be addressed.

To build a new large pressurised-water reactor (PWR) nuclear power station in the UK takes at least a decade, and that is after the project gets the go-ahead and finance is put in place. The UK has repeatedly had plans to build lots of nuclear, from the late 1970s with the advanced gas-cooled reactors (AGRs), to the plan for ten PWRs in the 1980s, at one per year, to now, as the plan for four large reactors has become twin reactors at Hinkley and Sizewell.[6] Even the promise of SMRs is too slow, and recall their key feature is in the name on the tin: 'small'. By definition, you need a lot more of them to meet a given capacity: 50 GW of SMRs at 200 MW each requires the construction of 250 reactors. That might cover, say, half of the UK's demand for electricity in 2050. It would be an enormous project, but not impossible. You can see the problem if the deadline is 2050, and it is a problem for even a state-directed economy like China.

Even if the SMRs could be built, where is the money going to come from? Whose savings are going to finance them? As noted, in the period before 1980, nuclear power stations were paid for largely out of current bills – pay-as-you-go – not financed by borrowing on the principle of pay-when-delivered. That is not likely to work now. Even if there are willing lenders, who is going to pay the interest and the capital back and the dividends?

When it comes to the protection of ecosystems, the money is a problem too. Who is going to pay the government of the DRC not to develop the Congo, and the Brazilians, the Columbians, the Ecuadorians, and the other countries around the Amazon to leave it alone? In several of these cases – notably the DRC – there is not even a functioning government. The DCR is in a state of civil war, and, at the heart of the Congo, there is continuous violence and expropriation a long way from the cities and the military, and that is before corruption is taken into account. Who is going to pay to stop the war? Who is going to regulate and control the DCR's mining industries? There are so far no credible answers.

What Would It Take to Mobilise the Necessary Actions?

A golden rule of energy policies is that they rarely change before a crisis; it is almost always afterwards. The problem for climate change (and for the destruction of ecosystems) is that there is no obvious sudden crisis for the period up to the targets in 2050. Nothing much at scale is likely to be hit. In the northern countries, many aspects of life may even be getting better. Fewer deaths from the cold, longer growing seasons, and less travel disruption from snow and ice. The day-to-day lived experience of most in the north is getting better. It is true that in Southern Europe and parts of the US, climate change is having its effects. There are hotter heatwaves and stronger hurricanes. But, again, it is not having much impact on their economies. It is the hotter Italy, Spain and Greece that are currently amongst the fastest-growing economies in Europe not the UK, Germany and France. Some crops are affected, but then agriculture is not that big a part of any of these economies, and some yields are rising.

Similar observations can be made about rainforest loss. Indigenous people are often badly hit, but not the Brazilian economy as a whole measured in GDP terms, whilst even the impacts of climate change and biodiversity loss in the DRC pale into insignificance against the immediate death and destruction of war. It is true that climate change may already be exacerbating wars and leaves terrible marks on local people from droughts. Think Somalia and Ethiopia. But sadly, these are not major economies and most of the developed world carries on regardless.

Multiple crises are probably on the way, but not yet. The unsustainable will not be sustained and if the fossil-fuel burn even stays constant and renewables only take up the new demand post 2050, things look a lot messier. Will this be enough to mandate action to switch to the sustainable economy described in my book, *Legacy*? That, as they say, remains to be seen. History is to be written; it is not written already.

CONCLUSION

There can be little doubt that the climate change outlook is bleak. This is neither optimistic nor pessimistic, but rather just brutally realistic. Climate realism is a wake-up call, but not for the usual reasons.

The climate community's reaction to the lack of progress is often to double down on existing policies and institutions, and then scare the public and the politicians with dire predictions of the consequences of even moderate climate change. Using social media and graphic pictures of fires, typhoons, floods and caving icebergs, the approach aims to frighten people into action.

Calling out every heatwave and flood as caused by climate change is just not convincing. Nor is the claim that these prove that climate change is, or will be, disastrous any time soon. Bad weather has happened in the past, and its impacts are typically transient. Bad things happen without any climate change. New Orleans flooded because the levies broke, and rising sea levels have not stopped the Netherlands reclaiming lands that remain below sea levels. The world is not 'on fire';[1] nor do we have only 12 years left.[2]

To be clear, the climate will deteriorate and particularly after 2 °C. But for most people most of the time, it is not what they see every day, and they have lots of other things to worry about. It is not the only bad thing going on.

Whatever the trajectory of damage, the real error of the climate community is to think that more of the same policies are going to crack the problem, and more COPs are the framework within which these will work out.

What climate realism reveals is that this is just not true. The policies aren't working and more of the same is unlikely to make much difference to the increase in the ppm in the atmosphere. Climate realism forces us to face up to unpleasant facts. There is no energy transition under way. There is no such thing as clean power. Renewables are not cheap on a system basis in many countries. COPs just don't deliver, nor will they, the holy grail of legally binding and enforceable agreements.

Faced with a wall of increasing demand for energy, and against the backdrop of a projected doubling of GDP by 2050, even if current policies were working, they are feeble against the scale of the challenge. Subsidised wind and solar, helpful though they generally are, remain bit-part players in global energy supplies, still overwhelmingly dominated by coal, oil and gas.

Remarkably, after 35 years of targets and 30 COPs, most in the climate community avoid facing up to the question of what is causing emissions to keep rising and the continuous destruction of natural sequestrations. It is easy to link emissions to ppm in the atmosphere, net of sequestration. But this is just the intermediate cause. The real issue is about what causes the emissions and ecosystem destruction to continue. Why are both happening?

The easy answer is that they are both caused by using the wrong energy technologies, by using coal and gas power stations and petrochemical plants, and by burning and clearing the rainforests. If only we could get the energy without the emissions, and the minerals and the food without clearing forests, all would be well.

We should of course try to change the supply side. But, in doing so, we should be mindful of crass simplicities, such as the idea that solar and wind are clean. They are not; they require massive mining activities and refining and then fabrication. Recycling is energy intensive and often associated with lots of additional pollution. It's a much longer slog to get from dirty to less dirty to cleaner energy on the supply side, and it will never be clean. Supply-side realities also include the unlikelihood that the world's economies could ever be powered predominantly by wind and sunshine – particularly once these economies have doubled by 2050. There are good places to do wind and solar, but for the most part both are likely to remain bit-part players, significant at decentralised and favoured locations, and where small scale is appropriate.

That means something else is needed to deliver firm and dense power at very large scale. So far, only hydro and nuclear offer this as a lower-carbon option. Hydro comes with all sorts of environmental problems. Nuclear has environmental problems too, and these add yet more costs and risks. This might change, but it will take a couple of decades to get there. The conclusion that follows is that modifying the supply side will not be enough, even if it is better than using fossil fuels. It is necessary but by no means sufficient.

The elephant in the room is the demand side. It is all that unsustainable economic growth that translates into unsustainable consumption. What too few are prepared to admit is that the real cause of climate change and biodiversity loss is that we are living beyond our environmental means, and the reason why is that we are not paying for the pollution we are causing. The already bad consequences will get a whole lot worse if and when the world economy doubles and with it the world's energy demands.

In the sustainable economy there is still growth – sustainable growth built on human ingenuity. We humans can and should aspire to greater things. But that is very different from naive economic ideas about growth being supported by maximising demand. Economists happily assume from their first engagement with the dismal science that we humans are insatiable. It might be true, but then all the more reason to hedge that insatiability with costs and prices that reflect the consequences to the environment of our consumption.

Climate realism offers a way out. It would be bracing, it would be painful and it would be disruptive. Moving from an unsustainable consumption path to a sustainable consumption path means we would have to pay to maintain the natural capital (and the physical infrastructure capitals) so that the next generation inherits a set of assets at least as good as the current generation inherited. No more borrowing to fix the current problems, but rather paying now so we don't commit the broken window fallacy. We are breaking the windows – our natural capital in the atmosphere and the ecosystems – and we should pay to mend them, rather than borrowing from the next generation and expecting them to pay for the maintenance needed to tackle the damage we are doing.

Paying the capital maintenance would hurt, but there is no escape from this responsibility, because not paying just makes the problems worse, and continues the unsustainability of our economies. Part of these costs could be paid for by pollution charges. A carbon tax is a classic example, applied uniformly across all the pollutant sources. It would be a massive step forward. It changes the relative prices between carbon-intensive and low-carbon goods and services, including food. It also has an income effect: we have less to spend as a result.

The polluters who should pay are not the obvious targets that many in the climate community go for, and especially some of the activists. They are deluded when they claim it is all the fault of big corporations, such as the oil companies. Climate realism says that it is *us*, the consumers, who buy these polluting products who are to blame. It is us who have to change our ways. It is us who have to face up to the costs of our unsustainable lifestyles. Corporations don't pollute for the fun of it; they do it because we buy the stuff.

Making polluters pay – us – would do much to straighten out our consumption in ways that render our economies more sustainable and go some way to ensuring we are good stewards of this planet and can look the next generation in the eye with clearer consciences. It is a first vital step to addressing the fundamental causes of all those emissions and ecosystem destructions.

It is still, however, not enough. We have remedial work to do on the damage we have already inflicted on the planet. We need to save, setting aside money that would have been used for our consumption, in order to create enhancements to the assets. Our consumption should be net of the costs of the pollution we cause and net of the savings for investment. We should borrow only when the next generation can be certain of inheriting better assets than we did. Remediation is a version of loss and damage.

Climate realism forces us to confront the failures of current policies, and to recognise that more of the same won't work. It requires us to strive to reduce the carbon content of the energy we turn into usable forms. It requires us to live within our environmental means. It allows for growth only through genuine enhancements and these derive from human ingenuity.

Would all this be enough? Probably not, notably given that there are no clean energies, and that implementing a polluter-pays principle is bound to be caught in the mess that is democratic politics. None of it on the supply or demand side is going to be textbook neat.

What more would be needed? The answer comes back to remediation and carbon removals. DACS technologies are not going to provide a comprehensive answer any time soon; neither is CCS going to be on the scale necessary to really fix the residual emissions. But they are a start, as is the evolving of new and better nuclear technologies.

What all this tells us is that it is realistic to assume that, even if the climate community changes its tone on defending the existing policies, and drops all the stuff about clean cheap energy, the temperatures are going to go on rising for some considerable time, and the ppm will go on rising accordingly. We will do well to slow the increase of the ppm before 2050.

Realism forces us to accept that conventional wisdoms, like the idea that increased energy efficiency reduces demand, just aren't true. Sure, efficiency is a good idea. Who could be against being efficient? But energy efficiency has progressively lowered the price of energy, which increases demand.

We are in for quite a lot more warming whatever we do, and, because of the policy mistakes, more warming than we would have had. We spend a lot already to address climate change, and a lot of this is wasted. We have the wrong targets which can create perverse consequences to the climate, and can mislead us into believing that progress is being made, whilst in fact we may be just shifting energy-intensive industries abroad.

With reasonable temperature limits, climate change will not be the end of the world. We have time to build up the globally directed policies to help with both limiting the warming and with the adaptation to a warmer world where some will gain and lots may lose. Instead of wasting time, effort (and lots of air miles) on COPs, it is better to start realistically on bottom-up coalitions of the willing. That is what the carbon tax route enables, through extending carbon pricing to imports and thereby encouraging exporters to have their own carbon prices back home. We know this idea would work because of the howls of protest from those who currently exploit the carbon pricing of others.

Again, the problems are not without solutions. But these will get traction only if the climate community would just start to admit that the COP processes, however well intentioned they are, are not going to deliver the goods. They haven't worked and they won't work.

Ironically, those most challenged by climate realism are not those who claim to care most about the problems. It is those in the climate community who want to push immediate radical politics upon the wider population. Gluing themselves to company head offices, blocking motorways, spraying paint on great works of art, and claiming that the world is on fire, is about as counterproductive a strategy as can be imagined. They speak to themselves in select groups like Extinction Rebellion, Just Stop Oil, and whatever the latest reincarnation of these small bands is named. They even frighten young women enough to put them off having children, for fear of the apocalypse that they predict.

Climate change is much too serious for these sorts of antics. They haven't worked. At worst, the apocalypse they paint encourages us to assume we are all doomed. 'Why bother?' is not an irrational response. Less extreme are the silly short-term targets and the slogans like 'clean-energy superpower', 'clean, home-grown and secure energy' coupled with slogans about 'unleashing' and 'unlocking' green finance. What these do is get found out, and when they are, they encourage cynicism and doubt when better, more effective policies are actually proposed.

ACKNOWLEDGEMENTS

Writing *Climate Realism* has been a process of learning from, and responding to, conversations with academic colleagues, politicians, the many embedded in think-tanks and government organisations, and the multiple practitioners who deliver our energy supplies. I have gained most from those who will probably disagree with much of what I have written, but who nevertheless have been willing to engage in what is much more than a rigorous and sometimes heated debate. With the destruction of biodiversity, climate change is existential in ways that so many other preoccupations of our times are not. It is too serious for crude positioning.

Amongst my academic friends and colleagues, Cameron Hepburn has continued to be a brilliant influence, puncturing weak arguments and presenting an optimism to counter my realism. It was he who invited me to give the Battcock Lecture in May 2025. Discussions with Jean-Paul Carvalho, Paul Collier, Diane Coyle, Doyne Farmer, Charles Godfrey, Michael Grubb, Paul Johnson, Colin Mayer, David Vines and Dimitri Zhengelis have proved particularly helpful. Murray Park kindly told me how plastic polyethylene, polypropylene and nylon are used in so many of our everyday fixtures and fittings.

Contrary to the claims made by the eminent head of the IPCC, Jim Skea, from which I have learned much, net zero is very much a political matter and it is in the political world where the policy decisions are set and implemented. I have been fortunate enough to have engaged across the political spectrum. On the Labour side, the Blair governments, struggling to create an energy policy that incorporated climate change, came up with the idea that it would be both cheap and green, as well as secure. The Brown government led the way to the Climate Change Act and the creation of the Department of Energy and Climate Change (DECC). In those early days, Ed Miliband toyed with the idea that the Department would drive through an activist policy, one which he returned to more than two decades later. In one way or another, I got to know all the Secretaries of State covering energy, from David Howell and Nigel Lawson onwards, and most of the shadow Secretaries of State. I even spent two weeks as Boris Johnson's energy adviser at No. 10, though precisely when this started or ended remains a footnote in the chaos of his premiership. I gained a lot from Andrew Chittenden, my colleague in this adventure, whose understanding of the detailed design of energy policy is unrivalled.

As Chair of the Natural Capital Committee, I benefited from discussions with Michael Gove, and more recently Greg Clark, Grant Shapps and Claire Coutinho. I wrote the *Cost of Energy Review*, highlighting the mistakes about costs and the weaknesses in the unbridled excesses of those who thought renewables would be as cheap as chips.

In Brussels, following on from my period as Special Adviser to the Energy Commissioner over a decade ago, I helped with the Draghi Report, and am grateful for conversations with Miguel Gil-Terre, Chief Economist at the DG Energy, European Commission, during its preparation.

I learnt something from all of the above, though maybe not always what they intended. Behind the policy twists and turns, there were the officials, regulators and heads of government agencies. At DECC and later at Ofgem, Jonathan Brearley first helped Miliband with market reform before 2010, and after a break from the public sector came back to lead Ofgem. We have discussed much, and not always disagreed. The stand-out person at the Climate Change

Committee was Chris Stark, later to lead the 'Mission Control' at the Department of Energy Security and Net Zero. These two are amongst the towering figures of UK climate policy over the last couple of decades. Conversations with both of them have shaped my arguments, and helped to sharpen up why I disagree with them on some of the core questions – and notably on costs and the net zero targets. Amongst the Ofgem team, Gavin Knott has been especially engaging. With the creation of NESO, a core recommendation of the *Cost of Energy Review*, Paul Golby (as chair), Claire Dykta and Omar Saeed have been very helpful.

It is the energy businesses that deliver the outcomes, not the politicians or the regulators. Despite the political spin, governments make very few direct investments, and regulators do not provide funding and finance. The private sector does most of this, as it tries to navigate the twists and turns of policy and regulation. Across Europe and in the UK, I am particularly grateful to Keith Anderson, John Armitt, John Browne, Alex Chisholm, Tom Glover, Greg Jackson, Sam Laidlaw, Chris O'Shea, Peter O'Shea, John Pettigrew and Simone Rossi.

Throughout the years since 2000, I have chaired the Energy Futures Group, and many of the issues and ideas set out in this book have been tried out in this forum. I have learned a lot from its members and participants, including Carl Arntzen, Harriet Arscott, Richard Bodal Hansen, Simon Bowen, Josh Buckland, Bill Bullen, Declan Burke, Alex Chisholm, Emily Clark, Katherine Collett, Tom Crotty, Kevin Dibble, Arthur Downing, Bill Eden, Alastair Evans, Philip Hemmens, Rhian Kelly, Matthew Knight, Pauline Lawson, Dan Lord, Alan McLaughlin, Andrew Mennear, Duncan Moore, Thomas Morstyn, Tony Nixon, Holly Pattenden, Tom Restrick, Iain Smedley, Paul Spence, Lawson Steele, Richard Sweet, Brian Tilley, Tom Tindall, Jake Tudge, David Wellard, Ian Whitfield and Ingmar Wilhelm.

Philip Good and Chris Burrows at Cambridge University Press have supported this book at every stage with a contribution of enthusiasm and very helpful guidance, continuing the great work they did on my previous book *Legacy*.

Cate Dominian has provided excellent and indispensable copyediting and research support. Her professionalism and enthusiasm pervade this book. Jenny Vaughan has as ever greatly helped keep the show on the road. I am very grateful to them both.

Finally, the Fellows of New College have once again continued to provide the best of all academic environments within which to write this book. It is the students and their contemporaries who will determine whether we deliver the sustainable radical change required to tackle climate change.

ABBREVIATIONS

ACST	aluminium conductor steel-reinforced
AD	anaerobic digester
AfD	Alternative für Deutschland (Alternative for Germany)
AGR	advanced gas-cooled reactor
AI	artificial intelligence
bcm	billion cubic metre
CBAM	carbon border adjustment mechanism
CCC	Climate Change Committee
CCS	carbon capture and storage
CCUS	carbon capture, utilisation and storage
CEGB	Central Electricity Generating Board
CfDs	contracts for differences
CO_2	carbon dioxide
COP	Conference of the Parties
Covid	Severe acute respiratory syndrome coronavirus 2 (SARS-CoV-2)
DACS	direct air capture and storage
DECC	Department of Energy and Climate Change
DE&I	diversity, equality and inclusion
DRC	Democratic Republic of the Congo
ESG	environmental, social and governance
EPR	ethylene propylene rubber
EU ETS	European Union Emissions Trading Scheme
EU	European Union
EV	electric vehicle
FOMO	fear of missing out
GDP	gross domestic product

GHG	greenhouse gas
Gt	gigatonne
HFO	heavy fuel oil
IAM	integrated assessment model
IEA	International Energy Agency
IP	intellectual property
IPCC	Intergovernmental Panel on Climate Change
kg	kilogram
LNG	liquefied natural gas
mbd	million barrels a day
NATO	North Atlantic Treaty Organization
NDCs	national determined contributions
NESO	National Energy System Operator
NGO	non-governmental organisation
OPEC	Organization of the Petroleum Exporting Countries
ppm	parts per million
PVC	polyvinyl chloride
PWR	pressurised-water reactor
RAB	regulatory asset base
R&D	research and development
SAF	sustainable aviation fuel
SMR	small modular reactor
SUV	sport utility vehicle
UN	United Nations
UNFCCC	United Nations Framework Convention on Climate Change
WHO	World Health Organization
XLPE	cross-linked polyethylene

NOTES

Preface

1. Helm, D. (2023), *Legacy: How to Build the Sustainable Economy*, Cambridge: Cambridge University Press.
2. The annual mean average for 2025 was 427.35, https://gml.noaa.gov/ccgg/trends/.
3. Energy Institute (2025), 'Statistical Review of World Energy', 74th edn, www.energyinst.org/statistical-review.
4. For ease, in the book where I refer to critical minerals, I am including the rare earth elements too.
5. 'It's true that my carbon footprint is absurdly high […] by 2020 I started buying sustainable jet fuel […] I'm buying offsets.' Gates, B. (2021), *How to Avoid a Climate Disaster: The Solutions We Have and the Breakthroughs We Need*, London: Allen Lane, pp. 14–15.
6. '[A]s we set an example to the world by showing that reaching Net Zero is entirely possible, so the likes of China and Russia are following our lead with their own net zero targets, as prices tumble and green tech becomes the global norm.' Boris Johnson, 'Foreword' in HM Government (2021), 'Net Zero Strategy: Build Back Greener', October, p. 8, www.gov.uk/government/publications/net-zero-strategy.

Introduction

1. The arguments in the lecture are summarised in Helm, D. (2024), 'Climate realism – time for a re-set', December, https://dieterhelm.co.uk/energy-climate/climate-realism-time-for-a-re-set/.

2. For an explanation of the paradigm approach, see Kuhn, T. (1962), *The Structure of Scientific Revolutions*, Chicago, IL: University of Chicago Press.
3. See Weart, S.R. (2003), *The Discovery of Global Warming*, Cambridge, MA: Harvard University Press for the history of climate change science. See also Arrhenius (1896), who linked falling carbon levels to falling water vapour levels and hence to the triggering of ice ages. Arrhenius, S. (1896), 'On the influence of carbonic acid in the air upon the temperature of the ground', *The London, Edinburgh, and Dublin Philosophical Magazine and Journal of Science*, 5th series, 41, 237–276.
4. In this book, we will focus on the CO_2 equivalent as a proxy for GHGs, and for stylistic ease simplify this to 'carbon'.
5. United Nations (2015), 'Paris Agreement', https://unfccc.int/sites/default/files/english_paris_agreement.pdf.
6. International Energy Agency (2025), 'Coal Mid-Year Update 2025', 24 July, www.iea.org/reports/coal-mid-year-update-2025. Institute for Energy Research (2025), 'Coal is still king – globally', 5 September, www.instituteforenergyresearch.org/fossil-fuels/coal/coal-is-still-king-globally/.
7. https://gml.noaa.gov/ccgg/trends/data.html.
8. Energy Institute (2025), 'Statistical Review of World Energy', 74th edn, p. 6.
9. See Bass (1969) and Geroski (2000). Bass, F. (1969), 'A new product growth for model consumer durables', *Management Science*, 15(5), 215–227; Geroski, P.A. (2000), 'Models of technology diffusion', *Research Policy*, 29(4–5), 603–625. Doyne Farmer has recently argued that when applied to solar, the result will be a rapid transition. See Way, R., Ives, M.C., Mealy, P. and Doyne Farmer, J. (2022), 'Empirically grounded technology forecasts and the energy transition', *Joule*, 13 September, www.sciencedirect.com/science/article/pii/S254243512200410X, and Baumgärtner, L. and Doyne Farmer, J. (2025), 'Will national renewable costs continue declining?', INET Working Paper, Institute for New

Economic Thinking, May, www.inet.ox.ac.uk/publications/no-2025-12-will-national-renewable-costs-continue-declining.

10. The 2025 future energy scenarios of the UK National Energy Supply Operator (NESO) now see the promised lower costs and prices in 2045 – just in time to meet the 2050 target. National Energy System Operator (2025), 'Future energy scenarios: pathways to net zero', v.5, www.neso.energy/publications/future-energy-scenarios-fes.
11. The alternative approach to scientific advance is Karl Popper's. He argued that progress is made by fabrication. See Popper, K.R. (1959), *The Logic of Scientific Discovery*, London: Hutchinson & Co. For an accessible summary, see Stokes, G. and Shearmur, J. (2016), 'Popper and his philosophy: an overview', pp. 1–29 in J. Shearmur and G. Stokes (eds), *The Cambridge Companion to Popper*, Cambridge: Cambridge University Press.
12. See Langengen, T. (2025), 'Cheaper Power 2030, Net Zero 2050: Resetting the UK's electricity strategy for the future', Tony Blair Institute for Global Changes, 23 October, www.institute.global/insights/climate-and-energy/cheaper-power-2030-net-zero-2050-resetting-UK-electricity-strategy. See also Gates, B. (2025), 'Three tough truths about climate: what I want everyone at COP30 to know', 28 October, www.gatesnotes.com/three-tough-truths-about-climate.
13. See BBC (2025), 'China's rare earths: the BBC visits the world's mining capital for the metals', 8 July. The claim is made that every 1 tonne of rare earth minerals processed produces 2,000 tonnes of toxic waste.
14. 'China's share in all the manufacturing stages of solar panels (such as polysilicon, ingots, wafers, cells and modules) exceeds 80%', Executive Summary, in International Energy Agency (2022), 'Solar PV global supply chains: an IEA special report', www.iea.org/reports/solar-pv-global-supply-chains.

1 There Is No Transition

1. Energy Institute (2025), 'Statistical Review of World Energy 2024', p. 6, www.energyinst.org/statistical-review. There is a distinction to be made between energy supplied and energy capacity and the losses in the processes of turning natural resources into delivered and usable energy. Nevertheless, the gulf between renewables and fossil fuels remains vast.
2. Fressoz, J.B. (2004), *More and More and More: An All-Consuming History of Energy*, London: Penguin Books.
3. See European Commission (2009), '2020 climate and energy package', https://eur-lex.europa.eu/legal-content/EN/TXT/?uri=legissum:2001_8. See also Helm, D. (2012), *The Carbon Crunch: How We're Getting Climate Change Wrong – and How to Fix It*, New Haven, CT: Yale University Press, Chapter 4, p. 91 et seq.
4. See Tilman, D., Hill, J. and Lehman, C. (2006), 'Carbon-negative biofuels from low-input high-diversity grassland biomass', *Science*, 314(5805), 1598–1600 and Tilman, D., Reich, P.B, Knops, J. et al. (2001), 'Diversity and productivity in a long-term grassland experiment', *Science*, 294(5543), 843–845. See also Searchinger, T.D., Hamburg, S.P., Melillo, J. et al. (2009), 'Fixing a critical climate accounting error', *Science*, 326(5952), 527–528 and Peng, L., Searchinger, T.D., Zionts, J. and Waite, R. (2023), 'The carbon costs of global wood harvests', *Nature*, 620, 110–115.
5. Department for Environment, Food and Rural Affairs (2025), 'Bioenergy crops in England and the UK: 2003–2023', updated 11 September, www.gov.uk/government/statistics/bioenergy-crops-in-england-and-the-uk-2008-2023/bioenergy-crops-in-england-and-the-uk-2008-2023.
6. Energy Institute (2025), 'Statistical Review of World Energy', 74th edn, https://ourworldindata.org/grapher/global-primary-energy-share-inc-biomass?overlay=sources.

7. It was until very recently burnt in power stations in Ireland. The last peat-fired power station in Ireland stopped burning peat in December 2023, when the Edenderry plant switched fully to biomass. Bord na Móna (undated), 'Bord na Móna to work with Irish farmers to produce energy crops for power stations', press release, www.bnm.ie/bord-na-mona-to-work-with-irish-farmers-to-produce-energy-crops-for-power-stations/.
8. There are various reports of figures, which include UK Steel (2024), 'UK steel sector sets out manifesto strategy to secure future of steel', www.uksteel.org/steel-news-2024/uk-steel-sector-sets-out-manifesto-strategy-to-secure-future-of-steel, GMK Center (2025), 'UK steel market: importers to brace themselves', https://gmk.center/en/posts/uk-steel-market-importers-to-brace-themselves/.
9. Statistisches Bundesamt (2026), 'Gross electricity production in Germany', www.destatis.de/EN/Themes/Economic-Sectors-Enterprises/Energy/Production/Tables/gross-electricity-production.html.
10. In August 2025, negotiations in Genova to agree a legally binding international instrument broke down. This had been the aim of the UN's Intergovernmental Negotiating Committee set in March 2022. Even the very limited attempt to include some words about fossil fuels at the Brazil COP30 failed.
11. International Energy Agency (2025), 'Global Energy Review', www.iea.org/reports/global-energy-review-2025/key-findings.
12. The Chernobyl accident in Ukraine is described in detail in Plokhy, S. (2018), *Chernobyl: History of a Tragedy*, London: Allen Lane.
13. See Weyler, R. (2002), *Greenpeace: How a Group of Journalists, Ecologists and Visionaries Changed the World*, London: Rodale.
14. The average age of currently operating nuclear reactors worldwide is 32 years. WNISR (2025), 'World nuclear industry status report 2025', www.worldnuclearreport.org/World-Nuclear-Industry-Status-Report-2025-HTML.

15. See www.world-nuclear.org/information-library/facts-and-figures/world-nuclear-power-reactors-and-uranium-requireme.

2 An Explosion of Energy Demand

1. A summary of the conventional arguments in the UK context can be found in Select Committee on Science and Technology (2005), 'Second Report', Session 2005–06, Chapter 3: The economics of energy efficiency, https://publications.parliament.uk/pa/ld200506/ldselect/ldsctech/21/2102.htm. For how this argument plugs into the conventional economic theory of economic growth, see Bergmann, T. and Kalkuhl, M. (2025), 'Decoupling economic growth from energy use: the role of energy intensity in an endogenous growth model', *Ecological Economics*, 230, 108519.
2. International Energy Agency (2025), 'World Energy Outlook', www.iea.org/reports/world-energy-outlook-2025.
3. International Energy Agency (2025), 'World Energy Outlook', www.iea.org/reports/world-energy-outlook-2025.
4. The term was famously used by Alan Greenspan, Chairman of the US Federal Reserve, in December 1996. See also Shiller, R.J. (2000), *Irrational Exuberance*, Princeton, NJ: Princeton University Press.
5. International Energy Agency (undated), 'Energy and AI', World Energy Outlook Special Report, www.iea.org/reports/energy-and-ai/energy-demand-from-ai.
6. McKinsey & Company (2024), 'How data centers and the energy sector can sate AI's hunger for power', 17 September, www.mckinsey.com/industries/private-capital/our-insights/how-data-centers-and-the-energy-sector-can-sate-ais-hunger-for-power#/.
7. Crownhart, C. (2024), 'Why Microsoft made a deal to help restart Three Mile Island', *The Spark*, MIT Technology Review, 26 September, www.technologyreview.com/2024/09/26/1104516/three-mile-island-microsoft/.

8. See www.neom.com/en-us.
9. Chen, L., Thorup, V.M., Kudahl, A.B. and Østergaard, S. (2024), 'Effects of heat stress on feed intake, milk yield, milk composition, and feed efficiency in dairy cows: a meta-analysis', *Journal of Dairy Science*, 107(5), 3207–3218.
10. UNESCO (2021), 'The United Nations world water development report 2021', www.un.org/sites/un2.un.org/files/un_world_water_dev._report_2021.pdf.
11. UNESCO (2021), 'The United Nations world water development report 2021', www.un.org/sites/un2.un.org/files/un_world_water_dev._report_2021.pdf.
12. Reverse osmosis is energy intensive and is impacted by intermittent power supplies. Thermal desalination requires firm power.
13. Some studies suggest the impact on the demand for electricity could be very significant, even if the overall demand for energy goes down. See Baruah, P.J., Eyre, N., Qadrdan, M. et al. (2014), 'Energy system impacts from heat and transport electrification', *Proceedings of the Institution of Civil Engineers – Energy*, 167(3), 139–151.
14. See Helm, D. (2004), *Energy, the State, and the Market: British Energy Policy since 1979*, Oxford: Oxford University Press, Chapter 1.
15. For 1970 and 2012, see Department of Energy & Climate Change (2013), 'United Kingdom housing energy fact file', www.gov.uk/government/statistics/united-kingdom-housing-energy-fact-file-2013.
16. 'Of the economy of fuel', Chapter 7 in Jevons, W.S. (1865), *The Coal Question: An Inquiry Concerning the Progress of the Nation, and the Probable Exhaustion of Our Coal-mines*, London: Macmillan & Co.
17. See Draghi, M. (2024), 'The future of European competitiveness – a competitiveness strategy for Europe', 9 September, European Commission, https://commission.europa.eu/document/97e481fd-2dc3-412d-be4c-f152a8232961_en.
18. Thanks to Murray Park for this list.

3 The Wrong Target

1. European Commission (2009), '2020 climate and energy package', https://eur-lex.europa.eu/legal-content/EN/TXT/?uri=legissum:2001_8.
2. Ackerman, F., Stanton, E. and Kartha, S. (2017), 'Inside the Integrated Assessment Models: Four Issues in Climate Economics', Chapter 8 in F. Ackerman and E.A. Stanton (eds), *Climate Change and Global Equity*, Cambridge: Cambridge University Press.
3. See Stern, N. (2007), *The Economics of Climate Change: The Stern Review*, HM Treasury, Cambridge: Cambridge University Press.
4. Nordhaus, W.D. (2007), 'A review of the Stern Review on the economics of climate change', *Journal of Economic Literature*, 45(3), 686–702.
5. World Meteorological Organization (2025), 'WMO confirms 2004 as warmest year on record at about 1.55°C above pre-industrial level', press release, 10 January, https://wmo.int/news/media-centre/wmo-confirms-2024-warmest-year-record-about-155degc-above-pre-industrial-level?
6. Intergovernmental Panel on Climate Change (2006), '2006 IPCC Guidelines for National Greenhouse Gas Inventories', www.ipcc-nggip.iges.or.jp/public/2006gl/, and (2019), '2019 Refinement to the 2006 IPCC Guidelines for National Greenhouse Gas Inventories', www.ipcc.ch/report/2019-refinement-to-the-2006-ipcc-guidelines-for-national-greenhouse-gas-inventories/.
7. Office for National Statistics (2025), 'Methodology note: measuring UK greenhouse gas emissions', 7 November, www.ons.gov.uk/economy/environmentalaccounts/methodologies/measuringukgreenhousegasemissions.
8. These include dust from the fabrication of the pellets and PM2.5 from burning them.
9. The UK government calculates something called the 'carbon footprint'. This is an incomplete addition of carbon emissions embedded in imports, but not of the full supply chain-associated emissions. See Department for Environment, Food and Rural Affairs (2025), 'Carbon

footprint for the UK and England to 2022', updated 14 May, www.gov.uk/government/statistics/uks-carbon-footprint/carbon-footprint-for-the-uk-and-england-to-2022.

10. Minerals Production Association (2025), 'Government building plans at risk as UK cement production falls to 75-year low', www.mineralproducts.org/News/2025/release28.aspx.
11. United Nations (1998), 'Kyoto Protocol to the United Nations Framework Convention on Climate Change', https://unfccc.int/resource/docs/convkp/kpeng.pdf.
12. See European Commission (2025), 'GHG emissions of all world countries – 2025 report', https://edgar.jrc.ec.europa.eu/report_2025.
13. Comparing current Chinese with historical UK emissions depends upon baselines, estimates of historical emissions and the period over which current emissions are measured. Small changes in the assumptions create a wide range of estimates. See Our World in Data (2025), 'Which countries have contributed the most to historical CO_2 emissions?', 17 March, www.ourworldindata.org/data-insights/which-countries-have-contributed-the-most-to-historical-co-emissions.
14. Ed Miliband post on X, 24 August 2022, www.x.com/Ed_Miliband/status/1562444641236316161. *Manchester Evening News*, 'Renewable energy such as solar and wind are nine times cheaper than gas', Direct Interview Statement, 24 November 2022, www.manchestereveningnews.co.uk/news/cost-of-living/renewables-can-help-cost-living-25574282. 'Labour's plan for a cheaper, zero carbon electricity system by 2030 will lower bills because renewables are far cheaper than gas.' Labour Party (2024), 'Make Britain a clean energy superpower', p. 6, www.gov.uk/missions/clean-energy. 'As the Climate Change Committee puts it very well, "British-based renewable energy is the cheapest and fastest way to reduce vulnerability to volatile global fossil fuel markets."', Energy UK Conference 2024: keynote speech by Ed Miliband. 'Homegrown clean energy from renewables and nuclear offers us a security that fossil fuels simply cannot provide.' – from

the same speech, www.gov.uk/government/speeches/energy-uk-conference-2024-keynote-speech-by-by-ed-miliband.

4 There Is No Such Thing as Clean Energy

1. ING (2025), 'Nickel still capped by surplus', 8 December, https://think.ing.com/articles/nickel-still-capped-by-surplus.
2. Indonesia is the third-largest coal producer in the world. International Energy Agency (2025), 'Coal 2025: Analysis and forecast to 2030', www.iea.blob.core.windows.net/assets/113a8274-500c-4684-951f-947d25bef3c9/Coal2025.pdf; Setiabudi, P. (2025), 'Green ambitions? Indonesia's smelters reveal the harsh reality of energy transition', www.petromindo.com/news/article/green-ambitions-indonesia-s-smelters-reveal-the-harsh-reality-of-energy-transition-1.
3. Rathore, S., Joy, J. and Kumar, A. (2025), 'Life cycle analysis of the simultaneous production of lithium hydroxide monohydrate and lithium carbonate from spodumene ore using electrodialysis', *Sustainable Materials and Technologies*, e01650.
4. See Hawken, P. (2025), *Carbon: The Book of Life*, Melbourne, Australia: Text Publishing Company.
5. See www.riotinto.com/en/operations/south-america/escondida.
6. Such materials cannot be re-used or recovered during the recycling process and contain toxic substances (e.g., heavy metals, solvents or persistent organic pollutants).
7. ACST, aluminium conductor steel-reinforced.
8. XLPE, cross-linked polyethylene, PVC, polyvinyl chloride and EPR, ethylene propylene rubber.
9. The load factor of a wind turbine is the ratio of the actual electricity generated in any period of time compared with what it could have generated if it ran all of the time at full power.
10. Harper, T. (2025), 'By building the world's biggest dam, China hopes to control more than just its water supply', *The Conversation*, 31 July, https://theconversation.com/by-building-the-worlds-biggest-dam-china-hopes-to-control-more-than-just-its-water-supply-261984.

11. See Tilman, D., Hill, J. and Lehman, C. (2006), 'Carbon-negative biofuels from low-input high-diversity grassland biomass', *Science*, 314(5805), 1598–1600 and Tilman, D., Reich, P.B., Knops, J., Wedin, D., Mielke, T. and Lehman, C. (2001), 'Diversity and productivity in a long-term grassland experiment', *Science*, 294(5543), 843–845. See also Searchinger, T.D., Hamburg, S.P., Melillo, J. et al. (2009), 'Fixing a critical climate accounting error', *Science*, 326(5952), 527–528, and Peng, L., Searchinger, T.D., Zionts, J. and Waite, R. (2023), 'The carbon costs of global wood harvests', *Nature*, 620, 110–115.

5 The Broken Window Fallacy

1. Reproduced in Bastiat, F. (2007), *The Bastiat Collection*, 2nd edn, Ludwig von Mises Institute, https://mises.org/library/book/bastiat-collection.
2. See Helm, D. (2023), *Legacy: How to Build the Sustainable Economy*, Cambridge: Cambridge University Press, Chapter 8.
3. In his General Theory, Keynes suggested that: 'If the Treasury were to fill old bottles with banknotes, bury them at suitable depths in disused coal mines which are then filled up to the surface with town rubbish, and leave it to private enterprise on well-tried principles of laissez-faire to dig the notes up again […] there need be no more unemployment.' Chapter 10, 'The marginal propensity to consume and the multiplier', in Keynes, J.M. (1936), *The General Theory of Employment, Interest and Money*, London: Macmillan,
4. In the UK, the government's fiscal rules positively encourage 'investment' and discourage current maintenance spend. For example, funding the new Sizewell C nuclear power station with state contributions does not count against the fiscal rules.
5. New buildings and accommodation have been added, and these bits are investment – the genuine enhancement of the college's assets.

6. See Helm, D. (2004), *Energy, the State, and the Market: British Energy Policy since 1979*, Oxford: Oxford University Press, Chapter 2.
7. See Helm, D. (2023), *Legacy: How to Build the Sustainable Economy*, Cambridge: Cambridge University Press.
8. World Business Council for Sustainable Development and World Resources Institute (undated), 'The Greenhouse Gas Protocol: A Corporate Accounting and Reporting Standard', revised edn, https://ghgprotocol.org/sites/default/files/standards/ghg-protocol-revised.pdf.
9. If an intermittent renewables generator had to purchase electricity from back-up suppliers to render its output firm power, then it would have very high scope 2 emissions.
10. World Business Council for Sustainable Development and World Resources Institute (undated), 'The Greenhouse Gas Protocol: A Corporate Accounting and Reporting Standard', revised edn, https://ghgprotocol.org/sites/default/files/standards/ghg-protocol-revised.pdf.
11. 'There is one and only one social responsibility of business—to use its resources and engage in activities designed to increase its profits so long as it stays within the rules of the game, which is to say, engages in open and free competition without deception or fraud.' Friedman, M. (1970), 'The social responsibility of business is to increase its profits', *New York Times Magazine*, 13 September. For a different view, see also C. Mayer (2024), *Capitalism and Crises: How to Fix Them*, Oxford: Oxford University Press.

6 Renewables and Nuclear Aren't Cheap

1. A model of how a competitive auction market for firm power would incorporate the costs of intermittency is set out in Helm, D. (2017), 'The cost of energy review', 25 October, https://assets.publishing.service.gov.uk/media/5a749c26ed915d0e8e39997a/Cost_of_Energy_Review.pdf.
2. The major reason for the falling costs of solar panels is the large-scale subsidies and over-production in China. The prices

that importers pay for Chinese solar panels are less than their full cost of production in China.

3. A CfD is, in effect, a fixed-price (the strike price) electricity contract, facilitated by an adjustment to the actual wholesale price of electricity. If the wholesale price goes above the strike price, there is a refund, and vice versa.
4. In the UK, nuclear provides an interesting case study. The new Hinkley C nuclear power station is supported by a CfD and hence is pay-when-delivered. The new Sizewell C nuclear power station is to be funded using pay-as-you-go, through a contract based on the regulatory asset base (RAB).
5. Even biomass such as Drax has fixed contract prices independent of the wholesale market, and therefore it can bid down towards zero too.
6. National Energy System Operator (2025), 'Future energy scenarios: pathways to net zero', v.5, November, www.neso.energy/publications/future-energy-scenarios-fes.
7. National Energy System Operator (2024), 'Our Clean Power 2030 advice to Government', 5 November, www.neso.energy/news/our-clean-power-2030-advice-government.
8. A panel set up to investigate the incident published a factual report in October 2025. ENTSO-E (2025), 'Grid incident in Spain and Portugal on 28 April 2025', ICS Investigation Expert Panel, factual report. See also Chapter 2 in this book, p. 32.
9. No register of private standby generation was kept until 2000. Twenty per cent of installed capacity is not an unreasonable estimate.
10. See National Energy System Operator (2025), 'North Hyde Review final report', 30 June, www.neso.energy/publications/north-hyde-review.
11. NESO adds a further cost methodology, which it calls 'economic resource cost'. It is not, however, the full system costs.
12. In the case of 'non-nuclear' Germany, it particularly relies on French nuclear reactors to meet demand peaks, notably in the south of the country and in winter.

13. National Energy System Operator (2024), 'Our Clean Power advice to Government', 5 November, www.neso.energy/news/our-clean-power-2030-advice-government.
14. Note that in the 'old system' which required around 60 GW total capacity, the interconnectors in 2030 would add nearly 17 per cent to total capacity.
15. See Department for Environment, Food and Rural Affairs (2025), 'Midstream gas system: update to the market', 30 June, Figure 1, www.gov.uk/government/publications/midstream-gas-system-update-to-the-market/midstream-gas-system-update-to-the-market.

7 Offsets, Buying Indulgences and Sequestration

1. In Indonesia, large areas of rainforest are being cleared to make way for rice, sugar cane and palm oil, the last for biofuels. See *Financial Times* (2025), 'Indonesia calls in military to help clear forests at rapid pace', 21 December, www.ft.com/content/27a6bd42-aa95-449f-97b7-7a086da42bac.
2. This is what, for example, Shell is doing, and it has at times been the largest buyer of voluntary carbon offsets, almost all of which are to stop rainforests from being chopped down. Fossil-fuel companies dominate the voluntary carbon offsets market (around 40 per cent), and amongst these, Shell was the largest buyer in 2024. See www.shell.com/motorist/oils-lubricants/helix-for-cars/our-carbon-neutral-aspiration/offsetting-remaining-emissions.html.
3. Eucalyptus are among the fastest-growing trees in the world, with high photosynthesis rates and short rotation cycles. See Chilton, K., Campoe, O., Allan, N. and Hinkle, H. (2025), 'Increasing carbon sequestration, land-use efficiency, and building decarbonization with short rotation eucalyptus', *Sustainability*, 17(3), 1281.
4. Field, C.B., Behrenfeld, M.J., Randerson, J.T. and Falkowski, P. (1998), 'Primary production of the biosphere', *Science*, 281, 237–240.

5. The Article 6.4 mechanism, also known as the 'Paris Agreement Crediting Mechanism', has a supervisory body tasked with developing and supervising the requirements and processes needed to operationalise the mechanism. This includes developing and/or approving methodologies, registering activities, accrediting third-party verification bodies and managing the Article 6.4 Registry.
6. For a survey of some of the schemes, see Kollmuss, A., Zink, H. and Polycarp, C. (2008), 'Making sense of the voluntary carbon market: a comparison of carbon offset standards', WWF Germany, www.sei.org/mediamanager/documents/Publications/SEI-Report-WWF-ComparisonCarbonOffset-08.pdf.
7. Article 6.4 of the Paris Agreement introduces a centralised carbon crediting mechanism, allowing countries, businesses and other stakeholders to engage in GHG reduction activities. This mechanism is designed to generate carbon credits that can be traded internationally, thereby supporting countries in achieving their NDCs while promoting sustainable development.
8. See Trencher, G., Nick, S., Carlson, J. et al. (2024), 'Demand for low-quality offsets and voluntary carbon market integrity', *Nature Communications*, 15, 6863, Chuang, Y. and Chung-En Liu, J. (2025), 'Assessing data integrity in voluntary carbon offsets using Benford's Law', *Energy Economics*, 152, 109021, and Science-Based Targets Initiative (2024), 'Evidence synthesis report: part 1: carbon credits', Version 1.0, July, https://files.sciencebasedtargets.org/production/files/Evidence-Synthesis-Report-Part-1-Carbon-Credits.pdf.
9. See Convention on Biological Diversity (2022), 'COP15: nations adopt four goals, 23 targets for 2030 in landmark UN biodiversity agreement', www.cbd.int/article/cop15-cbd-press-release-final-19dec2022.
10. See Helm, D. (2015), *Natural Capital: Valuing the Planet*, New Haven, CT: Yale University Press, Chapter 7, pp. 152–156.
11. For example, in the UK, the government applies a simple matrix of a few general criteria and then 'scores' the results,

which then feed into the planning system. The repeated claims by developers that bats and newts get in the way leads to the further claims that a few boxes for the bats to move to when their habitats are destroyed will address this problem, and a new pond to replace the old one sorts out the newts. Put aside the obvious point that biodiversity is about so much more than a few easy-to-observe mammals and reptiles, the results are often barely credible on their own terms and reflect the capture by the consultancy industry in providing the 'assessments' of sites and the extraordinary ignorance of the main parties.

12. See, for example, Calel, R., Colmer, J., Dechezleprêtre, A. and Glachant, M. (2025), 'Do carbon offsets offset carbon?', *American Economic Journal: Applied Economics*, 17(1), 1–40.

8 No Get-Out-Of-Jail Cards

1. One of the two environmental ethics embedded in Genesis has humans as custodians of the Earth and therefore constrained to act in its wider interests.
2. WHO defines obesity as a BMI of 30 or over. See World Health Organization, 'Obesity and overweight', www.who.int/news-room/fact-sheets/detail/obesity-and-overweight.
3. See also Osnos, E. (2025), *The Haves and the Have-Yachts*, London: Simon & Schuster; and Chapter 3, 'Compensation conservation', in Farrell, J. (2020), *Billionaire Wilderness: The Ultra-Wealthy and the Remaking of the American West*, Princeton, NJ: Princeton University Press.
4. www.spacex.com/mission.
5. See Royal Society & Royal Academy of Engineering (2018), 'Greenhouse gas removal', https://royalsociety.org/-/media/policy/projects/greenhouse-gas-removal/royal-society-greenhouse-gas-removal-report-2018.pdf.
6. Other notable DACS projects include STRATOS in Texas, US, BISON in Wyoming, US, and Deep Sky in Alberta, Canada.
7. Climeworks (2024), 'Climeworks switches on world's largest direct air capture plant', press release, 8 May, https://

climeworks.com/press-release/climeworks-switches-on-worlds-largest-direct-air-capture-plant-mammoth.

8. There may in due course be breakthroughs in geothermal. These include the greater application of fracking technologies to access pockets of hot water in rock structures.
9. Climeworks (2024), 'Pioneering the race to zero: Key strategies and innovations to scale up carbon dioxide removal', p. 6, https://climeworks.com/uploads/documents/2024_climeworks_pioneering_the_race_to_zero.pdf.
10. There is the question of the defence and the military protection of these cables, as there is too with oil and gas pipelines and shipping.
11. Jenkins, S., Kuijper, M., Helferty, H., Girardin. C. and Allen, M. (2023), 'Extended producer responsibility for fossil fuels', *Environmental Research Letters*, 18(1), 011005.
12. World Resources Institute (2025), 'World's forest carbon sink shrank to its lowest point in at least 2 decades, due to fires and persistent deforestation', 24 July, www.wri.org/insights/zero-amazondeforestation-can-grow-brazil-gdp.
13. The albedo effect is the reflection of solar radiation back into space.
14. The North Sea, with its depleted oil and gas wells and associated pipelines, is one of the best places to try CCS at scale.

9 The COP-outs

1. United Nations (2023), 'Programme budget for the biennium 2024–2025', 10 March, https://unfccc.int/sites/default/files/resource/sbi2023_02_adv.pdf.
2. Kennedy, P. (2006), *The Parliament of Man: The Past, Present, and Future of the United Nations*, New York: Random House.
3. United Nations (1992), 'United Nations Framework Convention on Climate Change', https://unfccc.int/process-and-meetings/united-nations-framework-convention-on-climate-change.
4. United Nations (1987), 'Report of the World Commission on Environment and Development: our common future'

(the Brundtland Report), www.un-documents.net/our-commonfuture.pdf.

5. Thatcher, M. (1989), 'Speech to the United Nation's General Assembly on the global environment', 8 November, www.margaretthatcher.org/document/107817.
6. Created by the World Meteorological Organization and the UN Environment Programme, its first assessment report came out in 1990. See World Meteorological Organization and the UN Environment Programme (1990), 'Climate Change: The 1990 and 1992 assessments'.
7. In 2024 China's share reached 58 per cent. See 'Coal' in International Energy Agency (2025), 'Global Energy Review 2025', www.iea.org/reports/global-energy-review-2025.
8. How German politics – and its *Energiewende*, the ongoing transition in Germany to renewable energy, energy efficiency and energy demand management – became captured by renewables is set out in Helm, D. (2012), *The Carbon Crunch: How We're Getting Climate Change Wrong – and How to Fix It*, New Haven, CT: Yale University Press.
9. Legislative support for the *Energiewende* was passed in late 2010 and includes GHG reductions of 80–95 per cent by 2050 (relative to 1990) and a renewable energy target of 60 per cent by 2050.
10. Canada withdrew in December 2012. Japan did not formally withdraw, but opted out of the second commitment period targets from December 2012.
11. Under Article 55, the Annex 1 Parties (those taking targets) had to represent at least 55 per cent of total CO_2 emissions. It was met when Russia ratified in November 2004.
12. In 2025, the US was assessed to contribute 22 per cent of the UN's regular budget, which amounts to approximately $820.4 million out of a $3.5 billion total. Pew Research Center (2025), 'How the United Nations is funded, and who pays the most', 31 July, www.pewresearch.org/short-reads/2025/07/31/how-the-united-nations-is-funded-and-who-pays-the-most/.
13. See Helm, D. (2012), *The Carbon Crunch: How We're Getting Climate Change Wrong – and How to Fix It*, New Haven, CT: Yale University

Press, Chapter 8; United Nations (2012), 'Report of the Conference of the Parties on its seventeenth session, held in Durban from 28 November to 11 December 2011: Addendum. Part Two: Action taken by the Conference of the Parties at its seventeenth session', Decision 1/CP.17 – Establishment of an Ad Hoc Working Group on the Durban Platform for Enhanced Action, FCCC/CP/2011/9/Add.1, https://unfccc.int/documents/7110.

14. United Nations (2015), 'Paris Agreement', https://unfccc.int/sites/default/files/english_paris_agreement.pdf.
15. Here is a sample of what they said: 'This agreement represents the best chance we have to save the one planet that we've got.' (Barack Obama); 'Today the world gets a lifeline ... a healthier planet, fairer societies and more prosperous economies.' (Jean-Claude Juncker); 'This generation has taken vital steps to ensure that our children and grandchildren will see that we did our duty.' (David Cameron); 'It is a victory for all of the planet and for future generations.' (John Kerry); 'This is a herculean task ... a complete transformation of the way we do business.' (Angela Merkel); 'The Paris agreement is humanity's life insurance.' (Ursula von der Leyen); 'We must treat nature as our root. Respect it, protect it, and follow its laws.' (Xi Jinping).
16. President Biden attended in person. President Xi did not attend, but submitted a written statement and a video message. President Putin also did not attend, citing Covid-19 concerns. Russia was represented by other officials.
17. 'In 2050, we will still be driving cars, flying planes and heating our homes, but our cars will be electric gliding silently around our cities, our planes will be zero emission allowing us to fly guilt-free, and our homes will be heated by cheap reliable power drawn from the winds of the North Sea.' Boris Johnson, 'Foreword from the Prime Minister' in HM Government (2021), 'Net Zero Strategy: Build Back Greener', October, p. 9, www.gov.uk/government/publications/net-zero-strategy.
18. India Ministry of Coal (2025), 'Enhancement of Coal Production', 28 July, https://coal.gov.in/sites/default/files/2025-08/PIB2149193.pdf.

19. *Financial Times* (2025), 'Indonesia calls in military to help clear rainforests at rapid pace', 21 December.
20. The Belt and Road Initiative was launched in 2013. The 'Belt' is the land corridors to Central Asia, the Middle East and even Europe. The 'Road' is actually the sea links, including strategic ports in Sri Lanka and Pakistan.
21. In 2009, there was a scientific determination that climate change was a threat to public health and welfare. This is the 'endangerment finding'. It enabled the Environment Protection Agency to regulate GHG emissions under the 1970 Clean Air Act.
22. Joe Machin as a centrist Democrat watered down the Biden Administration's 'Build Back Better' legislation, forming an energy policy based upon 'all of the above', including coal.
23. https://worldpopulationreview.com/country-rankings/oil-production-by-country.
24. Block 59 is the first in this process.
25. Saudi Aramco's dividend in 2024 was $124 billion compared to the COP25 commitment of $100 billion Climate Action Fund by 2020. In 2025, Saudi Aramco's dividend fell back to $85 billion.
26. U.S. Energy Information Administration, https://www.eia.gov/dnav/pet/hist/LeafHandler.ashx?n=PET&s=MCRFPUS2&f=M.

10 Unilateralism, Bottom-Up and No Regrets

1. The classic statement on reciprocal altruism is by Robert Trivers, in Trivers, R.L. (1971), 'The evolution of reciprocal altruism', *Quarterly Review of Biology*, 46(1), 35–57.
2. 'By reducing emissions produced in the UK to zero, we also end our contribution to rising global temperatures.' Climate Change Committee (2019), 'Net zero: the UK's contribution to stopping global warming', May, p. 8, www.theccc.org.uk/publication/net-zero-the-uks-contribution-to-stopping-global-warming/.
3. Marx, K. and Engels, F. (1848), *Manifesto of the Communist Party*, www.marxists.org/archive/marx/works/download/pdf/Manifesto.pdf.

4. See Pearce et al. for an early exposition. Pearce, D.W., Markandya, A. and Barbier, E.B. (1989), *Blueprint for a Green Economy*, London: Routledge.
5. See Wang, D. (2025), *Breakneck: China's Quest 2025 to Engineer the Future*, London: Allen Lane. On some of the early environmental consequences, see Economy, E.C. (2005), *The River Runs Black: The Environmental Challenge to China's Future*, Ithaca, NY: Cornell University Press.
6. It also invests in posts in Sri Lanka and Pakistan along the shipping pathways for Middle Eastern oil.
7. European Council (2025), 'Council and Parliament strike a deal on rules to phase out Russian gas imports for an energy secure and independent Europe', 3 December, www.consilium.europa.eu/en/press/press-releases/2025/12/03/council-and-parliament-strike-a-deal-on-rules-to-phase-out-russian-gas-imports-for-an-energy-secure-and-independent-europe/.
8. In the UK, raising employer National Insurance Contributions in the Autumn 2024 Budget is a tax on labour and an example of how to increase rather than diminish distortions of the economy.
9. An early example is the UK proposal to introduce a charge per mile for EVs.
10. See Helm D., Hepburn, C. and Ruta, G. (2012), 'Trade, climate change, and the political game theory of border carbon adjustments', *Oxford Review of Economic Policy*, 28(2).
11. European Parliament and European Council (2023), 'Regulation (EU) 2023/956 establishing a carbon border adjustment mechanism', https://climate-laws.org/document/regulation-eu-2023956-establishing-a-carbon-border-adjustment-mechanism-5063.

11 What Happens If We Don't Act?

1. World Resources Institute (2023), 'Ending deforestation in the Amazon can grow Brazil's GDP – but that's not the only reason to do it', 19 June, www.wri.org/insights/zero-amazon-deforestation-can-grow-brazil-gdp.

2. International Panel on Climate Change (2023), 'Climate Change 2023: synthesis report. Contribution of Working Groups I, II and III to the Sixth Assessment Report of the Intergovernmental Panel on Climate Change', www.ipcc.ch/report/ar6/syr/downloads/report/IPCC_AR6_SYR_FullVolume.pdf.
3. The hurricane that hit Jamaica in late October 2025 gave rise to an example of extreme reporting.
4. Bjorn Lomborg, President of the Copenhagen Consensus Center, got castigated for making this observation. Lomborg, B. (2001), *The Skeptical Environmentalist: Measuring the Real State of the World*, Cambridge: Cambridge University Press.
5. Saudi Vision 2030, www.saudipedia.com/en/article/1242/government-and-politics/vision-2030/.
6. Gates, B. (2025), 'Three tough truths about climate: what I want everyone at COP30 to know', 28 October, www.gatesnotes.com/three-tough-truths-about-climate.
7. See Bauch, M. and Büntgen, U. (2025), 'Climate driven changes in Mediterranean grain trade mitigated famine but introduced the Black Death to medieval Europe', *Communications Earth & Environment*, 6, Article 986.
8. See Macfalane, R. (2025), *Is a River Alive?*, London: Penguin Books.
9. Pilgrimages by the likes of Sidney Webb led to claims about Joseph Stalin's new Jerusalem. See Webb, S. and Webb, B. (1935), *Soviet Communism: A New Civilisation?* London: Longmans, Green & Co.
10. In 2025, European gas prices fell by 40 per cent. Since the gas price spike associated with Putin's invasion of Ukraine, they had fallen by 90 per cent by the end of 2025. For data, see Trading Economics (2025), 'TTF prices fall to 1–1/2-year low', 13 November, https://tradingeconomics.com/commodity/eu-natural-gas/news/501792.
11. Perhaps with the exception of sunshine-rich countries like Spain.
12. Stern, N. (2007), *The Economics of Climate Change: The Stern Review*, HM Treasury, Cambridge: Cambridge University Press.
13. Fressoz, J.B. (2004), *More and More and More: An All-Consuming History of Energy*, London: Penguin Books.

14. Stanley, S.M. (1990), 'The general evolutionary theory of species duration', *Paleobiology*, 16(4), 372–391.

12 How Not to Waste Another 25 Years

1. The Spanish government in 2025 has flirted with the same approach, with a formal policy to exit between 2027 and 2035.
2. See Merkel's attempts to justify the volte-face in her autobiography, Merkel, A. and Baumann, B. (2024), *Freedom: Memories 1954–2021*, New York: St. Martin's Press.
3. LNG has to be first liquefied, then shipped and then re-gasified. It is roughly 10–15 per cent worse than pipeline gas.
4. Exxon (2024), 'ExxonMobil Global Outlook: Our view to 2050', Executive Summary, p. 3, https://corporate.exxonmobil.com/-/media/global/files/global-outlook/2024/global-outlook-executive-summary.pdf.
5. This 30-by-30 target was adopted in December 2022 in the Kunming-Montreal Global Biodiversity Framework, agreed by most at the COP15 Convention on Biodiversity.
6. For the history, see World Nuclear Association (2025), 'Nuclear development in the United Kingdom', www.world-nuclear.org/information-library/appendices/nuclear-development-in-the-united-kingdom.

Conclusion

1. 'Our house is on fire', Greta Thunberg, Speech at the World Economic Forum, Davos, January 2019, https://awpc.cattcenter.iastate.edu/communication/address-davos-our-house-fire-jan-25-2019.
2. In 2019, at a Martin Luther King Day forum in New York City, US Congresswoman, Ocasio Cortez, claimed that there are only about 12 years left before catastrophic impacts are very likely, www.discoverthenetworks.org/individuals/alexandria-ocasio-cortez/.

WEBSITES

www.discoverthenetworks.org/individuals/alexandria-ocasio-cortez/

www.eia.gov/dnav/pet/hist/LeafHandler.ashx?n=PET&s=MCRFPUS2&f=M

www.gml.noaa.gov/ccgg/trends/data.html

www.neom.com/en-us

www.riotinto.com/en/operations/south-america/escondida

www.saudipedia.com/en/article/1242/government-and-politics/vision-2030/

www.shell.com/motorist/oils-lubricants/helix-for-cars/our-carbon-neutral-aspiration/offsetting-remaining-emissions.html

www.spacex.com/mission

www.world-nuclear.org/information-library/facts-and-figures/world-nuclear-power-reactors-and-uranium-requireme

www.worldpopulationreview.com/country-rankings/oil-production-by-country

www.x.com/Ed_Miliband/status/1562444641236316161

BIBLIOGRAPHY

Ackerman, F., Stanton, E. and Kartha, S. (2017), 'Inside the integrated assessment models: four issues in climate economics', Chapter 8 in F. Ackerman and E.A. Stanton (eds), *Climate Change and Global Equity*, Cambridge: Cambridge University Press.

Arrhenius, S. (1896), 'On the influence of carbonic acid in the air upon the temperature of the ground', *The London, Edinburgh, and Dublin Philosophical Magazine and Journal of Science*, Series 5, 41, 237–276.

Baruah, P.J., Eyre, N., Qadrdan, M. et al. (2014), 'Energy system impacts from heat and transport electrification', *Proceedings of the Institution of Civil Engineers-Energy*, 167(3), 139–151.

Bass, F. (1969), 'A new product growth for model consumer durables', *Management Science*, 15(5), 215–227.

Bastiat, F. (2007), *The Bastiat Collection*, 2nd edn, Ludwig von Mises Institute, https://cdn.mises.org/The per cent 20Bastiat per cent20Collection_4.pdf.

Bauch, M. and Büntgen, U. (2025), 'Climate driven changes in Mediterranean grain trade mitigated famine but introduced the Black Death to medieval Europe', *Communications Earth & Environment*, 6, Article 986.

Baumgärtner, L. and Doyne Farmer, J. (2025), 'Will national renewable costs continue declining?', INET Working Paper, Institute for New Economic Thinking, May, www.inet.ox.ac.uk/publications/no-2025-12-will-national-renewable-costs-continue-declining.

BBC (2025), 'China's rare earths: the BBC visits the world's mining capital for the metals', 8 July, www.bbc.co.uk/news/resources/idt-66cdf862-5e96-4e6e-90b8-a407b597c8d9.

Bergmann, T. and Kalkuhl, M. (2025), 'Decoupling economic growth from energy use: the role of energy intensity in an endogenous growth model', *Ecological Economics*, 230, 108519.

Bord na Móna (undated), 'Bord na Móna to work with Irish farmers to produce energy crops for power stations', press release, www.bnm.ie/bord-na-mona-to-work-with-irish-farmers-to-produce-energy-crops-for-power-stations/.

Calel, R., Colmer, J., Dechezleprêtre, A. and Glachant, M. (2025), 'Do carbon offsets offset carbon?', *American Economic Journal: Applied Economics*, 17(1), 1–40.

Carbon Brief (2024), 'Analysis: wind and solar added more to global energy than any other source in 2023', 20 June, https://www.carbonbrief.org/analysis-wind-and-solar-added-more-to-global-energy-than-any-other-source-in-2023/.

Chen, L., Thorup, V.M., Kudahl, A.B. and Østergaard, S. (2024), 'Effects of heat stress on feed intake, milk yield, milk composition, and feed efficiency in dairy cows: a meta-analysis', *Journal of Dairy Science*, 107(5), 3207–3218.

Chilton, K., Campoe, O., Allan, N. and Hinkle, H. (2025), 'Increasing carbon sequestration, land-use efficiency, and building decarbonization with short rotation eucalyptus', *Sustainability*, 17(3), 1281.

Chuang, Y. and Chung-En Liu, J. (2025), 'Assessing data integrity in voluntary carbon offsets using Benford's Law', *Energy Economics*, 152, 109021.

Climate Change Committee (2019), 'Net zero: the UK's contribution to stopping global warming', May, www.theccc.org.uk/publication/net-zero-the-uks-contribution-to-stopping-global-warming/.

Climeworks (2024), 'Climeworks switches on world's largest direct air capture plant', press release, 8 May, https://climeworks.com/press-release/climeworks-switches-on-worlds-largest-direct-air-capture-plant-mammoth.

Climeworks (2024), 'Pioneering the race to zero: key strategies and innovations to scale up carbon dioxide removal', https://climeworks.com/uploads/documents/2024_climeworks_pioneering_the_race_to_zero.pdf.

Convention on Biological Diversity (2022), 'COP15: nations adopt four goals, 23 targets for 2030 in landmark UN biodiversity agreement', www.cbd.int/article/cop15-cbd-press-release-final-19dec2022.

Crownhart, C. (2024), 'Why Microsoft made a deal to help restart Three Mile Island', *The Spark*, MIT Technology Review, 26 September, www.technologyreview.com/2024/09/26/1104516/three-mile-island-microsoft/.

Department for Environment, Food and Rural Affairs (2025), 'Bioenergy crops in England and the UK: 2003–2023', updated 11 September, www.gov.uk/government/statistics/bioenergy-crops-in-england-and-the-uk-2008-2023/bioenergy-crops-in-england-and-the-uk-2008-2023.

Department for Environment, Food and Rural Affairs (2025), 'Carbon footprint for the UK and England to 2022', updated 14 May, www.gov.uk/government/statistics/uks-carbon-footprint/carbon-footprint-for-the-uk-and-england-to-2022.

Department for Environment, Food and Rural Affairs (2025), 'Midstream gas system: update to the market', 30 June, Figure 1, www.gov.uk/government/publications/midstream-gas-system-update-to-the-market/midstream-gas-system-update-to-the-market.

Department of Energy & Climate Change (2013), 'United Kingdom housing energy fact file', https://www.gov.uk/government/statistics/united-kingdom-housing-energy-fact-file-2013.

Draghi, M. (2024), 'The future of European competitiveness – a competitiveness strategy for Europe', 9 September, European Commission, www.commission.europa.eu/document/97e481fd-2dc3-412d-be4c-f152a8232961_en.

Economy, E.C. (2005), *The River Runs Black: The Environmental Challenge to China's Future*, Ithaca, NY: Cornell University Press.

Energy Institute (2025), 'Statistical Review of World Energy', www.energyinst.org/statistical-review.

Energy UK (2024), Keynote speech by Ed Miliband, Energy UK Conference 2024, www.gov.uk/government/speeches/energy-uk-conference-2024-keynote-speech-by-by-ed-miliband.

ENTSO-E (2025), 'Grid incident in Spain and Portugal on 28 April 2025', ICS Investigation Expert Panel, Factual Report, https://eepublicdownloads.blob.core.windows.net/public-cdn-container/clean-documents/Publications/2025/iberian-blackout/entso-e_incident_report_ES-PT_April_2025_06.pdf.

European Commission (2009), '2020 climate and energy package', https://eur-lex.europa.eu/legal-content/EN/TXT/?uri=legissum:2001_8.

European Commission (2025), 'GHG emissions of all world countries – 2025 Report', https://edgar.jrc.ec.europa.eu/report_2025.

European Council (2025), 'Council and Parliament strike a deal on rules to phase out Russian gas imports for an energy secure and independent Europe', 3 December, www.consilium.europa.eu/en/press/press-releases/2025/12/03/council-and-parliament-strike-a-deal-on-rules-to-phase-out-russian-gas-imports-for-an-energy-secure-and-independent-europe/.

European Parliament and European Council (2023), 'Regulation (EU) 2023/956 establishing a carbon border adjustment mechanism', https://climate-laws.org/document/regulation-eu-2023956-establishing-a-carbon-border-adjustment-mechanism-5063.

Exxon (2024), 'ExxonMobil global outlook: our view to 2050', Executive Summary, www.corporate.exxonmobil.com/-/media/global/files/global-outlook/2024/global-outlook-executive-summary.pdf.

Farrell, J. (2020), *Billionaire Wilderness: The Ultra-Wealthy and the Remaking of the American West*, Princeton, NJ: Princeton University Press.

Field, C.B., Behrenfeld, M.J., Randerson, J.T. and Falkowski, P. (1998), 'Primary production of the biosphere', *Science*, 281, 237–240.

Financial Times (2025), 'Indonesia calls in military to help clear forests at rapid pace', 21 December, www.ft.com/content/27a6bd42-aa95-449f-97b7-7a086da42bac.

Fressoz, J. B. (2004), *More and More and More: An All-Consuming History of Energy*, London: Penguin Books.

Friedman, M. (1970), 'The social responsibility of business is to increase its profits', *New York Times Magazine*, 13 September.

Gates, B. (2021), *How to Avoid a Climate Disaster: The Solutions We Have and the Breakthroughs We Need*, London: Allen Lane.

Gates, B. (2025), 'Three tough truths about climate: what I want everyone at COP30 to know', 28 October, www.gatesnotes.com/three-tough-truths-about-climate.

Geroski, P.A. (2000), 'Models of technology diffusion', *Research Policy*, 29(4–5), 603–625.

GMK Center (2025), 'UK steel market: importers to brace themselves', https://gmk.center/en/posts/uk-steel-market-importers-to-brace-themselves/.

Harper, T. (2025), 'By building the world's biggest dam, China hopes to control more than just its water supply', *The Conversation*, 31 July, https://theconversation.com/by-building-the-worlds-biggest-dam-china-hopes-to-control-more-than-just-its-water-supply-261984.

Hawken, P. (2025), *Carbon: The Book of Life*, Melbourne, Australia: Text Publishing Company.

Helm, D. (2004), *Energy, the State, and the Market: British Energy Policy since 1979*, Oxford: Oxford University Press.

Helm, D. (2012), *The Carbon Crunch: How We're Getting Climate Change Wrong – and How to Fix It*, New Haven, CT: Yale University Press.

Helm, D. (2015), *Natural Capital: Valuing the Planet*, New Haven, CT: Yale University Press.

Helm, D. (2017), 'The cost of energy review', 25 October, https://assets.publishing.service.gov.uk/media/5a749c26ed915d0e8e39997a/Cost_of_Energy_Review.pdf.

Helm, D. (2023), *Legacy: How to Build the Sustainable Economy*, Cambridge: Cambridge University Press.

Helm, D. (2024), 'Climate realism – time for a re-set', December, https://dieterhelm.co.uk/energy-climate/climate-realism-time-for-a-re-set/.

Helm D., Hepburn, C. and Ruta, G. (2012), 'Trade, climate change, and the political game theory of border carbon adjustments', *Oxford Review of Economic Policy*, 28(2).

HM Government (2021), 'Net Zero Strategy: Build Back Greener', October, www.gov.uk/government/publications/net-zero-strategy.

India Ministry of Coal (2025), `Enhancement of Coal Production', 28 July, https://coal.gov.in/sites/default/files/2025-08/PIB2149193.pdf.
ING (2025), 'Nickel still capped by surplus', 8 December, https://think.ing.com/articles/nickel-still-capped-by-surplus.
Institute for Energy Research (2025), 'Coal is still king – globally', 5 September, www.instituteforenergyresearch.org/fossil-fuels/coal/coal-is-still-king-globally/.
Intergovernmental Panel on Climate Change (2006), '2006 IPCC Guidelines for National Greenhouse Gas Inventories', www.ipcc-nggip.iges.or.jp/public/2006gl/.
Intergovernmental Panel on Climate Change (2019), '2019 Refinement to the 2006 IPCC Guidelines for National Greenhouse Gas Inventories', www.ipcc.ch/report/2019-refinement-to-the-2006-ipcc-guidelines-for-national-greenhouse-gas-inventories/.
International Energy Agency (2022), 'Solar PV global supply chains: an IEA special report', www.iea.org/reports/solar-pv-global-supply-chains.
International Energy Agency (2025), 'Coal 2025: analysis and forecast to 2030', www.iea.blob.core.windows.net/assets/113a8274-500c-4684-951f-947d25bef3c9/Coal2025.pdf.
International Energy Agency (2025), 'Coal Mid-Year Update 2025', 24 July, www.iea.org/reports/coal-mid-year-update-2025.
International Energy Agency (2025), 'Global Energy Review 2025 – Coal', www.iea.org/reports/global-energy-review-2025/coal.
International Energy Agency (2025), 'Global Energy Review 2025', https://www.iea.org/reports/global-energy-review-2025/key-findings.
International Energy Agency (2025), 'World Energy Outlook', https://www.iea.org/reports/world-energy-outlook-2025.
International Energy Agency (undated), 'Energy and AI', World Energy Outlook Special Report, https://www.iea.org/reports/energy-and-ai/energy-demand-from-ai.
International Panel on Climate Change (2023), 'Climate Change 2023: Synthesis Report. Contribution of Working Groups I, II and III to the Sixth Assessment Report of the Intergovernmental Panel on Climate Change', www.ipcc.ch/report/ar6/syr/downloads/report/IPCC_AR6_SYR_FullVolume.pdf.

Jenkins, S., Kuijper, M., Helferty, H., Girardin. C. and Allen, M. (2023), 'Extended producer responsibility for fossil fuels', *Environmental Research Letters*, 18(1), 011005.

Jevons, W.S. (1865) *The Coal Question: An Inquiry Concerning the Progress of the Nation, and the Probable Exhaustion of Our Coal-mines*, London: Macmillan & Co.

Kennedy, P. (2006), *The Parliament of Man: The Past, Present, and Future of the United Nations*, New York: Random House.

Keynes, J.M. (1936), *The General Theory of Employment, Interest and Money*, London: Macmillan.

Kollmuss, A., Zink, H. and Polycarp, C. (2008), 'Making sense of the voluntary carbon market: a comparison of carbon offset standards', WWF Germany, www.sei.org/mediamanager/documents/Publications/SEI-Report-WWF-ComparisonCarbonOffset-08.pdf.

Kuhn, T. (1962), *The Structure of Scientific Revolutions*, Chicago, IL: University of Chicago Press.

Labour Party (2024), 'Make Britain a clean energy superpower', www.gov.uk/missions/clean-energy.

Langengen, T. (2025), 'Cheaper Power 2030, Net Zero 2050: Resetting the UK's electricity strategy for the future', Tony Blair Institute for Global Changes, 23 October, www.institute.global/insights/climate-and-energy/cheaper-power-2030-net-zero-2050-resetting-UK-electricity-strategy.

Lomborg, B. (2001), *The Skeptical Environmentalist: Measuring the Real State of the World*, Cambridge: Cambridge University Press.

Macfalane, R. (2025), *Is a River Alive?*, London: Penguin Books.

Manchester Evening News (2022), 'Renewable energy such as solar and wind are nine times cheaper than gas', Direct Interview Statement, 24 November, www.manchestereveningnews.co.uk/news/cost-of-living/renewables-can-help-cost-living-25574282.

Marx, K. and Engels, F. (1848), *Manifesto of the Communist Party*, www.marxists.org/archive/marx/works/download/pdf/Manifesto.pdf.

Mayer, C. (2024), *Capitalism and Crises: How to Fix Them*, Oxford: Oxford University Press.

McKinsey & Company (2024), 'How data centers and the energy sector can sate AI's hunger for power', 17 September, www.mckinsey.com/industries/private-capital/our-insights/how-data-centers-and-the-energy-sector-can-sate-ais-hunger-for-power#/.

Merkel, A. and Baumann, B. (2024), *Freedom: Memories 1954–2021*, New York: St. Martin's Press.

Minerals Production Association (2025), 'Government building plans at risk as UK cement production falls to 75-year low', www.mineralproducts.org/News/2025/release28.aspx.

Ministry of Coal (2025), 'Enhancement of coal production', 28 July, www.coal.gov.in/sites/default/files/2025-08/PIB2149193.pdf.

National Energy System Operator (2024), 'Our clean power 2030 advice to government', 5 November, www.neso.energy/news/our-clean-power-2030-advice-government.

National Energy System Operator (2025), 'Future energy scenarios: pathways to net zero', v.5, November, www.neso.energy/publications/future-energy-scenarios-fes.

National Energy System Operator (2025), 'North Hyde review final report', 30 June, www.neso.energy/publications/north-hyde-review.

Nordhaus, W.D. (2007), 'A review of the Stern Review on the economics of climate change', *Journal of Economic Literature*, 45(3), 686–702.

Office for National Statistics (2025), 'Methodology note: measuring UK greenhouse gas emissions', 7 November, www.ons.gov.uk/economy/environmentalaccounts/methodologies/measuringukgreenhousegasemissions.

Osnos, E. (2025), *The Haves and the Have-Yachts*, London: Simon & Schuster.

Our World in Data (2025), 'Which countries have contributed the most to historical CO_2 emissions?', 17 March, www.ourworldindata.org/data-insights/which-countries-have-contributed-the-most-to-historical-co-emissions.

Pearce, D.W., Markandya, A. and Barbier, E.B. (1989), *Blueprint for a Green Economy*, London: Routledge.

Peng, L., Searchinger, T.D., Zionts, J. and Waite, R. (2023), 'The carbon costs of global wood harvests', *Nature*, 620, 110–115.
Pew Research Center (2025), 'How the United Nations is funded, and who pays the most', 31 July, www.pewresearch.org/short-reads/2025/07/31/how-the-united-nations-is-funded-and-who-pays-the-most/.
Plokhy, S. (2018), *Chernobyl: History of a Tragedy*, London: Allen Lane.
Popper, K.R. (1959), *The Logic of Scientific Discovery*, London: Hutchinson & Co.
Rathore, S., Joy, J. and Kumar, A. (2025), 'Life cycle analysis of the simultaneous production of lithium hydroxide monohydrate and lithium carbonate from spodumene ore using electrodialysis', *Sustainable Materials and Technologies*, e01650.
Royal Society & Royal Academy of Engineering (2018), 'Greenhouse gas removal', https://royalsociety.org/-/media/policy/projects/greenhouse-gas-removal/royal-society-greenhouse-gas-removal-report-2018.pdf.
Science-Based Targets Initiative (2024), 'Evidence synthesis report: Part 1: carbon credits', Version 1.0, July, https://files.sciencebasedtargets.org/production/files/Evidence-Synthesis-Report-Part-1-Carbon-Credits.pdf.
Searchinger, T.D., Hamburg, S.P., Melillo, J. et al. (2009), 'Fixing a critical climate accounting error', *Science*, 326(5952), 527–528.
Select Committee on Science and Technology (2005), 'Second Report', Session 2005–06, Chapter 3: The economics of energy efficiency, https://publications.parliament.uk/pa/ld200506/ldselect/ldsctech/21/2102.htm.
Setiabudi, P. (2025), 'Green ambitions? Indonesia's smelters reveal the harsh reality of energy transition', www.petromindo.com/news/article/green-ambitions-indonesia-s-smelters-reveal-the-harsh-reality-of-energy-transition-1.
Shiller, R.J. (2000), *Irrational Exuberance*, Princeton, NJ: Princeton University Press.
Stanley, S.M. (1990), 'The general evolutionary theory of species duration', *Paleobiology*, 16(4), 372–391.

Statistiches Bundesamt (2026), 'Gross electricity production in Germany', www.destatis.de/EN/Themes/Economic-Sectors-Enterprises/Energy/Production/Tables/gross-electricityproduction.html.

Stern, N. (2007), *The Economics of Climate Change: The Stern Review*, HM Treasury, Cambridge: Cambridge University Press.

Stokes, G. and Shearmur, J. (2016), 'Popper and his philosophy: an overview', pp. 1–29 in J. Shearmur and G. Stokes (eds), *The Cambridge Companion to Popper*, Cambridge: Cambridge University Press.

Thatcher, M. (1989), 'Speech to the United Nation's General Assembly on the global environment', 8 November, www.margaretthatcher.org/document/107817.

Thunberg, G. (2019), 'Our house is on fire', Speech at the World Economic Forum, Davos, January, https://awpc.cattcenter.iastate.edu/communication/address-davos-our-house-firejan-25-2019.

Tilman, D., Hill, J. and Lehman, C. (2006), 'Carbon-negative biofuels from low-input high-diversity grassland biomass', *Science*, 314(5805), 1598–1600.

Tilman, D., Reich, P.B, Knops, J. et al. (2001), 'Diversity and productivity in a long-term grassland experiment', *Science*, 294(5543), 843–845.

Trading Economics (2025), 'TTF prices fall to 1-1/2-year low', 13 November, www.tradingeconomics.com/commodity/eu-natural-gas/news/501792.

Trencher, G., Nick, S., Carlson, J. et al. (2024), 'Demand for low-quality offsets and voluntary carbon market integrity', *Nature Communications*, 15, 6863.

Trivers, R. L. (1971), 'The evolution of reciprocal altruism', *Quarterly Review of Biology*, 46(1), 35–57.

UK Steel (2024), 'UK steel sector sets out manifesto strategy to secure future of steel', www.uksteel.org/steel-news-2024/uk-steel-sector-sets-out-manifesto-strategy-to-secure-future-of-steel.

UNESCO (2021), 'The United Nations world water development report 2021', www.un.org/sites/un2.un.org/files/un_world_water_dev._report_2021.pdf.

United Nations (1987), 'Report of the World Commission on Environment and Development: our common future' (the Brundtland Report), www.un-documents.net/our-common-future.pdf.

United Nations (1992), 'United Nations Framework Convention on Climate Change', https://unfccc.int/process-and-meetings/united-nations-framework-convention-on-climate-change.

United Nations (1998), 'Kyoto Protocol to the United Nations Framework Convention on Climate Change', https://unfccc.int/resource/docs/convkp/kpeng.pdf.

United Nations (2012), 'Report of the Conference of the Parties on its seventeenth session, held in Durban from 28 November to 11 December 2011: Addendum. Part Two: Action taken by the Conference of the Parties at its seventeenth session', Decision 1/CP.17 – Establishment of an Ad Hoc Working Group on the Durban Platform for Enhanced Action, FCCC/CP/2011/9/Add.1, https://unfccc.int/documents/7110.

United Nations (2015), 'Paris Agreement', adopted 12 December, https://unfccc.int/sites/default/files/english_paris_agreement.pdf.

United Nations (2023), 'Programme budget for the biennium 2024–2025', 10 March, https://unfccc.int/sites/default/files/resource/sbi2023_02_adv.pdf.

Wang, D. (2025), *Breakneck: China's Quest 2025 to Engineer the Future*, London: Allen Lane.

Way, R., Ives, M.C., Mealy, P. and Doyne Farmer, J. (2022), 'Empirically grounded technology forecasts and the energy transition', *Joule*, 13 September, www.sciencedirect.com/science/article/pii/S254243512200410X.

Weart, S.R. (2003), *The Discovery of Global Warming*, Cambridge, MA: Harvard University Press.

Webb, S. and Webb, B. (1935), *Soviet Communism: A New Civilisation?* London: Longmans, Green & Co.

Weyler, R. (2002), *Greenpeace: How a Group of Journalists, Ecologists and Visionaries Changed the World*, London: Rodale.

WNISR (2025), 'World nuclear industry status report 2025', www.worldnuclearreport.org/World-Nuclear-Industry-Status-Report-2025-HTML.

World Business Council for Sustainable Development and World Resources Institute (undated), 'The Greenhouse Gas Protocol: A Corporate Accounting and Reporting Standard', revised edn, https://ghgprotocol.org/sites/default/files/standards/ghg-protocol-revised.pdf.

World Health Organization, 'Obesity and overweight', www.who.int/news-room/fact-sheets/detail/obesity-and-overweight.

World Meteorological Organization (2025), 'WMO confirms 2004 as warmest year on record at about 1.55°C above pre-industrial level', press release, 10 January, https://wmo.int/news/media-centre/wmo-confirms-2024-warmest-year-record-about-155degc-above-pre-industrial-level?

World Meteorological Organization and the UN Environment Programme (1990), 'Climate Change: The 1990 and 1992 assessments', www.ipcc.ch/report/climate-change-the-ipcc-1990-and-1992-assessments/.

World Nuclear Association (2025), 'Nuclear development in the United Kingdom', www.world-nuclear.org/information-library/appendices/nuclear-development-in-the-united-kingdom.

World Resources Institute (2023), 'Ending deforestation in the Amazon can grow Brazil's GDP – but that's not the only reason to do it', 19 June, www.wri.org/insights/zero-amazon-deforestation-can-grow-brazil-gdp.

World Resources Institute (2025), 'World's forest carbon sink shrank to its lowest point in at least 2 decades, due to fires and persistent deforestation', 24 July, www.wri.org/insights/forest-carbon-sink-shrinking-fires-deforestation.

INDEX

accidents, nuclear, 20
activists, climate, 3
adaptations, temperature, 49–51
aggregate electricity demand, 42–43
agriculture
  air conditioning, 34
  effects on atmospheric carbon, 53–54
  fertilisers, 35–36
  intensive, 32–33, 113
  use of robots, 31
AI
  electricity demand, 22, 27–29, 129
  future growth, 191–192
air conditioning, 26–27, 33–34, 49–51
Allen, Myles, 137
altruistic countries, 163–166
aluminium smelting, 35–36
always-on economy, 32
Amazon rainforest, 158–159
  loss, 177–178, 182
  protection, 201
American Carbon Registry, 121
anaerobic digesters, 16
anti-net zero perspective, 4, 185–186
anti-nuclear movement, 20, 149–150
Arctic melting, 7, 179, 182
Argentina, lithium mining, 66, 158–159, 161
artificial fertilisers, 16, 18–19, 128
artificial intelligence. *See* AI
aviation, 77–78, 126.
  See also 'sustainable aviation fuel' (SAF)
Azerbaijan, oil producing, 154

Bastiat, Frédéric, 82–83, 94
batteries
  charging for EVs, 36–37
  critical minerals, 4, 72
  disposal, 9
  need to cover intermittency, 70–72
  nickel requirements, 65–66
Belt and Road subsidies, 155–156, 167
benefits of climate change, 49, 179, 204–205
Betts, Pete, 2–3
Bezos, Jeff, 11–12
Biden, Joe, 2–3
Big Tech companies, 90, 129
biodiversity
  carbon offsetting, 118–119
  framework, COP15, 122
  increasing, 189–190
  natural sequestration, 138
  biodiversity loss, 12, 46–47, 63, 192, 189, 202
  carbon sequestration, 53–54, 113
  copper production, 67
  nickel production, 65–66
  river ecology, 73

biomass burning, 13–14, 15–17, 53–56, 73–76, 120, 197
Bolivia, lithium mining, 158–159, 161
borrowing, for capital maintenance, 88–89
bottom-up versus top-down approaches, 161–162, 188, 211
Brahmaputra River, 73
Brazil
  COP30, 158–159
  GDP growth, 204–205
  oil production, 18–19, 154, 161
broken window fallacy, 82–85, 94, 209–210
bronze, uses, 64
Brundtland Report, 145–147, 160
Bush, George Jr, 2–3

cables, international, 109
cabling, 69–70, 107–109, 136
Canada
  climate change benefits, 49
  oil production, 18–19
  thawing north, 49–51
  wood producing, 75
capacity requirements, intermittent energy, 100–109
capital costs, renewables, 98
capital maintenance, 109–111, 210
  current spending, 86–87
  versus investment, 81–82, 86–89, 98
car industry, use of robots, 31
carbon concentration, atmosphere, 4–5, 45, 60–61
  targets, 45–60, 199
  likely increase, 177
carbon capture and storage (CCS), 9–10, 136–137, 202, 210
  biomass burning, 74
  North Sea, 192–194
carbon consumption, 8–9, 11, 54–56, 60–61, 211
  need to reduce, 202, 209–210
  personal, 165
  versus production, 54–60, 149–150, 164–165
carbon contracts, 124
carbon credits, pricing, 123
carbon embedded in exports, 164–165
carbon offsets. *See* offsetting
carbon taxes, 11, 23–24, 58–59, 96, 116, 165–170, 172–175, 209–210. *See also* polluter-pays principle
  carbon border adjustment mechanism, 174–175
  distortions, 170
  economic efficiency, 166–167
  EU Emissions Trading System, 96
  World Trade Organization, 169–170
'carbon-free' energy, 4
CCC (Climate Change Committee), 164
CCS. *See* carbon capture and storage (CCS)
cement making, 35–36
Chernobyl, Ukraine, 20, 78
Chile
  copper mining, 67
  lithium mining, 66, 158–159
China
  batteries and EVs, 167
  climate leadership aspiration, 155–156

China (cont.)
coal burning, 2–3, 4, 9, 17–18, 49–51, 63, 65, 154, 166
emissions, 54–56, 133, 148–149, 155–156
energy demand, increase, 25
energy-intensive exports, 58–59
environmental damage, 128, 168
hydroelectricity, 72–73
intensive agriculture, 32–33
minerals mining, 9, 67
nuclear power stations, 21–22
resistance to COPs, 143
rivalry with US, 148–149, 156–158
subsidies, 89–90, 166–167
Christian philosophy, 165
'clean' energy, 4, 49–51, 62–63, 208, 210. *See also* renewable energy; 'sustainable aviation fuel' (SAF)
aviation and shipping, 77–78
biomass burning, 73–76
cabling and infrastructure, 69–70
electric vehicles, 76–77
versus fossil fuels, 79–80
hydroelectricity, 72–73
intermittency and the need for batteries, 70–72
nuclear power stations, 78–79
pollution from mining, 64–68
'recycling', 68–69
Climate Action Reserve, 121
climate activists, 3
climate change
avoidance of mistakes, 194–198
benefits, 49, 179, 204–205
broken window fallacy, 86
consequences of inaction, 177–178, 189–190, 205–206
denial, 2, 146
designing systems changes, 203–205
economics, 47–49
future actions, 191–192
global impacts focus, 192–194
mitigation, avoidance of mistakes, 194–198
mobilisation, 205–206
modelling, 3, 47–49, 110, 145–147, 183–187
paradigm, 1–2, 5–8, 9–10
political divides, 183–187
progressive left and UN, 187–189
sceptics, 2
system approach, 198–202
temperature rise, 178–181
tipping points, 181–183
variable impacts, 204–205
Climate Change Committee (CCC), 164
climate change community, 1, 7–8, 49
broken window fallacy, 84
dire warnings, 207
failure of COPs, 159–162
flying, 77
green finance, 89
green growth, 81–82
misleading language, 62–63
renewables, cost, 95
system energy costs, 110
technological progress, 127–128
time wasted, 191
unrealistic policies, 207
wrong targets, 211–212
Clinton, Bill, 59–60
cloud seeding, 34, 138–140

coal burning, 17–18
  China, 2–3, 4, 17–18, 65, 154
  for data centres, 27–29
  increasing, 4
  for solar panels, 9, 49–51, 63
  for steel, 17–18, 166
coalition of the willing, 175–176
cobalt mining, 4, 9, 161
Communist Manifesto (Marx and Engels), 165
Conference of the Parties. *See* COPs
Congo, Democratic Republic of, 64
  cobalt mining, 9, 161
  ecosystems, 204–205
consumption
container ships, 77–78, 128–129
cooling. *See* air conditioning
Copenhagen Accord, 2009, 143, 148
copper
  mining, 4, 67, 128
  uses, 64
COPs (Conference of the Parties), 141–143
  carbon, atmospheric concentration, 60–61
  climate change global, 143–147
  COP15 biodiversity framework, 122
  COP30, 158–159
  failings, 10, 153–158, 159–162, 191, 208, 211
  Kyoto Protocol, 147–150
  legally binding treaty, aim, 151–153
  Paris Agreement, 2, 4–5, 48, 89, 121
  US withdrawal, 156–158
critical minerals. *See* minerals, critical
cruise ships, 77–78, 130
DACS (direct air carbon capture and storage), 9–10, 202, 210
data centres
  energy demands, 22, 27–29
  future growth, 191–192
  Iceland, 136
decoupling energy demand from GDP, 25
deep-sea mining, 64
de-growth, 11–12, 129–130
deindustrialisation, 56–57, 186–187
  UK, 37–38, 88–89
demand side, 71–72, 105
  changes needed, 209–210
desalination, 49–51, 179–180
  electricity demand, 26–27
  energy demand increases, 33–34
developing countries
  emissions, 132–134
  environmental disaster, 168
  GDP growth, 40
  mercantile approach, 168–169
direct air capture and storage. *See* DACS (direct air carbon capture and storage)
domestic heating, 33
Drax power station, 54–56, 75, 197

economic growth argument, 81–82
  broken window fallacy, 82–85
  capital maintenance versus investment, 82–85
  ESG-directed ‘investments’, 91–93
  green finance, 89–91
  net zero targets, 94
Economics of Climate Change (Stern), 48–49, 188

ecosystems, 47–51, 53–54, 189
damage to, 63, 73
protection, 192, 201, 202, 204–205
efficiency, energy, 32–33
Egypt, gas producing, 154
electric-arc process, 68–69
electric vehicles, 36–37, 76–77, 105
electricity demand, increases, 13–14, 26–27, 38–39, 42–43, 106–107
desalination, 34–35
electric vehicles, 36–37
new sources of demand, 31
post Second World War, 87
security of supplies, 32
emissions
biofuels, 15–17, 73–76
caused by offsetting, 117–118
causes of increases, 208
CCS, 202
China, 54–56, 133, 148–149, 155–156
versus consumption, 54–60, 149–150
COPs, 143
developing countries, 154–155
global problem, 8, 143–147, 192–194
national targets, 45, 149–150
reductions in UK, 54–56, 152–153
renewables supply chain, 63, 79–80, 90–91
scope classifications, 90–91
sequestration of carbon, 53–54, 57, 140
sequestration offsetting, 117–123
US, 156–158
zero emissions, 63
Emissions Trading System (EU), 96
Energiewende ('energy transition'), 149–150, 194–196
energy costs, 187
energy demand, increase, 5, 13–14, 25–26, 177, 189, 191–192
aggregate electricity demand, 42–43
air conditioning and desalination, 33–34
electrification, 26–27
energy efficiency argument, 41–42, 211
existing heavy industry, 35–36
GDP growth, 37–41
information technologies, 27–31
oil, gas and coal, 43–44
robots, 31–33
transport, 36–37
energy demand management, 71–72
energy efficiency, 32–33, 41–42, 211
energy 'transition'. *See* transition, energy
environment, social and governance. *See* ESG
environmental damage
biomass burning, 74–75
'clean' energy, 62
limits exceeded, 10–11
mining, 64
nuclear power stations, 78
recycling, 68–69
technology, 128–131
environmental remediation, 210
Escondida copper mine, 67
ESG (environment, social and governance), 'investments', 85, 91–93

ethics, individual, 144
European Union (EU)
  carbon border adjustment mechanism, 174–175
  deindustrialisation, 186–187
  Emissions Trading System, 96
  high energy prices, 37–38
  Kyoto Protocol, 1997, 149–150
  Russian gas versus US shale gas, 169
EVs. *See* electric vehicles

far-right parties
  Alternative für Deutschland, AfD 196
  anti-net zero, 185–186
  European, 4
fertilisers, artificial, 16, 18, 128
Figueres, Christiana, 2–3
finance versus funding, 81–82
financial considerations, government, 170–172
flexible demand for energy, 104–105
flying. *See* aviation
forest burning, 113, 114–115
fossil fuels, 9, 185
  continued use, 93
  versus energy, 79–80
  falling prices, 39
  future use, 42–43, 191–192, 200–201, 203
  lobbyists, 142
  price advantage, 23
  use for electricity generation, 22
fresh water, scarcity, 26–27, 33–34
Fressoz, Jean-Baptiste, 13–14
Fukushima, Japan, 20, 78
funding versus finance, 81–82

gas
  reliance on, 194–198
  price volatility, 37
  use for electricity generation, 21
Gates, Bill, 11–12, 181
GDP growth, 81–82, 190
  energy demand, increase, 37–41
  future growth, 200
  tempering, 11–12
  unsustainable, 209–210
geoengineering, 10, 114, 120, 131–134, 183, 202
  carbon capture and storage, 136–137
  dangers, 140
  direct air carbon capture and storage, 134–136
  solar reflectors, 138–140
  time period, 140
geothermal energy, 136
Germany
  Alternative für Deutschland, AfD 196
  Energiewende 149–150, 194–196
  Green Party, 149–150, 194
  renewables, 194–196
  use of coal in steel making, 17–18
Glasgow, COP 2021, 152–153
global
governance, 159–162
  impacts focus, 192–194
  versus national targets, 54–60, 143–147, 163
  problem of climate change, 8, 143–147, 192–194
  temperature rise, 45–51, 178–181
  treaty, aim, 151–153

global warming, 4–5. *See also* climate change; global, temperature rise
government-to-government transfers, 116
Grand Coulee Dam, United States, 73
Grasberg copper mine, 67
green
  finance, 89–91, 202
  growth, 40–41, 81–82
  political movement, 149–150
Green Party, Germany, 149–150, 194
green steel, 68–69
Greenpeace, 20
greenwashing, 90, 93
  carbon contracts, 124
  offsetting, 120–123
groupthink, 3
growth. *See* economic growth argument

Haber–Bosch process, 128
human causation, 131–134, 184, 190
human ingenuity, 10–11, 209–210
hydroelectricity, 72–73, 208–209
  future use, 203
  Norway, 107
hydrogen production, 100

IAMs (integrated assessment models), 47–49, 147
ice ages, 182
Iceland
  direct air carbon capture and storage, 134–135
  geothermal energy, 28–30, 136
immigration
  large-scale, 180–181
  policies, 187
India
  coal burning, 4, 17–18, 154
  energy demand, increase, 25
  GDP growth, 154–155, 177
  nuclear power stations, 21–22
  resistance to COPs, 143
Indonesia
  coal burning, 4, 65
  copper production, 67
  energy demand, increase, 25
  GDP growth, 154–155, 177
  nickel mining and production, 9
  peat fires, 17
information technologies, electricity demand, 26–27. *See also* AI; data centres
integrated assessment models (IAMs), 47–49, 146–147
interconnectors, 107–109
Intergovernmental Panel on Climate Change (IPCC), 60–61, 145–147, 159, 178, 183–184
intermittent energy, 6–7. *See also* managing intermittency
  cost, 100–109
  extra transmission capacity, 69–70
  Germany, 195
  impact on economics of gas, 99
  impact on economics of nuclear, 99–100
  need for batteries, 70–72
internationalism, 187
IPCC. *See* Intergovernmental Panel on Climate Change
Iran
  cloud seeding, 34
  effects of war, 22

Jevon's Law, 41–42
Just Stop Oil, 3, 13–14, 18–19, 93

Kennedy, Paul, 144–145
Kenya, carbon tax, 173
Kerry, John, 2–3
Keynes, John Maynard, 83–84
Keynesianism, 83–84
Korea, South, nuclear power stations, 21–22
Kyoto Protocol, 1997, 142–143, 147–150

labour-intensive industries, use of robots, 31
Langeled pipeline, 109
left-wing perspectives. *See* progressive left
lifestyle changes, 11–12, 209–210
lithium mining, 4, 66
living beyond our means, 209–210

maintenance, capital. *See* capital maintenance
maize, 16
managing intermittency
  active demand, 104–105
  batteries and storage, 106–107
  interconnectors, 107–109
marginal costs, solar panels/wind turbines, 96–97
marine cloud brightening, 139–140
markets, offsetting, 124–125
Mars, colonising, 10, 130–131, 181
Marx, Karl, 13–14
Medog Hydropower Station, Tibet, 72–73
Mekong River/rainforest, 73, 128, 177–178
mercantile approach, developing countries, 168–169
Merkel, Angela, 196
methane emissions, 16, 181–182
migration. *See* immigration
mineral ages, 64
minerals, critical
  for batteries, 4, 72
  China, 148–149, 154–155
  US dependency, 168–169
minerals mining. *See also* pollution from mining
  all energy production, 63
  dominance of China, 2–3, 9
  embedded in renewables, 62–63, 90–91, 200–201
  environmental damage, 50
  transportation and refining, 65
Mongolia, copper mining, 9, 161
Musk, Elon, 10, 11–12, 181

national
  territorial emissions, 45
  versus global targets, 54–60, 143–147, 163
Neom, Saudi Arabia, 33, 49–51, 180–181
net zero
  carbon consumption, 164–165, 174–175
  debts, 89
net zero targets, 2, 57–58, 89
  consumption versus production, 8–9
  economic growth argument, 94
  UK, 197–198
nickel mining, 4, 9, 65–66
non-renewable natural resources, 64
Nordhaus, 48
north–south divide, 145–147, 160, 179–181
Norway
  gas supplies to UK, 109
  hydroelectricity, 107
nuclear accidents, 20

nuclear energy, 19–22
  economics, 99–100
  fusion, 128, 183
  future use, 204
  Germany, 194–195
  new construction, 21–22
  power stations, 78–79
  small modular reactors, 22, 30
  waste management, 79

Obama, Barack, 2–3, 59–60
obesity epidemic, 129–130
ocean
  acidification, 178, 182
  pollution, 12
offsetting, 112–116
  general versus sequestration, 114, 115, 117–120
  greenwashing, 120–123
  ineffectiveness, 125–126
  markets, 123–125
  verification difficulties 116
oil, use in plastics, 18–19
Orwell, George, 62
over-consumption, 129–130

palm oil, 128
paradigm, climate change, 1–2, 5–8, 9–10
Paris Agreement 2015, 2, 4–5, 48, 89, 121, 143, 152
pay rather than borrow, 209–210
peak oil, 7, 37–41, 185
peat bogs exposure, 113
peat burning, 17
petrochemicals, 18–19, 35–36, 177
pipelines, security issues, 109
plastics, use of oil, 18–19, 177
political perspectives, 7–8, 37, 175–176, 183–187
  carbon taxes, 174–175
  EU, 149–150
  IPCC, 145–147
  US, 156–158
polluter-pays principle, 11, 85, 113, 114, 166, 209–210
pollution from mining, 64–68
  copper, 67
  lithium, 66
  nickel, 65–66
  rare earths, 67
popularist right, 184. *See also* far-right parties
ppm (parts per million). *See* carbon concentration, atmosphere
progressive left, 4, 185–187
  UN, 151–153, 187–189
pumped storage, 107
Putin, Vladimir, 2–3, 184

quantum computing
  electricity demand, 30–31, 129
  future growth, 191–192

rainforest
  loss, 12, 177–178, 204–205
  protection, 122, 201
rare earths, 2–3, 59, 67
rearmament, and GDP, 82–83
'recycling', 68–69
renewable energy, 2. *See also* 'clean' energy
  carbon footprint, 9
  costs, 23, 60, 95–98, 109–111, 165–166, 208
  Germany, 194–196
  impact on cost of gas, 96–98
  impact on cost of nuclear, 99–100
  intermittent energy, 100–109
  lobbyists, 142
  marginal costs versus system cost, 6–7

repair of damage, as part of GDP, 82–83
research and development (R&D), 11, 128, 131–134, 140, 224
robotics, electricity demand, 31–33
'rocks-to-rocks' pathway, 137
rubber plantations, 128
Russia
benefits of climate change, 49
gas producing, 196
invasion of Ukraine, 21, 37
Kyoto Protocol, 1997, 150
oil producing, 161

Saudia Arabia
adaptation to high temperatures, 49–51
air conditioning, 33
living with climate change, 180–181
scope classifications of emissions, 90–91
scrap metal, 68–69
sea levels, rising, 49, 142, 178
security of supplies, 102–103
seeding the atmosphere, 34, 138–140
self-sufficiency, 129–130
sequestration, 113
baselines, 118
biomass burning, 54–56
versus emissions of carbon, 53–54
ignored by COPs, 159–162
loss, 177–178
natural, 138
sequestration offsetting versus general offsetting, 114, 115, 117–120
shale gas, 148–149
shipping, 77–78
small modular reactors (SMRs), 22, 30
smart metering, 41–42, 71–72
charging electric vehicles, 36, 105
solar energy, 13
costs, 95–96
desalination, 34
Germany, 195–196
UK, 192–193
solar panels
Chinese competition, 89–90
coal burning, 9, 17–18, 63
costs, 96–98
intermittency, 70–72
materials, 49–51
solar reflectors, 138–140
South China Sea, 128
South Korea, nuclear power stations, 21–22
space tourism, 130–131
species extinction, 189
standby capacity, intermittent energy, 102–103
steel making
carbon taxes, 166, 172
green steel, 35–36, 68–69
UK, 56–57
use of coal, 17–18, 43–44, 63
Stern, Nick, 2–3, 48–49, 188
storage of renewable energy, 100, 106–107
subsidies, renewables, 95–96
supply-side changes, inadequacy, 208–209
'sustainable aviation fuel' (SAF), 16, 53–54, 77, 126
sustainable economic growth, 40–41, 130, 164–165, 190, 205–206, 209–210

system approach, 198–199
correct objectives, 199
designing systems changes, 203–205
energy costs, 109–111

Taiwan, 168–169
'take-back' rule, 137
Tanzania, copper mining, 161
tariffs
against China, 167–168
proxies for carbon taxes, 171
technological solutions, 2, 10–11, 127, 183
carbon capture and storage, 136–137
direct air carbon capture and storage, 134–138
environmental damage, 128–131
geoengineering, 131–140
natural sequestration, 138
technological succession, 13–14
temperature increase. *See* global, temperature rise
temperature variability, 51
Thatcher, Margaret, 145–147
theory of value, 13–14
Three Gorges Dam, China, 72–73
Three Mile Island, 20, 78
Thunberg, Greta, 3, 13–14
tin, uses, 64
tipping points
Amazon drying out, 182
Arctic melting, 182
geoengineering, 183
ice ages, 182
technology breakthrough, 183
tundra melting, 181–182
volcanic activity, 182
top-down versus bottom-up approaches, 161–162, 188, 211
transition, energy, 5, 22–24, 200–201, 208
coal burning, 17–18
current predicament, 22–24
Energiewende, 149–150, 194–196
fossil fuels to renewables, 2, 85
historical perspective, 13–15
nuclear, 19–22
oil, 18–19
renewables, 22–24
wood, peat, biomass burning, 15–17
transmission network, 69–70
transport, energy demand increases, 36–37
tree-planting, 112, 117–120
tropics, impacts of climate change, 49, 179–181
Trump, Donald, 2–3, 4, 186
attitude to COPs, 59–60
climate change 'hoax', 41, 156–158, 184
tariffs, 167–168, 174–175
tundra, melting, 181–182
Turkey, use of coal in steel making, 17–18

Ukraine, 21, 22, 37, 79, 83, 145, 169, 176, 186
unilateralism, 163
carbon imports, 172–174
carbon taxes, 166–170, 172–175
governmental financial considerations, 170–172
persuading the voters, 175–176
pure altruism, 163–166

United Arab Emirates, living with climate change, 180–181
United Kingdom
  CCS, 192–194
  'clean' energy, 42–43, 54–56
  Climate Change Committee, 164
  coal consumption, 17–18
  coal mining, ended, 196–198
  deindustrialisation, 186–187
  domestic heating, 33
  electricity generation, 100–109
  energy costs/prices, 5, 41, 187
  energy demand, 25, 37–38
  imported gas, 186–187
  net zero targets, 197–198
  nuclear power, 204
  offshoring manufacturing, 37–38, 152–153
  R&D, 192–194
  renewables, 111, 192–193
United Nations
  general remit, 151–153
  governance, 145
  internationalism, 187
United Nations COPs. *See* Conference of the Parties
United Nations Framework Convention on Climate Change (UNFCCC) Secretariat, 121, 141–143, 145–147, 183–184
United States
  attitude to COPs, 59–60, 143, 156–158
  Big Tech companies, 90
  coal burning, 27–29
  intensive agriculture, 32–33
  oil producing, 161
  rivalry with China, 148–149, 156–158
  shale gas, 148–149, 169
  tariffs, 167–168, 174–175
uranium mining and processing, 79

VERRA, 122
Vietnam, 25
virtue taxes, 171
volcanic activity, 182
voluntary power cuts, 104–105

'waste' wood, 75–76
weather events, extreme, 179, 207
wind energy, costs
  onshore/offshore, 95–96
wind turbines, 13
  coal burning for manufacture, 17–18, 63
  costs, 96–98
  future use, 203
  intermittency, 70–72
  materials, 49–51
Windscale disaster, 20, 78
wood burning, 13–14
World Health Organization (WHO), 129–130
World Trade Organization (WTO), 169–170

Xi Jinping, 2–3

zero emissions, 4
Zuckerberg, Mark, 11–12

www.ingramcontent.com/pod-product-compliance
Lightning Source LLC
LaVergne TN
LVHW020342240926
848761LV00033B/276
* 9 7 8 1 0 0 9 8 8 0 6 1 9 *